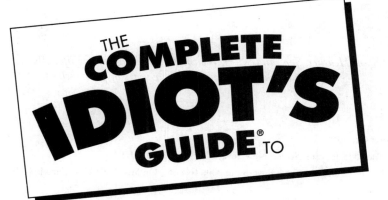

THE COMPLETE IDIOT'S GUIDE® TO

Sewing

Illustrated

by Carole Ann Camp

ALPHA

A member of Penguin Group (USA) Inc.

D1401839

To Morgan, Heather, Jen, and Nicki, the thirtysomethings in my life, who never learned how to thread a needle in all their years of public school.

ALPHA BOOKS

Published by the Penguin Group

Penguin Group (USA) Inc., 375 Hudson Street, New York, New York 10014, USA

Penguin Group (Canada), 90 Eglinton Avenue East, Suite 700, Toronto, Ontario M4P 2Y3, Canada (a division of Pearson Penguin Canada Inc.)

Penguin Books Ltd., 80 Strand, London WC2R 0RL, England

Penguin Ireland, 25 St. Stephen's Green, Dublin 2, Ireland (a division of Penguin Books Ltd.)

Penguin Group (Australia), 250 Camberwell Road, Camberwell, Victoria 3124, Australia (a division of Pearson Australia Group Pty. Ltd.)

Penguin Books India Pvt. Ltd., 11 Community Centre, Panchsheel Park, New Delhi—110 017, India

Penguin Group (NZ), 67 Apollo Drive, Rosedale, North Shore, Auckland 1311, New Zealand (a division of Pearson New Zealand Ltd.)

Penguin Books (South Africa) (Pty.) Ltd., 24 Sturdee Avenue, Rosebank, Johannesburg 2196, South Africa

Penguin Books Ltd., Registered Offices: 80 Strand, London WC2R 0RL, England

Copyright © 2005 by Carole Ann Camp

International Standard Book Number: 1-59257-154-9
Library of Congress Catalog Card Number: 2004115790

10 09 08   8 7

Interpretation of the printing code: The rightmost number of the first series of numbers is the year of the book's printing; the rightmost number of the second series of numbers is the number of the book's printing. For example, a printing code of 05-1 shows that the first printing occurred in 2005.

Printed in the United States of America

Note: This publication contains the opinions and ideas of its author. It is intended to provide helpful and informative material on the subject matter covered. It is sold with the understanding that the author and publisher are not engaged in rendering professional services in the book. If the reader requires personal assistance or advice, a competent professional should be consulted.

The author and publisher specifically disclaim any responsibility for any liability, loss, or risk, personal or otherwise, which is incurred as a consequence, directly or indirectly, of the use and application of any of the contents of this book.

Most Alpha books are available at special quantity discounts for bulk purchases for sales promotions, premiums, fund-raising, or educational use. Special books, or book excerpts, can also be created to fit specific needs.

For details, write: Special Markets, Alpha Books, 375 Hudson Street, New York, NY 10014.

Publisher: *Marie Butler-Knight*
Product Manager: *Phil Kitchel*
Senior Managing Editor: *Jennifer Bowles*
Senior Acquisitions Editor: *Randy Ladenheim-Gil*
Development Editor: *Christy Wagner*
Production Editor: *Megan Douglass*
Copy Editor: *Krista Hansing*

Cartoonist: *Chris Eliopoulos*
Cover/Book Designer: *Trina Wurst*
Indexer: *Heather McNeil*
Layout: *Becky Harmon*
Proofreading: *Mary Hunt*
Graphics: *Tammy Graham, Laura Robbins*

Contents at a Glance

Contents

Foreword

I remember when I was in high school and making an outfit I wanted to wear to school the next day. It was close to midnight, and I was almost finished sewing my new outfit. It only needed some hand-stitching and a final pressing to be complete. My mother insisted that I go to bed so I'd be alert in school; however, at that time, I was more concerned about "looking good" than learning. When I woke the next morning, my outfit was hanging in my room, ready to wear. Mom had finished it while I slept. Years later, upon holding my daughter on my lap and teaching her to sew, I hoped to pass on the passion. Growing up with four sisters, and all who sew, we would fight over whose turn it was to use the sewing machine. All of us have continued to sew throughout our adult lives, and when we visit, sewing is often the conversation topic of choice.

Sewing is a skill, an art, a stress reducer, and a great hobby. It's never too late to begin sewing. This book, *The Complete Idiot's Guide to Sewing Illustrated*, comes recommended for a beginner or even an experienced seamstress looking to refresh her or his skills.

As a beginner, you may be overwhelmed with the idea of getting the right equipment and supplies. Relax. Carole Ann Camp takes you step by step through the process of getting started and staying organized. You can start with the basic tools and expand as you are ready. *The Complete Idiot's Guide to Sewing Illustrated* will introduce you to simple projects that will get you started. You are shown how to use your creative ideas to embellish and personalize your projects. In a short time, you will be tackling any sewing project. Just be sure to learn the basics first!

You will be amazed at the ideas in this book that will rekindle your interest in sewing. Those who have sewn for years will enjoy this book. I chuckled as memories were triggered by Carole Ann's writing. With renewed motivation, I found a few projects to finish and even started a few new ones. With that, I'm off to the fabric store in search of the perfect fabric for sash belts.

You will enjoy this book. *The Complete Idiot's Guide to Sewing Illustrated* is motivational, funny, and informational. It is a great resource to help you learn everything you need to become a successful sewer. You will also learn some creative touches so you can personalize items you make for yourself, for your home, and to give as even gifts. Enjoy your journey!

Paula Lee

Paula Lee is a sixth-grade communication arts and science teacher in Bozeman, Montana. She has also taught family and consumer science at both the middle and high school level. Paula has a B.S. in home economics from the University of Minnesota and her elementary education certification from the University of St. Thomas, St. Paul, Minnesota. Prior to teaching, she worked as an extension educator for the University of Minnesota in Lyon, Douglas, and Goodhue counties. Paula was a contributing writer for the national 4-H youth development curriculum "A Stitch in Time," which included three youth manuals and a leaders' guide.

Introduction

Creating home furnishings and body coverings began when the first humans twisted two fig leaves together to make a loin cloth or kept the cold away by throwing a wooly mammoth skin around their shoulders.

Designing with fabrics is an ancient skill that's both creative and practical. In addition, sewing is fun as well as meditative. Hemming a long hem is relaxing and gives you a time to sit and think as stitch after stitch leaves your needle.

Sewing might at first appear complex, but in fact, you need to master only a few basic skills—sewing seams and making hems. Like our ancient ancestors, you can make anything you want without ever touching a sewing machine. All it takes is time and a little practice.

During the last four decades, fewer young people have learned even these simple sewing skills. Fortunately, sewing is experiencing a revival today. More young people are learning the satisfaction of being able to say, "I made this myself!"

The Complete Idiot's Guide to Sewing Illustrated will help you learn all the basic skills necessary to start on your way to being part of this new renaissance in sewing and the fabric arts. It's my hope that the book will also dispense any fears you might have about your own lack of skill and inspire you to create your own clothes, gifts, home furnishings—whatever you can think of.

Even if you already know how to sew, you'll find many helpful tips and hints throughout. If you're an experienced sewer and have been looking for just the right book to give to someone new to sewing, this is the book that will guide them on their journey.

Soon they, too, will see that creating home furnishings and a closet full of new clothes is only a matter of mastering a few basic skills and combining them with the selection of fabrics and trim.

A whole new world awaits! Let's get sewing.

How to Use This Book

This book is divided into six parts:

Part 1, "What Your Home Economics Teacher Didn't Teach You," gives an overview of all the tools and fabrics you'll need to create the projects in this book.

Part 2, "Starting Simply—Simply Starting," takes you from hand-stitching to machine-stitching through all the basic types of seams and hems.

Part 3, "Easy Home Projects," helps you start redecorating your home right away with directions for everything from pillows to drapes.

Part 4, "Creating Your New Wardrobe," teaches you everything you need to start creating garments from a pattern.

Part 5, "No Pattern? No Problem!" gives you the basics for creating basic garments without patterns. Here's where you can let your imagination go!

Part 6, "The Joy of Giving," contains patterns for nine easy gifts to make for your friends and family.

You'll also find several appendixes filled with other helpful information and resources.

Extras

Many sidebars in this book provide additional information and helpful tips:

Sew You Say
Here you find the definitions of frequently used words spoken by people who sew.

Cut It Out!
In sewing, you're bound to hit a few snags. These warnings might help keep you from getting all tangled up.

Fringe Benefits
There's usually more than one way to do the same thing. Some are tips your grandmother might have taught you; some might come about because of new technologies. Check out the Fringe Benefits for hints and helps on alternative strategies.

I'll Be Darned
The history of sewing is as old as humankind. Here you'll find some interesting snippets and stories about people and events that have influenced the current art of sewing.

Acknowledgments

Thanks and appreciation go to Calico Fabrics of Hatfield, Massachusetts, who invited my photographer and me to freely wander around their great fabric store and take pictures, many of which are found in the first few chapters. Also thanks and appreciation to Clotilde for allowing us to use pictures of notions from her website catalog.

Thanks to Barbara Conn of Yes Photography, who took more than 500 pictures for this book. I could not have written this book in such a timely fashion if she hadn't been there at any time of the day or night to take more pictures.

Thanks also go to John Maruskin, who helped with some of the illustrations.

I would also like to thank two young women, Jennifer Turner and Morgan Lobo, who took the time from their busy schedules of work and mothering to read the first few chapters and help me get off on the right track.

Special Thanks to the Technical Reviewer

The Complete Idiot's Guide to Sewing Illustrated was reviewed by an expert who double-checked the accuracy of what you'll learn here, to help us ensure that this book gives you everything you need to know about sewing. Special thanks are extended to Phyllis Van De Keere.

Phyllis Van De Keere is a graduate of Purdue University with a degree in home economics education. She has been a 4-H clothing instructor for 15 years and has owned her own custom clothing and alterations business for about 20 years.

Trademarks

All terms mentioned in this book that are known to be or are suspected of being trademarks or service marks have been appropriately capitalized. Alpha Books and Penguin Group (USA) Inc. cannot attest to the accuracy of this information. Use of a term in this book should not be regarded as affecting the validity of any trademark or service mark.

In This Part

What Your Home Economics Teacher Didn't Teach You

It's impossible to paint a house without a paintbrush, paint, and a ladder. So it is with sewing. Before you begin, you need some basic tools. You can't sew a seam if you don't have a needle, some thread, and some fabric.

In Part 1, you'll learn about the basic tools you need for sewing plus some fun extras that will help you fill your sewing basket. There's also an overview of the wide variety of fabrics available to you.

In This Chapter

- ◆ Discovering the joys of sewing
- ◆ Claiming your creative talents
- ◆ Adorning yourself
- ◆ Decorating your home

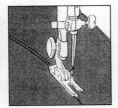

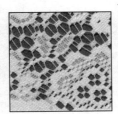
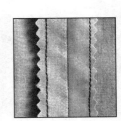

Chapter 1

Why Sew?

People ask me how I have time to sew. We all have time or should take time from our busy lives for some personal recreation time. One way to do that is to find a satisfying and exciting hobby. Sewing is my hobby. Not only can I be creative and design and make beautiful or fun outfits for myself, but I can also decorate my home with unique and wonderful not-to-be-found-in-any-store creations. You can, too.

If you have never sewn a stitch in your life or do not own a spool of thread or a sewing machine, this book will get you started making something for yourself or your home. Even if you know how to sew, you will find many handy hints and several do-it-now projects in these pages. If you have put away your sewing machine because you can't seem to find time to use it, it's time to get it out. Find your sewing machine in the back of the closet, dust it off, oil it up, and get back in the seam of things.

Sewing Is Part of the Human Story

Sewing is more than just making something to wear. Sewing is one of humanity's most ancient skills. For more than 20,000 years, our ancestors have decorated their bodies and their living spaces. At first, they used their bodies as canvases, covering themselves with intricate, dyed artwork. As time went on, other materials, primarily animal skins, became popular as high fashion. Early people used these skins as clothing, from simple leg coverings tied with a piece of leather to elaborately decorated tunics, as well as loincloths, shoes, boots, pants, gloves, and head coverings. They also made walls and covered their doorways with hangings.

In every civilization and throughout all of history, men and women have adorned themselves and their homes; sometimes simply, sometimes in the most flamboyant ways. We today are no different!

Sewing Is Fun and Practical

Clothing serves two primary functions. First, it's functional. Clothes not only protect people from the weather, but in some cases, clothing also protects people from harm, like bulletproof vests and firefighters' uniforms.

Second, we wear clothes as a means of decorating our bodies. Clothes are a way of making a statement about who we are. Certainly, during our dating years, we dress to be noticed, especially by potential partners.

Today the fashion industry provides good-quality clothes in every price range. So why sew when it is so easy to go to the mall or go online and select from a nearly infinite array of different types of clothes from fancy shoelaces to shirts, from wedding dresses to baby bibs?

The same is true with home décor. Why make something when you can buy almost anything at the mall or online?

One reason to sew is because it is fun. It is intoxicating to take a few yards of fabric and create a dress, a pair of pants, a pillow, or a table runner and then be able to say, "Look what I made." There is something natural about making your own clothes and home decorations, whether you make them from the skins of animals or from materials woven from wool, flax, cotton, or silk.

Sewing for the holidays adds color to your home.

Sewing, along with knitting, crocheting, needlework, and a host of other crafts using fabrics and fibers, is experiencing a renaissance. For a few decades, some of the home economic skills were seen as "women's work" and were shunned by the younger generations. Many high schools offered home economics courses, but they were electives, and not chosen by many students. Many modern women turned away from learning the skills their grandmothers used every day. Thankfully, the tide is turning. Now, under the glorious title of "fiber arts," these ancient skills are regaining popularity.

One of the joys of sewing is that it is both creative and practical. With just a few basic sewing skills, anyone can add a creative touch to his or her home décor. In an hour or two, and using the most basic skills, you can make a pillow to add color and style to any room in your home. You can even easily make elaborate-looking draperies.

I'll Be Darned

Believe it or not, drapes and curtains are some of the simplest items to make. If you can measure and sew a straight seam by hand or with a machine, you can make simple drapes and curtains. Most curtains and drapes are only hemmed rectangles of fabric.

In many cases, sewing for yourself saves money. This isn't always the case, but if you are a good shopper and enjoy looking for sales on fabrics and patterns, you should be able to make most clothes and home decorations for less than what you would pay in the store or online. Believe it or not, you can make an elegant wedding dress for around $300.

Fringe Benefits

You can save money by using one pattern many times and varying the fabric or style. Most patterns include variations such as a choice of different necklines or sleeves. Some even include directions for a blouse, a skirt, long pants, maybe even short pants, a jacket, or a vest—all in the same envelope.

Sewing Is Creative and Inventive

Looking back over the centuries of fashion, it is hard to imagine that most clothes were made by hand by a few tailors and seamstresses without the aid of sewing machines and with very few *notions*. There were no zippers until the 1930s. Snaps and hook and eyes are also relatively recent inventions. As technology changed, so did the art of sewing.

Sew You Say

Notions include a wide variety of items and tools, such as pins, thread, zippers, buttons, and scissors, that help you with your sewing projects. (See Chapter 2 for more on notions.)

Creating isn't limited to designing a unique skirt or blouse. People invent tools and notions that make sewing easier all the time.

In 1797, Mrs. Samuel Slater of Rhode Island developed a new way to spin thread. A decade later, Mary Kies of Killingly, Connecticut, invented an efficient way to weave straw hats. Sarah Boone, one of the first African Americans to receive a patent, invented an ironing board that made it easier to press collars and cuffs for dresses and very similar to ones still in use today. (Sarah received her patent in 1892.) In 1966, Stephanie Kwolek created the process that led to the discovery of a material named Kevlar. Sewing machines did not become popular until the mid-1850s, and machines powered by electricity did not go on the market until the early 1900s.

Many fabric stores display all their notions on a wall.

Hundreds of inventions over the years have made sewing easier. My great-grandmother and yours probably never heard of *iron-on no-sew* hems or *liquid glue* for putting together all kinds of seams and hems. With these inventions, it is now possible to make a pair of exotic drapes for your living room in about 45 minutes—without ever touching a needle, a sewing machine, or thread!

Sewing Is Meditative

Sewing can be meditative and relaxing. It's not the same as sitting in a hot bath with lots of sweet-smelling bubbles, but it can be relaxing and soothing nonetheless. Hand-sewing especially provides a great opportunity to sit, listen to quiet music, think, and rest. As a meditative practice, hand-sewing works best when sewing long, uncomplicated seams, hemming curtains, or quilting. What could be more wonderful than having an excuse to sit by yourself for an hour in a comfortable chair with a cup of hot tea, listen to music, and be able to say to all the demanding voices in one's life, "Don't bother me, I'm busy sewing!" Even if no voices are demanding your time, there is still something incredibly relaxing and meditative about hand-sewing.

No One Else Has Anything Like It

Another enticing reason to sew is the satisfaction of knowing that no one else on the planet will be wearing what you are wearing. Every clothing chain store in the United States carries the same lines. Granted, there are some regional variations (it's unlikely that you will find heavy winter jackets in shopping malls in Miami!) and also some color variations (the lighter, brighter colors tend to show up in stores located in warmer climates). For the most part, though, the clothes are all the same. If you want to really express the unique you, making your own clothes is one of the ways you can do it.

The pockets in these pants go all the way to the bottom cuff and hold lots of stuff.

What Do You Want to Create?

The sky is really the limit! You can make anything you want. You can use any fabric you want. You can make something plain or fancy. You can start with a quick and easy project like a pull-on hang-around-the-house dress. You can make something for your home, like new drapes or a few throw pillows. Go to your local fabric store, look through the pattern books, pick a pattern and some fabric, and get sewing.

You can sew many projects in very little time. This pillow only took 30 minutes to make.

The Least You Need to Know

◆ With minimal skill, you can make a pair of drapes—or almost anything else you can think of or find a pattern for.

◆ Sewing can help you save money on a new wardrobe.

◆ You can dazzle your friends with your creativity.

◆ Sewing can be a meditative practice.

In This Chapter

◆ Filling your sewing basket

◆ Finding old sewing accessory standbys

◆ Getting new notions

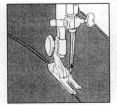

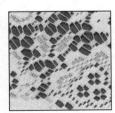
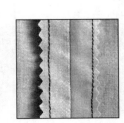

Chapter 2

A Paper of Pins and Other Necessities

No matter what the activity, it is always a good idea to have everything you need on hand before you start a project. It can be frustrating to have to keep running out to the store when you're in the middle of something—not to mention it's a waste of precious time. Sewing is no different.

If you have a large space designated for your sewing supplies, you might want to acquire everything you will ever need for sewing—if you haven't done that already. I'm a notion junkie. Every day I find new *gizmos* and *gotta-haves*. However, many of us have only a small space or a tiny closet for our sewing tools and supplies. In this case, you will need to be more selective.

For those of you who are new to sewing and somewhat overwhelmed by the incredible array of sewing notions and tools available, let's begin with the very basics you'll need.

Your Sewing Basket

First, you'll need some sort of container. In the old days, baskets were the container of choice. Today we have many choices. A clear plastic box about the size of a shoe box and with a snap-on lid is a good choice. You can start with one. It will hold everything you need to begin with. Then, as you gather more notions, you can acquire more boxes and begin to put similar things together.

Fringe Benefits

In spite of our good intentions to label, things do get in the wrong boxes. With clear containers, you can see in without having to open every box. You can also get small, clear plastic boxes that will fit in the larger box and hold pins, needles, or other small objects.

Start by selecting a sewing basket for all your notions and equipment.

Now you have your sewing basket (or clear plastic box). Time to stock it. At a minimum, it should contain the following:

- A good pair of sharp shears that are used only for cutting fabric
- A small pair of scissors for clipping and trimming
- Straight pins
- A tape measure
- A variety pack of hand-sewing needles
- A variety pack of sewing machine needles, if you have a sewing machine
- A spool of white all-purpose cotton-wrapped polyester thread

Some other handy items to put in your box include the following:

- A pincushion with an emery strawberry
- A thimble
- A seam ripper
- Other colors of thread, including black
- A ruler
- A seam gauge
- A needle threader

Every person who has ever sewn will have a different list of what he or she thinks are sewing-basket essentials. Eventually, you will know what items you absolutely need and which ones you can live without.

Cut It Out!

To keep your scissors sharp, do not use them to cut paper, cardboard, or aluminum foil. Also, try not to use them as pliers or wire cutters. If you have children or other people living in your home, you might even want to hide your sewing scissors!

On Pins and Needles

On one hand, pins are pins and needles are needles, and as a beginner sewer, you don't need every design of pin or needle. On the other hand, if you are planning to start your sewing career by making something that requires some fancy materials, you might want to buy specific pins to help you with that project. For example, using a big fat pin in satin might leave a hole in the fabric when the pin is removed.

Pins and Their Uses

Over the centuries, the names of pins have changed, as have the materials pins have been made of. The first pins were made out of bone, and today you'll find them in metals such as steel, stainless steel, and brass. Different pin manufacturers use the words *straight pins, dressmaker's pins,* and *silk pins* interchangeably, but don't let this confuse you. In most cases, it doesn't really matter!

The following is a brief description of the types of pins available and some of their uses. As with most aspects of sewing, you will find the ones that work best for you and the types of projects you want to make.

- For the all-purpose sewing basket, use *straight pins.* These pins are made from steel, stainless steel, or brass, are about $1\frac{1}{16}$ inches (2.6 cm) long, and usually have a flat head.

- If you are planning to use some delicate material such as silk or chiffon, *pleating pins* are a good choice. They are only 1 inch (2.5 cm) long and can be easily inserted into a *seam allowance.* They can be found with round or flat metal heads.

- For medium-weight fabrics, use *silk pins.* They come in a variety of lengths, from $1\frac{1}{16}$ inches to $1\frac{1}{4}$ inches, with a variety of different heads. Some heads are the typical flat heads, and others have different colored round glass (or plastic) heads. The latter are easier to grab and see when you drop them on the floor. Pins with large heads sometimes get stuck under the presser foot if you don't pull them out in time.

- Quilting pins are $1\frac{1}{4}$ inches long and are used for heavier materials.

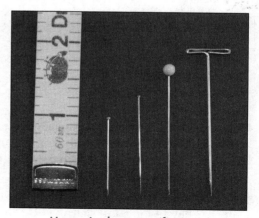

Many pins have specific uses.

Needles and Their Uses

The first needles were made out of animal bones. Today, most needles are made from brass, stainless steel, or nickel-plated steel. When looking for needles, be sure the ones you buy are rustproof.

Hand-sewing needles are numbered according to length—but counterintuitively. The smaller the needle, the larger the number, so a #4 is larger than a #9.

Some good hand-sewing needle choices include the following:

◆ *Sharps* are the best choice for general hand-sewing, with their round eyes, sharp points, and medium length.

◆ *Betweens* make some types of hand-sewing easier because they are shorter. Use a #5 for tacking and sewing on buttons, #7 or #8 for normal hand-sewing, and #9 or #10 for working on fine fabric. Betweens are the favorite choice of quilters because you can make fine stitches in heavy quilts.

◆ *Milliner's needles* are great to use for gathering stitches and *basting* because they are long with a round eye.

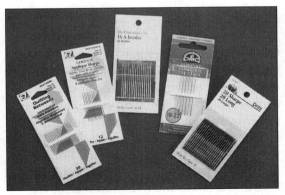

Always keep a variety of hand-sewing needles in your sewing basket.

When selecting sewing machine needles, buy a variety pack that includes fine needles for fine materials (9/65), medium needles (12/80), and heavier needles for heavier fabrics (18/110). The needles also have to fit the type of machine you have. Read the package. All sewing machine needles are not interchangeable. Many needles are color coded, so save the packages.

Some sewing machines are equipped to use a twin needle, which is two needles on one shaft. If your machine is so equipped, use this kind of needle for sewing decorations.

As with hand-sewing, use a ballpoint sewing machine needle when sewing on knits, stretchy material, and silk satin.

> **Sew You Say**
>
> **Basting** is a type of sewing that uses long stitches to hold several pieces of fabric together temporarily. Because the temporary stitches are so long, it's easier to remove them after the permanent stitches have been made.

◆ *Ballpoint needles* are used when sewing on knits. Other needles tend to cut the fibers, whereas ballpoint needles slip between the threads.

◆ *Crewel needles* are used mostly for embroidery. They're long and sharp, with a long eye.

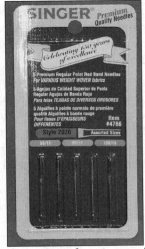

You will need a variety of sewing machine needles.

Cut It Out!

Throw out your dull pins and needles. Dull needles and pins cause some fibers to break or split, creating holes in the fabric. Throw out sewing machine needles after you've sewn a few projects, and especially after you have hit a pin!

Through the Eye of the Needle

If you want a fun party game, give everyone a needle and some thread, and see who can thread the needle first. Be sure the needles are the same size and the thread is cut, not broken.

Threading needles is either fun or frustrating. As a game among your friends, it can be quite hilarious, but it becomes very frustrating after several minutes of poking, sucking, licking, and cutting, when you *still* can't get the thread through the eye of the needle. Fortunately, inventive minds have come up with several needle-threading solutions.

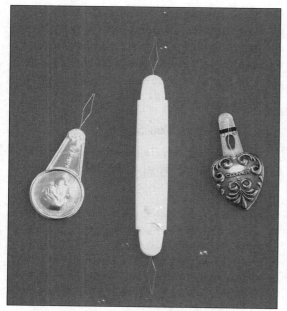

Needle threaders save you time (and sometimes your eyes!) when you're trying to thread a needle.

Pincushions

You have a variety of ways to keep your pins handy. The traditional pincushion looks like a red tomato. However, creative people have designed a host of different kinds of pincushions, all with the purpose of keeping pins ready for use, in one place, and not on the floor. The red tomato pincushion often comes with an attached emery strawberry. The emery strawberry is used to clean and sharpen needles and pins.

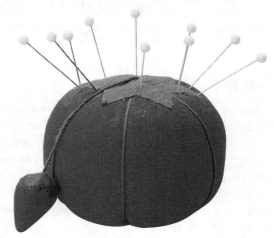

The red tomato is a traditional pincushion. Note the attached emery strawberry.

Many sewers like to use a wrist pincushion. These are great if you are using a lot of pins that you keep putting in and taking out of the fabric. Wrist pincushions are also great if your cutting table is far away from your sewing table and the pincushion always seems to be in the other place!

Cut It Out!

Don't store hand-sewing needles in your pincushion. Because they do not have heads, the needles often slide all the way into the cushion. You'll lose the needles in the cushion, and they'll poke out in odd places, creating a finger-pricking danger.

Wrist pincushions are great if you need to move around while you work.

Thimbles

Thimbles come in a variety of designs and sizes, from 6 to 12. The thimble most people imagine is the metal "cap" worn snugly on the middle finger of the sewing hand, but that's not the only kind available. Some thimbles are made of leather with a small metal circle that you use to push the needle. Others are made of plastic and are open in the back.

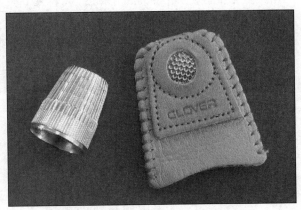

Find a thimble you like and that fits well.

I'll Be Darned

Thimbles were originally made of stone, bronze, bone, or ivory, and early humans used them to push bone needles through animal skins. In the sixteenth and twentieth centuries, thimbles were valued as objects of art. They served as love tokens during Victorian times and were given as engagement gifts. Often a woman's status could be determined by the type of thimble she wore. Paul Revere made a gold thimble for his daughter, Maria. In 1856, with the addition of some acid and zinc, a thimble became a miniature electric cell that generated enough current to send a signal across the Atlantic Ocean in a second.

If you have very long fingernails, it might be difficult to keep the traditional thimble on your finger. Try one of the other designs.

A Cut Above

Good-quality cutting tools are essential for good sewing. It is also necessary to keep your cutting tools sharp. There is almost nothing worse or more frustrating than trying to cut a piece of fabric with dull *scissors* or *shears*.

Sew You Say

Scissors and *shears* differ slightly. The finger holes on scissors are the same size, but the finger holes on shears are different sizes. One is round (for your thumb), and the other is oblong (for the rest of your fingers). Scissors are straight from the handle to the point, but shears are bent where the handles meet the blade so it is easier to cut fabric that's lying on a surface. The bent design also helps relieve pain in the thumb joint from extended use.

Shears and Scissors

Look at the cutters section of your fabric store, and you'll find all sizes and styles of scissors and shears. You need at least one pair of dressmaker's shears. They range in size from 7 to 12 inches. The idea is that smaller shears fit smaller hands, but some people with small hands prefer the longer blades. Choose shears or scissors that fit your hand and feel good to you.

Shears also have different weights. Heavierweight shears work better for heavier materials. Shears with a serrated edge, like a serrated kitchen knife, work well on knits.

You'll also find a variety of shears with nonstraight blades. Pinking shears, for example, have a jagged edge and are often used to finish seams and help prevent fraying. There are also shears with a scalloped edge rather than the traditional zigzag edge. These are used mostly for paper cutting and scrapbooking.

Pinking shears are easily recognizable by their jagged teeth.

Every sewing basket needs a pair of small, sharp scissors, especially a pair that has one pointed blade and one rounded blade. These are easier to use than shears for trimming seams, particularly *facings*. They are also easier to use when clipping a curved seam.

Newcomers to the scissors market are electric scissors. They do zip along, but it takes some practice not to slip or slide off the line, especially on curves.

Rotary Cutters and Cutting Mats

Rotary cutters are used for cutting many straight pieces at the same time. They are particularly useful for cutting pieces for quilts and save time by cutting through many layers at once. Rotary cutters look like pizza cutters, and you line them up next to a thick ruler and can easily cut straight lines in fabric.

When using a rotary cutter, you also need a cutting mat to protect your table or work surface. A cutting mat is made of a special material that "heals" itself when it's cut. Cutting mats come in a variety of sizes and are marked in inch grids, making it easy to cut strips and squares. Many have diagonal lines to aid in cutting bias strips, and some are marked with different shapes like triangles, squares, hearts, and diamonds.

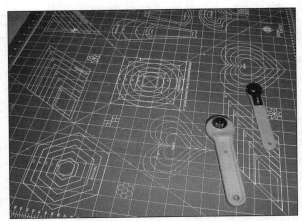

Rotary cutters are great for cutting stacks of cloth in straight lines.

Seam Rippers

Seam rippers might sound menacing, but you really have to have one in your basket. Everyone sews a seam in the wrong place. Everyone has put wrong pieces of patterns together. Everyone has been confused about which side was the right side of the material. Everyone has made two right fronts of a blouse. The only solution is to rip it out or unsew the seam. The easiest way to do that is with a seam ripper. This little gadget is very sharp with a very sharp point!

Seam rippers are also helpful for cutting the hole in a button hole, if you are very careful.

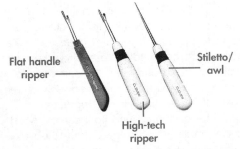

Flat handle ripper

Stiletto/ awl

High-tech ripper

Seam rippers can be a sewer's best friend.

> **Cut It Out!**
> Be careful when using a seam ripper because it is easy to cut the fabric instead of the thread.

All Snarled Up: Thread

When you decide on a sewing project, you'll need to find the fabric you want to use to make the project and then find the right thread. The best all-around, all-purpose thread is cotton-wrapped polyester. It is good for hand-sewing and machine-sewing on almost all fabrics. You can also use 100 percent *mercerized cotton thread* on all natural fibers. The 100 percent cotton is not good for knits because it doesn't have much stretch.

> **Sew You Say**
> **Mercerized cotton thread** is thread that has been chemically treated to shrink it and make it take dye more easily.

If you are using a very lightweight fabric or are doing machine embroidery, try an extra-fine cotton-wrapped polyester thread.

Quilters tend to choose a strong cotton thread because it does not tangle, knot, or unravel during hand-sewing.

Extra-heavy-duty thread is used for upholstery and drapes and for sewing on buttons.

> **Cut It Out!**
> I recommend beginning sewers stick to the basic types of thread.

In most store thread displays, the thread is organized first by kind and then by color. Find the kind of thread you want and then look for the color. If you can't find exactly the right color and you are confronted with a slightly darker or a slightly lighter shade, go with the slightly darker shade.

Verify the kind of thread by reading the label on the top of the spool. Sometimes threads get put back in the wrong place. It is frustrating to get home with the perfect color of thread, only to discover that you accidentally picked up the wrong weight thread for your project.

When picking thread from the wide variety available, select the one that works best with the fabric you're using.

Measuring Up

"Measure twice, cut once" is a good rule to keep in mind. One cannot measure too often! There are many things to measure when sewing and many tools to help do the measuring. Although it is possible to live and sew with only a 12-inch ruler, sewing is a lot more fun—and a lot easier—if you invest in some good and accurate measuring tools.

I'll Be Darned

Don't assume every measuring tool measures up. Once when I was making a quilt, I couldn't figure out why the border didn't fit the top I'd made. I measured and remeasured. I used a ruler to measure each quilt square. They appeared to be exactly right. I used a tape measure to measure the border, and those appeared to be exactly right, too. I finally figured out that the tape measure was off by $\frac{1}{32}$ inch. That meant it was off by more than 3 inches for the 108 inches of the quilt!

Measuring Tools

When you're making clothes, you'll need a tape measure to determine the size of the body you are sewing for. Use a fabric or flexible plastic tape measure, not the metal kind used by carpenters!

You'll need yard sticks or meter sticks when you lay out the pattern on a piece of fabric and you want to be sure the grain line is correct. Rulers can also be used for this purpose, but they might be too short for some applications.

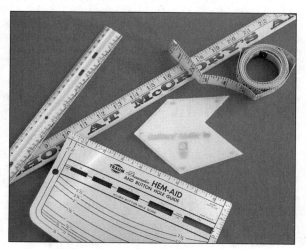

Use good-quality and accurate measuring tools. (You'll be glad you did!)

Cut It Out!

Check the end of your measuring tools nearest the 1 inch mark. Sometimes the zero mark is not at the very edge of the ruler. It is better to use a measuring tool where the edge of the tool is zero.

Seam Gauges

Seam gauges are useful when you're pinning hems and making pleats. They are usually made of plastic or metal and have a sliding marker.

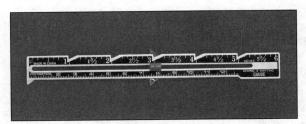

A seam gauge is a handy tool to have in your sewing basket.

See-Through Rulers

See-through rulers are made of clear plastic, with the markings etched into or painted onto the plastic. These are great for seeing what you are doing! Use them for straight rotary cutting or for checking grain lines. They also help with button hole placement.

On the Mark

When you're working with a pattern, you'll need to transfer the markings from a pattern to the fabric. One way to do this is to use a marking tool. The type of fabric determines, to some extent, which kind of marking tool you should use.

Chalk is easy to use when transferring pattern marks to your fabric. However, it is best used when you are going to immediately sew what you have just cut out. If you plan to mark now and sew later, try a different marker because chalk easily brushes off and the marks might disappear or at least be blurred by the time you get back to it.

Marking pencils contain a special lead made for marking fabric. The pencils are particularly good if you have only small marks, such as dots or crosses, to make. They are not so good for drawing lines because the fabric often wrinkles if the pencil is dragged along the fabric for a long distance. The pencil usually has a brush on the end, which is useful for removing marks.

Some marking pens contain ink that is supposed to disappear within 48 hours or wash out easily. Read the package! If in doubt, test the marking pen or pencil on a scrap of fabric before using it on your project.

Cut It Out!

Some marking tools are not good on material that is dry clean only, and some liquid marking pencils set in when the article is pressed. Read the package!

All Steamed Up

It is difficult to say which tool is the most important tool you need to create professional and satisfying sewing projects, but my vote might have to go to the iron. Pressing as you go is very, very important. Whenever a pattern says "Press," do it. Do not skip this step.

To press as you go, you will need a very good steam iron and an ironing surface that is available for the whole time you are sewing. It also helps to have your pressing area close to your sewing area.

Irons and Pressing

Find a good steam iron that will work for all kinds of fabrics. Always press every seam open or to one side if instructed to so by the pattern. Also always press on the wrong side of the fabric. This prevents "iron shine" on the good side. Be sure to remove all pins before pressing so you will not scratch the surface of your iron.

Test a small sample of any fabrics you are unsure of before pressing the whole garment. Some synthetics and silks will shrivel up or even melt if the iron is too hot. Not only will you destroy your fabric, but you will also wreck the surface of your iron.

Cut It Out!

Do not press velvet! If you need to press velvet, use a special velvet ironing board. These are covered with vertical steel needles, and the velvet is placed, pile side down, on top of the needles and then pressed from the back. This prevents squashing of the velvet pile.

Pressing Cloths

Use pressing cloths to prevent iron shine on fabrics such as wool. Pressing cloths are also useful when pressing fusible interfacings. You might want to purchase a special pressing cloth, but you can also use a clean, nonpile dish towel or a single-layer diaper (if you can find a fabric one).

Ironing Boards

You have to have an ironing board! If you do not have a traditional ironing board or do not have room for one, there are small ironing boards that sit on the table. Ironing boards also come in large and rectangular sizes. These are terrific for large projects such as quilts, but they do not work so well for getting into corners, such as the top of a sleeve.

For corners and seams, try a small, hardwood point presser. The wood holds the steam and heat and helps make really crisp-looking points and seams.

Hamming It Up!

Ironing boards or pressers allow you to press crisp seams, but they really work well only on straight seams. For curves, darts, and tops of sleeves, you need a ham, a roll, or a mitt.

A sewing ham is a very hard, rounded cushion. Some are shaped like a real ham, hence the name. One side is covered with cotton; the other side is covered with wool. Hams make pressing curves much easier. Mitts work the same way, although it is possible to put a mitt on one hand to increase your flexibility. A seam roll is similar to a ham but is roll-shape instead to ham-shape.

Use a ham when you need to press a curved surface, like the top of a sleeve.

What a Notion!

In addition to the tools described earlier in this chapter, many more notions can help you with your sewing projects. Again, as with almost everything related to sewing, there are myriad options. Don't be afraid to experiment! Find what works for you, then more or less stick with that and don't worry about everything else.

Tapes and Trims

Bias tape and seam binding are two different notions:

◆ *Bias tape* is strips of woven material cut at a 45-degree angle to the *selvage*. Because the tape is cut on an angle—or on the bias—it has give and will go around curves easier. Bias tape does not fray, is preshrunk, and is pressed and folded from each side so the edges meet in the center. Common widths range from ⅜ to ⅞ inches. Bias tape is used when finishing edges, especially curves. It also can be used to make *casings*, trim, and facings.

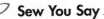

Sew You Say

The fabric **selvages** are the edges of the material that run the length of the fabric. They come already finished and will not unravel or fray.

A **casing** is made by turning over a hem or by attaching a piece of bias tape to an article so that a ribbon, cord, or elastic can be threaded through. Casings are also made at the top of curtains for the curtain rod to fit through.

◆ *Seam binding* is not cut on the bias, and, therefore, it has no give. The primary use of seam binding is to finish a hem. It is also used on a seam or a corner that might need reinforcement.

◆ *Lace seam bindings* are similar to seam binding, only they look like lace and add a decorative touch to the hem.

◆ *Twill tape* is used to reinforce seams.

◆ *Elastic* comes in many different widths and is used for waist, ankle, and wrist bands as well as necklines. Usually sold in black or white, it comes in a variety of types, depending on the intended use. For example, nonroll elastic works well in waistbands.

◆ *Piping* is a cord that's been covered with bias strips and is used to trim pillows and other items where you want an emphasized or decorative edge. Piping comes in a variety of colors and thicknesses. It is easy to place the piping in a seam before it is sewed.

A wide variety of laces, ribbons, braids, beading, and other trims is available to add texture, interest, and a unique touch to any article you create. Take a field trip to your local fabric store and just get acquainted with all the possible trims and tapes. Push the limits of your imagination. Pick out some interesting trim and figure out what you can make with it!

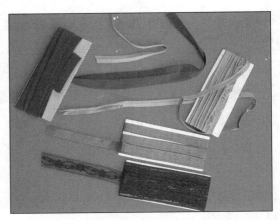

You'll find a wide variety of tapes at your fabric or craft store.

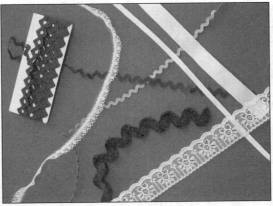

The number of trims available is almost infinite!

I'll Be Darned

In the early days of iron-on tapes, I tried a seam binding that was supposed to save all the trouble of sewing. It consisted of two tiny parallel strips of adhesive: one line to go on the hem, the other on the garment. It worked fine—until the first washing! Today's iron-on hem material is much more durable, and if it does come undone in the wash, it can be reapplied with a little pressing.

Fasten Up!

Buttons come in two basic styles: with holes and with shanks. The buttons with holes usually have either 2 or 4 holes.

Find a nice jar with a wide mouth, like a mayonnaise jar, and keep all your extra buttons in it. You can also put in all the buttons that come with store-bought clothes. Knowing where the extra buttons are comes in handy if you lose one.

I'll Be Darned

Fabric stores used to carry loose buttons. A few independent stores still do, but now buttons are carded and hang on a display stand. I always seem to need one more button than is on a card, so I have to buy more buttons than I need.

Buttons add decoration to any project.

Hooks and Eyes

Hooks and eyes usually come in black or silver and a variety of sizes. They are also available in white for wedding dresses. Hooks and eyes come in three varieties: hooks with rounded or looped eyes, hooks with straight eyes called bars, and flat hooks with bars. Use large sizes for heavy materials that get a lot of use and small ones for lighter fabrics. Use round eyes when two edges of fabric just come together. Use straight bars when the edges overlap. Hooks with bars work better on waistbands. If you need to use a hook and eye where the eye is going to be seen, it may be desirable to make a hand-worked thread eye (I'll tell you how in Chapter 4).

I'll Be Darned

Sometime during the thirteenth century, British commoners developed eyelets through which they laced rope or cord to hold their clothes together and their pants up. These eyelets and brooches prevailed as fasteners until the seventeenth century, when a German goldsmith turned the eyelets into buttons. Gradually, buttons were made from many natural elements, including shells, polished rocks, and fine-grained wood. Many buttons also held precious stones.

British sailors are credited with the invention of the hook-and-eye fastener. American Puritans claimed buttons were too gaudy and soon condemned them as sinful, preferring to use only hook-and-eye fasteners.

In 1893, Whitcomb Judson patented the Clasp Lock, which was complicated and not as durable as the hook-and-eye fastener but was the precursor to the zipper for shoes.

Snaps

Snaps also come in a variety of sizes and three colors: black, silver, and white. Snaps are used when fabrics overlap and when there is not much strain constantly pulling on them.

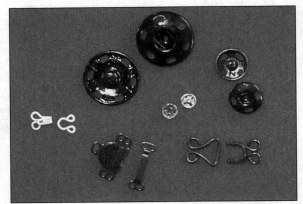

Fasten it up with snaps and also hooks and eyes.

I'll Be Darned

In 1948, after watching plant burrs stick to themselves, George DeMaestal accomplished the same thing by using strips of nylon and a strip of uncut pile. This led to the 1955 invention of hook and loop tape under the brand name Velcro.

Hook and Loop Tape

Hook and loop tape is great for some types of enclosures, but not all. For example, hook and loop tape would be a poor choice on silk or satin. The hooks are very indiscriminate; they grab at everything. This causes some fabrics to fray or to get a run when one of the fibers is caught and pulled.

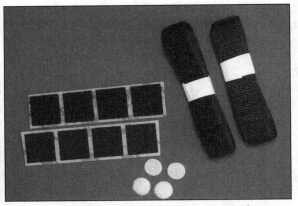

You can use hook and loop fasteners as an alternative fastening option in many situations.

Zippers

Zippers came into fashion as a fastener in the 1930s—less than 100 years ago. Original zippers were made of metal, but now they are mostly polyester. Metal zippers are still used in jeans and jackets and on other heavier materials. Zippers are usually closed or stopped at one end and open at the other. Some zippers are stopped at both ends and are used in side seams and sometimes on pillows. Some zippers are open at both ends; these are called separating zippers and are used mostly for jackets and coats. There are also invisible zippers. These zippers are put into the article being sewed in such a way that the zipper stitching doesn't show and it's hard to tell that a zipper is in the seam at all.

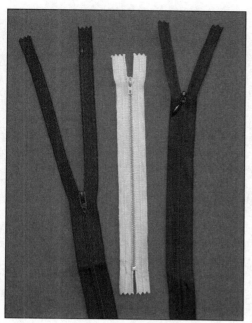

Zippers are very popular fastening options.

I'll Be Darned

In 1930, B. F. Goodrich coined the word *zipper* and used them on boots and tobacco pouches. French tailors soon began putting zippers instead of buttons in men's trousers.

The Least You Need to Know

◆ Every sewer needs a sewing basket of essential supplies. (What you consider *essential* is up to you.)

◆ To keep your sewing scissors and shears sharp, use them only to cut fabric.

◆ Hundreds of notions are available to help with your sewing projects.

◆ Throw out your pins and needles as soon as they lose their sharpness.

◆ Seam rippers are a sewer's best friend.

In This Chapter

◆ Discovering the wide variety of available textiles

◆ Identifying different kinds of fabrics

◆ Selecting fabrics appropriate for your project

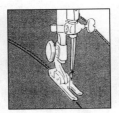

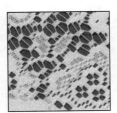

Chapter 3

It's All Material

Go to a fabric store, and you can easily be overwhelmed by the wide variety of types of material that are available to you. It's difficult to know what to look for or where to begin. There are so many colors, patterns, and textures!

Since World War II, with the introduction of synthetic-fiber fabrics, the number of different kinds of materials has sky-rocketed. To help make your selection simpler, most fabric can be categorized into a few groups. The fibers that are used to make fabrics—and, therefore, the fabrics themselves—are either all natural, all synthetic, or a combination of both.

Fabric Facts

There are hundreds of fabric choices, many variations on a theme, and new kinds of fabrics being created all the time. It is impossible to remember the names and properties of all of them, but don't worry—you don't have to. To make fabric selection a little less daunting, though, it is important to get an overview of a few fabric facts.

Natural fibers are those made directly from plants or animals, namely cotton, flax, wool, or silk (from silkworms). Some synthetic fibers include acetate, acrylic, nylon, Olefin, polyester, rayon, and triacetate. Many materials manufactured from synthetic fibers are made to simulate the natural fabrics.

Fibers are made into fabric in three basic ways: woven, nonwoven, and knitted.

I'll Be Darned

Flax, the fiber that is woven into linen, is considered the oldest natural textile fabric. It has been used as a textile since 5000 B.C.E. and was used by the ancient Egyptians for burial shrouds.

Northern Ireland and Belgium are the largest exporters of linen.

The oldest manufactured fiber is rayon, developed in 1910 by the American Viscose Company.

Warps, Wefts, and Weaves

Woven fabrics are made on looms. The fibers that get woven into fabric are first spun into yarn or thread. Some of this yarn is spun with long fibers, some with short fibers, and some with medium-length fibers.

On the loom, the lengthwise yarns are the *warp*. The across-the-loom threads are the weft (or *woof* or *fill*).

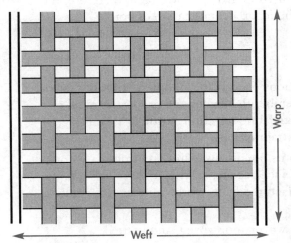

Woven fabric is made of warp and weft threads.

You can vary the weaving pattern to create different textures. Although the possibilities are almost endless, there are only a few basic weaves most commonly used for home decorating and clothing construction:

◆ *Plain weave* is the simplest of weaves. The warp and weft yarns are evenly spaced and interlaced in an alternating pattern. The weft yarn goes over one warp yarn and under one warp yarn across the width of the fabric. The weight of the fabric is determined by the weight of the yarn and the compactness of the weave. Some common plain weave materials include cotton calico, silk organza, and wool challis.

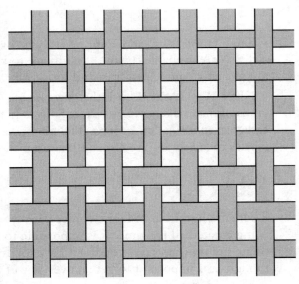

In plain weave, the warp and weft yarns are evenly spaced.

◆ *Basket weave* is the same as plain weave, except that two or more yarns are interlaced together, for example, over two and under two or over three and under three. The number of weft yarns woven over the warp is the same number as those gone under. The warp threads follow the same pattern.

In basket weave, two or more yarns are interlaced.

◆ In *twill weave,* instead of the yarns passing over and under an equal number of yarns as in plain weave or basket weave, the yarns pass over one yarn and then under two or more yarns. This makes the fabric look like it has a diagonal pattern woven into it and produces a very strong, durable fabric. Denim and gabardine are popular fabrics made in the twill weave pattern.

In twill weave, the yarns pass over one yarn and then under two or more yarns.

◆ *Ribbed weave* is the same as plain weave, except that the warp and weft yarns are of different weights. Broadcloth and poplin are common examples used in ribbed weave.

◆ *Satin weave* creates a smooth, lustrous fabric. The over and under pattern of the warp and woof yarns is set randomly. This causes the surface to look very smooth and shiny.

◆ *Pile weave* creates a fabric that has depth. Loops are woven into the fabric to create the pile. The loops can be left uncut like terrycloth or cut like velvet.

Terrycloth is an example of loop weave.

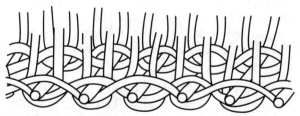

When the loops are cut, you get a velvetlike fabric.

◆ *Jacquard weave* is a patterned design that is produced on a special "jacquard-equipped" loom. Combinations of plain, twill, and satin weaves are used to create the design on a plain or satin-weave background.

In addition to the kind of weave, the weaves vary by how tightly or loosely the fabric is woven and what fiber is used. You can find natural fibers, synthetic fibers, or some sort of combination of those woven in a variety of ways and with different weights of threads and various tightness of weave. This creates a large number of possible variations of fabric. In addition, some fabrics are smooth, while others are rough. Some fabrics are stiff to the touch, and some are very soft. Some are heavyweight and some are light-weight; some are see-through, some opaque, and some translucent.

I'll Be Darned

In 1964, DuPont set a challenge to its chemists to make a fabric that would be as strong as Superman's. Stephanie Kwolek created the synthetic fiber that resulted in Kevlar. This material is so strong that it's used for bulletproof vests, fire fighters' uniforms, and even canoes!

Not only does every kind of fabric have a unique name, but there are even more variations within the same kind of fabric. For example, some cottons are labeled according to where the cotton was grown, and some silks differ depending on the diet of the silkworms. Some fabrics are named by the town where the fabric was first woven or by the name of the weaver who invented the weave. Don't let all these names scare you off.

One of the best things to do to familiarize yourself with fabric is to feel the fabric. It would be a rare event to go into a fabric store and find signs that said, "Do not touch." People who sew are by nature touchy-feely types. Don't be surprised if you hear something like this in a fabric store:

Clerk: May I help you?

Customer: Oh no, thank you, I'm just here for a feel.

With a little practice, you'll soon be able to tell one kind of fabric from another. Before synthetics, this was much easier to do. Still, with practice, you, too, can develop enough

skill to be able to say, "Oh, that's chintz!" or "Oh, that's chambray!" or "Oh, that's challis!"

Although creativity knows no limit, some fabrics work better for a given project than others. For example, pure silk satin is very expensive and works better for wedding dresses than for a toddler's play clothes!

Most woven fabric comes in two standard widths: 42 to 44 inches and 56 to 60 inches. You can occasionally find material that is narrower. There is also some very wide material called sheeting that's usually 70 or 90 inches and is used for making bed sheets.

I'll Be Darned

Broadcloth got its name because it was woven in widths wider than the at-the-time standard of 29 inches.

For all woven fabrics, it is very important to identify the *straight* of the material and the *bias*. The uncut, finished edge of the material is called the *selvage*. The selvage is presumed to be straight, but this isn't always true. The straight of the material is usually on the warp (lengthwise) threads. The weft threads are considered to be on the crosswise straight of the material. Sometimes the straight of the material is called the *grain* of the material. You can tell the grain or straight of the material by pulling on the fabric. If you pull on the straight of grain, the fabric will not give or stretch.

Sew You Say

The **grain** or **grain line** of woven fabric runs parallel to the edge of the fabric.

If there is give, then you have pulled on a bias. The bias is any direction that is not on the line of the warp or weft threads. If you pull on the bias, you will notice that the fabric stretches. The maximum stretch is at a 45-degree angle to the edge or selvage of the fabric. When directions call for cutting on the bias or laying the pattern on the bias or true bias, you should work on a line at a 45-degree angle to the edge of the material.

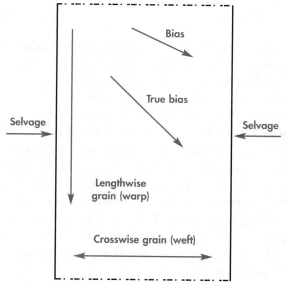

You must be able to identify the grain and bias of fabric.

Nonwoven Fabrics

Nonwoven fabrics are just that—nonwoven. The fabric is created by matting together fibers, either chemically by gluing, bonding, or melting, or mechanically by tangling the fibers together. Many *interfacings* are made from nonwoven material.

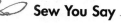

Sew You Say

An **interfacing** is a fabric layer used to stiffen and shape collars, cuffs, waistbands, tops of curtains, and other areas that need to stay crisp after several washings.

Knits

Knits are relatively recent arrivals on the fabric market. Although people have been knitting for eons, manufactured knitting is relatively new. Rather than have two yarns woven together as with woven fabric, knits have only one yarn that's knitted together just as a knitted scarf is.

Knits have stretch in all directions, and one advantage to knits is that an article of clothing made from a knit is usually very comfortable to wear. Because knits have a tendency to lose their shape after a while, they are probably not the best choice for items that should keep their shape, such as fitted trousers or long draperies.

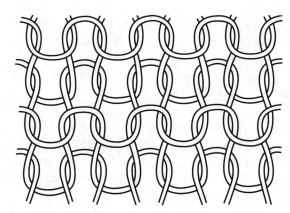

As the name suggests, knit weave looks like knitting.

There are several kinds of knits:

◆ *Single knits* include jersey, tricot, and cire. Use single knits if you want a lightweight, nicely draping look. Tricot is used mostly for lingerie. Single knits have a right and wrong side.

◆ *Double knits* are heavier and do not have a right side; both sides look exactly the same. Because double knits fall nicely, they are suitable for dresses, some kinds of pants, and skirts.

◆ *Sweater knits* look just like a knitted sweater.

◆ *Raschel knits* look like crochet or lace and usually need a lining.

Cut It Out!

If you're thinking of a knit for a pattern you're working on, be sure to check the pattern envelope to see if the project is suitable for knits. Most patterns will label the pattern as "suitable for knits" or "not recommended for knits." Knits do not work well for biased cut or circular skirts.

Cut It Out!

If material has been on a cardboard rectangular bolt for a long time or is in a dusty mill outlet store, it is often difficult to get the crease out of the fabric, especially if it has a dirt line. Be sure to check the creased edge by unrolling the fabric a few turns before you buy it. Check to see how dirty the crease is, too.

Reading Bolt Ends

Fabric comes on bolts. Bolts are either long rolled tubes about 60 inches long or rectangular cardboard frames about 10 inches wide and 24 inches long. Some fabrics, like satin, come on the long rolls to eliminate fold lines fabrics wrapped on the rectangular bolts get. Velvet is usually loosely hung by the selvage, not rolled or wrapped or folded, to prevent the pile from getting crushed.

Somewhere in most fabric stores, you will find fabric that is not on a bolt and might be labeled *flat fold*. Often these materials are upholstery fabrics, and sometimes they are ends of runs. Very often they are in a jumble and hard to look through.

On the end of the cardboard bolt is a label that gives most of the properties of the fabric. For example, you will find the name of the manufacturer, the type of material (100 percent cotton), how wide the fabric is, and usually something about how to care for it (Easy Care).

Don't get discouraged by the wide variety of fabric found in many stores. Most patterns make suggestions for the materials that will work best for a particular pattern. But remember, these are only suggestions. Be brave, move out of the groove, and follow your creative leanings.

Some fabric stores specialize in certain types of materials. For example, quilt stores mainly carry 100 percent cotton in thousands of colors and designs, but mostly only cotton. Some fabric stores specialize in only fancy fabric for weddings and evening wear.

If you don't really have time to shop around, or if going to a fabric store is problem, you can buy fabrics online. It helps to really know what you are looking for, though, because there are so many sites, just looking takes almost as much time as going to the store. On many sites, the colors that show on your screen aren't quite the same as they are when you open the package when you get it. Find a site you like and stick with it. That will save you time, and you will be pretty sure you will know what you are getting.

Most fabric is displayed on bolts. Be sure to check out the bolt end when picking fabric. It contains a great deal of helpful information.

I'll Be Darned

In some larger cities, you might be able to find factory outlets. In many of these outlets, tidiness is not a priority. Bolts of this and that are lined up floor to ceiling. These places are great if you just want to poke around, looking for the odd bargain.

Finishes

When you're selecting fabrics, consider the following:

- Will it wrinkle?
- Will it shrink?
- Does it need to be washed in any special way? Hand-wash only? Dry clean only? Warm water or cold water?
- Can it go in the dryer? Hot, cool, or warm setting?
- Does it need to be pressed? Can it be pressed?
- Is it flameproof? Flame retardant?
- What about stain-resistant qualities?

Your project might help you determine the kind of fabric finish you select. On the other hand, some fabric might dictate the project. If you fall in love with the color or pattern on a fabric that wrinkles badly, don't use it for a skirt. Make curtains with it instead.

Also, how much do you press your laundry? If you like to iron, then making a blouse out of a piece of fabric that needs pressing after every washing is great. However, if you hate to iron or have a tendency to put off ironing until next week, find material for your blouse that doesn't need a lot of extra care.

Making a pair of pajamas out of a dry-clean-only material is probably not the most practical of ideas. If you send your clothes out for dry cleaning every week, then go for it.

When making curtains or drapes, consider how much the material will fade. Almost all materials fade some, but some definitely will fade more than others. Even whites fade into yellow. If you find the perfect fabric for your drapes but are afraid it will fade, consider lining the curtains. This will cut down on the fading.

Fringe Benefits

The fabric bolt should give you an idea of the care the fabric needs, but here's a quick chart of some basic care instructions:

Fiber	Care
Acetate	Dry clean.
Acrylic	Hand- or machine-wash.
Cotton	Machine-wash.
Linen	Machine-wash, some dry clean.
Nylon	Hand- or machine-wash.
Polyester	Hand- or machine-wash.
Rayon	Hand- or machine-wash.
Silk	Dry clean; some hand-wash.
Wool	Dry clean; some are hand-wash in a soap designed for wools. Read the label!

When you go to the fabric store, look for some of these fabric finishes:

- *Bonding* is a process that makes fabric stronger by fusing together two kinds of fabric.
- *Carding and combing* removes dirt and other impurities from the fibers.
- *Colorfast* materials fade or run less than other fabrics.
- *Mercerized* fabrics are made from yarns that have been chemically treated to shrink them and to make them more able to hold dye.
- *Mildew-resistant* fabrics have been chemically treated to make them mold resistant.

- *Permanent press* fabrics require little or no pressing. It is difficult or nearly impossible to press out little puckers in fabric that has been treated with a permanent press finish. Even natural cotton acts like a synthetic when treated with this finish.
- *Soil-resistant* fabrics make particularly good tablecloths and napkins.
- *Waterproof* fabrics are usually coated with some form of rubber, resin, or plastic.
- *Water-resistant* fabrics do not absorb water, but instead allow it to pass through.

Special Fabric Considerations

When you start looking for fabric, in addition to the suggestions I gave you earlier in this chapter, you have a few considerations to ponder before making the first cut in the fabric.

Having a Nap

Corduroy is a good example of a fabric with a nap. If you run your hand down the grain of the material and then run your hand up the grain, you'll notice that the corduroy feels smooth in one direction and feels like you're pushing against the fabric in the other direction. It is just like rubbing the back of a cat: One way is smooth, and the other way is rough. This is called a *nap*, which means that one end is considered the top and the other end is the bottom. On fabric that doesn't have a nap, it doesn't matter which end is up.

On a pair of drapes, for example, it is important to have the nap going in the same direction on both panels and on all pairs if you're making more than one pair. For fabrics like corduroy or velvet, the color looks slightly different if one nap goes up and one nap goes down because the light is reflected differently from the smooth surface than from the rough.

Patterns will tell you if the article of clothing you are about to make is suitable for napped materials. More often than not, if you are using a fabric with a nap, you will have to buy more material. The back of the pattern envelope will tell you how much to buy.

> ### Fringe Benefits
>
> If you are using a pattern to make a pair of pants with material with a nap, it is important that all the tops of the pattern pieces are in the direction of the top of the material.

Other materials are treated as if they have a nap, but you can't feel the difference with your hand. Fabrics with pictures, especially flowers, often have a top or a bottom. Hold up a length of the fabric. Does it look right side up or upside down? Turn the fabric around and look again. If you can't tell a difference, it probably doesn't have a nap. However, if all the dinosaurs printed on the fabric are standing on their heads, then the fabric has a nap (and it's probably upside down, in this case—unless the dinosaurs are supposed to be standing on their heads!). You will have to plan how much you buy accordingly.

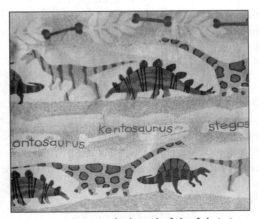

Be sure you know which end of the fabric is up and which is down.

Border Designs

Some fabrics have a decorative border along one selvage. The straight of the grain is then crosswise of the material, and this changes what is normally thought of as the width and the length. The pattern might be printed, woven, or embroidered.

Depending on your project, it is important to know where the bottom of the fabric is. With a border design, you probably want the bottom of the border to be the bottom of the skirt or curtain. Be sure to take into consideration the width of the border pattern. You might have to recalculate how much material you need. The pattern envelope might or might not tell you how much is required for a border design. It also might advise about whether the pattern is suitable for a border design.

Above the border, the fabric might be plain or might have an evenly placed smaller pattern. Fabric pieces that do not incorporate the border pattern should be placed here on the straight of the grain.

Cut border prints on the crosswise grain.

Stripes and Plaids

With stripes and plaids, it is important to place pattern pieces on the fabric so the plaids or stripes meet in an attractive way on seams. This requires some juggling of pattern pieces on the material—be sure to take the seam allowances into consideration, too. In some cases, you might want a certain line to be exactly at the bottom of a skirt or along the front edge opening of a jacket. Again, as with napped material, it will be necessary to buy extra yardage to have enough fabric for matching.

Remember to always keep the grain line straight, even though you might want to fudge on the grain line to keep the plaid or stripe lines straight. Resist the temptation. Always keep the grain line straight!

The Least You Need to Know

- Most fabric is all natural, all synthetic, or a combination of both.
- Fabric is woven, knitted, or nonwoven.
- Certain fabrics are better suited to a given project than other fabrics, and vice versa.
- Read the back of the pattern envelope to help determine what fabric to use.

In This Part

2

Starting Simply—Simply Starting

Part 2 begins with the basics of hand-stitching and nine patterns you can make by hand without a sewing machine.

If you'd rather sew by machine, I also describe the basic sewing machine, keeping in mind that there's a plethora of makes and styles today, including computer-driven embroidery machines.

From sewing a seam, to putting in a hem, to putting in a zipper, Part 2 covers all the basics you'll need to get started.

In This Chapter

- ◆ Learning a variety of hand-sewing stitches
- ◆ Mending store-bought clothes
- ◆ Sewing on buttons, snaps, hooks, and eyes

 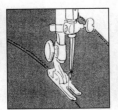   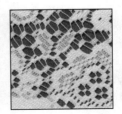 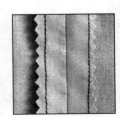

Chapter 4

In Stitches

Sewing is like walking. Once you get the hang of it, you wonder what all the fuss is about. Just like with walking, once you have mastered that basic skill, you then can run, jump, skip, and dance. So it is with taking up a needle and thread. At first, threading a needle might feel awkward. It might be overwhelming the first time you step foot in a fabric store. But here's the secret: There really are only a few very basic skills to practice.

In the next few chapters, you learn those few basic skills. With these skills, like threading a needle and sewing a simple seam, you will be equipped to run, jump, skip, and dance even if you do not have a fancy, well-stocked sewing room or an expensive machine.

The Ancient Art of Hand-Sewing

One thing we keep forgetting in this incredible age of technology and electronic devices is that, before all this stuff, we did things by hand! Everything a sewing machine can do, someone did by hand not too many years ago. Believe it or not, some things are easier to do by hand than with a sewing machine.

Granted, it might be true that using a sewing machine is faster, but it is also true that hand-sewing is soothing and meditative. I always look forward to the hand-sewing parts of a project. I would rather appliqué by hand than with a sewing machine. And although it is possible to quilt by machine, thousands of people love to sit and quilt by hand.

You don't need a sewing machine to make wonderful things for yourself and for your home. You might find that it is very pleasant to sit in a comfortable chair in the garden drinking a cup of hot tea, listening to the birds, smelling the flowers, and sewing a seam.

Needles and Thread

When hand-sewing, you need a needle, some thread, a small pair of scissors, and a thimble. Select a needle and some thread that will be appropriate for your project. Choose a needle that makes a hole as small as possible but is heavy enough to go through several layers of fabric without breaking.

When cutting a piece of thread for your needle, longer is not necessarily better. Cut the thread about 24 inches and definitely no longer than your arm. If the thread is too long, you run the risk of spending most of your time trying to untangle it! Also thread often wears out if it is pulled through the fabric too many times.

Thread the needle with or without a needle threader. If you're not using a threader, cut off any frayed ends. Cutting the thread on the diagonal helps. Thread the end that came off the spool first through the eye of the needle. For most sewing projects, you will use a single thread. Pull the thread through, but do not make them the same length. One should be about one-third shorter.

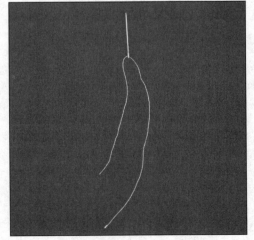

When you're threading a needle, the ends of the thread should be different lengths.

As you sew, you will begin to use up the long thread. Allow the shorter thread to slide through the needle gradually, keeping the shorter thread about one third shorter than the longer thread. If the shorter thread gets too long, you will soon discover that you're sewing with a double rather than single thread, and if it gets too short, the thread might slip out of the eye of the needle.

If you haven't finished the seam but are running out of thread, it's easy enough to stop and get more thread. Before you come to about 3 inches from the end of your thread, secure this length of thread and repeat the process with another thread (see the next section, "Making a Knot" for tips on tying off).

Occasionally, the thread will become twisted and start to tangle and knot with each stitch. Lift and hold the fabric upside down, let go of the needle, and let it spin to unravel itself. If the thread is short, be careful not to let the needle fall off the end of the thread!

> **Fringe Benefits**
>
> Many people run thread through beeswax. This makes the thread stronger and helps prevent tangles. Beeswax is available in most fabric stores.

Tying a Knot

Except when basting and gathering, you will want to secure your thread at the beginning and end of your seam. You'll want a knot at the end of the thread that came off the spool last. This should be on the longer thread. Here's how:

1. With the thumb and index finger of your nonprimary hand, hold the thread about .75 inch from the bottom. Hold the rest of the thread in your primary hand about 1 inch from your other hand.

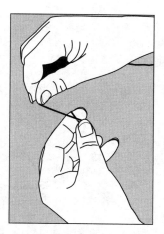

2. With your primary hand, wrap the thread around your index finger once and hold the thread up and taut for the rest of the steps.

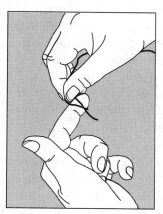

3. Gently secure the place of overlap with the thumb of your nondominant hand and roll the overlapped place toward the tip of your index finger, but don't let it fall off.

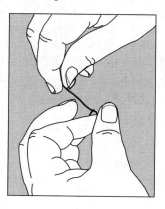

4. Just before it is about to fall off, move your thumb and middle finger above your index finger and gently pinch the taut thread.

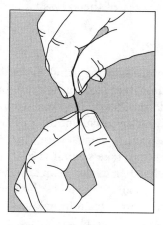

5. With your thumb and middle finger still on the thread, gently slide the twisted thread down toward the end of the thread.

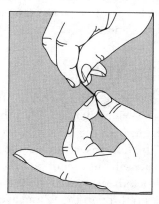

6. You should have formed a small knot.

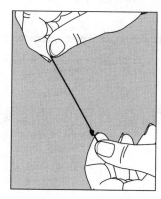

If your tail wasn't long enough, the twists will slide off the end. If that happens, try again with a longer tail. After you've formed the knot, you can cut off most of the excess tail.

Back-Tacking

Another method of securing the end of the thread is not to make a knot at all, but to back-tack. To do this, take a few small running stitches in the seam allowance, ending just before the point you want to start sewing. Just before you enter the seam, take several very tiny stitches on top of each other in the seam allowance very close to the seam. This locks the end of the thread and eliminates lumpy knots.

At the finished end, make a small stitch, but just before you pull the thread taut, slip the needle under the loop and then pull it taut. Repeat this process several times in the same place. It is also possible to use the back-tack method at the end.

Running Stitch

To make a running stitch, working from right to left, if you are right-handed, hold the fabric in your left hand with the edge you are going to be sewing to the left. Insert the needle into the layers of material, but do not pull the needle through. Rock the needle so the tip of the needle pokes back up through the fabric layers on the seam line and to the left of where you started.

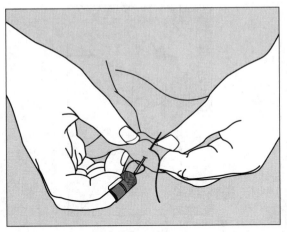

If you're right-handed, hold the fabric in your left hand with the edge you're going to be sewing to the left.

Repeat the rocking process until you have 3 or 4 stitches on the needle, then push the needle with your thimbled middle finger. When most of the needle is through, use your index finger and thumb to pull the needle through until the thread is taut, but not too tight. The fabric should remain flat with no puckers.

A stitch is considered to be the visible thread on the top side of the fabric facing you. In the running stitch, the length of the visible stitch should be the same length as the space between the stitches, so the stitches on the top side and under side should be the same length and should be the length appropriate to the job you are doing.

The running stitch can be used for any type of seam. Quilters use the running stitch for hand-quilting. The running stitch also works if you want to add a decorative topstitch to your project. However, unless your stitches are quite close together, you would do better to use the backstitch for any seams that are going to have to hold up to wear.

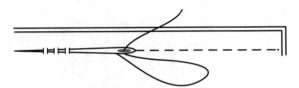

When you're sewing the basic running stitch, the stitch length and the space between the stitches should be the same.

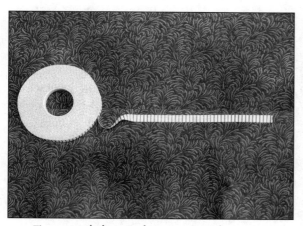

Tiger tape helps you keep your stitches even.

Basting Stitch

A basting stitch is the same as a running stitch, except that it is temporary and the stitch length is long. It is used to hold pieces of fabric together while you put in other, finer hand-stitching or machine-stitching. For example, you would often hand-baste a zipper in place to keep it from slipping while you sew the zipper in on the machine. Generally, you do not knot the end, but leave a long tail instead. This makes it easier to pull out the thread when you have finished.

Even though you are basting and the thread is going to be pulled out and thrown away, choose thread color that won't show if some pieces accidentally get left behind. Basting threads are sometimes caught up in the machine threads, especially in darts and zippers. A pair of tweezers helps get the basting threads out, but sometimes even the tiniest piece of fuzz is left behind. You don't want this to show on your finished project.

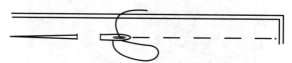

A basting stitch is the same as a running stitch, except it's temporary and the stitch length is longer.

Gathering Stitch

The gathering stitch is nearly the same as the running stitch but with longer stitches—but not as long as basting stitches. You use a longer thread than usual for the gathering stitch, as well as a longer needle. When sewing a gathering stitch, this is one of the few times that it helps to sew with a double thread because, when you make the gathers, you are going to slide the fabric along the thread. If you have a lot of fabric to gather, or if the fabric is heavy, there is a chance that the thread will break if it is only single.

Also it is better not to rely on just a knot on the end. Instead, put a pin at the right end of the seam you are going to gather. Run a few stitches; pull the thread through, leaving about a 2-inch tail. Wrap the thread securely around the pin in a figure-8 fashion. When you reach the other side of the seam, pull the fabric along the thread until you have the gathered piece to the width you want. Secure the left end of the thread in a figure-8 pattern around another pin. Distribute the gathers evenly along the thread. The gathered piece of fabric is then sewn to another, usually not gathered, piece. For example, the gathered panel of a skirt is sewn to a straight waistband, or a gathered ruffle is sewn to the straight panel of a curtain. (See Chapter 7 for more on gathering with a sewing machine.)

To lessen the chance of the thread breaking when you move the fabric along, use double thread when making a gathering stitch.

Fringe Benefits

Before putting in the gathering thread, mark the fabric in the seam allowance and at the halfway point. If the width is very wide, also mark the quarter and eighth points. Then, when you attach the gathered piece to another piece that has also been marked, you can be sure the gathers are evenly distributed.

Backstitch

You will use a backstitch for most seams. It is stronger and more durable than the running stitch. Using a single thread, and sewing from right to left, if you are right handed, make a single stitch by putting the needle down into the layers of fabric and back up through the layers and pulling the needle and thread taut, but not tight. Instead of continuing to the left to make another stitch, as with the running stitch, move the needle back to the right halfway between where the thread went in and came

out of the fabric on the last stitch. Put the needle into the fabric and then up a stitch length to the left of the first stitch. Insert the needle back to the right where the last stitch ends. Repeat the process always inserting the needle "back" to the right next to the last stitch made.

You cannot put several stitches on the needle at one time as with the running stitch. The thread needs to be pulled taut with each stitch.

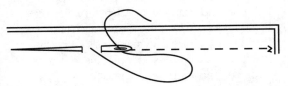

The backstitch is stronger and more durable than the running stitch.

Overcast/Overhand/Whip Stitch

The overcast stitch, sometimes called the whip stitch, was mainly used to keep fabric from raveling and fraying. It is also sometimes called the overhand stitch when you are joining two finished or folded edges. When sewing two edges together, the edges to be sewn should line up and be exactly even.

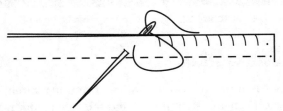

You can use overcast stitches to keep edges from fraying.

The length of the overcast stitch depends on the material and the tendency of the material to fray. Overhand stitches are very fine, taking up only a few threads of each fold so they barely show on the right side.

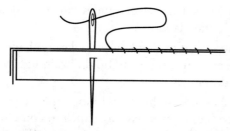

Overcast stitches are also good for sewing together two folded edges.

Blind Hem Stitch

The blind stitch is used for hems. It is called the blind stitch because when it's done correctly, the stitches do not show on the right side of the finished article. The edge of the hem is finished in some way, either by machine zigzag or by folding over a ¼ inch and basting on a machine or by hand. The hem is then folded to a given width and pinned. After the hem is pinned to the appropriate width, the finished edge of the hem is sewn to the underside of the fabric.

To blind stitch a hem, fold back the hem edge ¼ inch. Using small, slanting stitches, catch just a few threads of the material, being careful not to let the threads show on the right side. Then bring the needle up through the folded edge of the hem. Keep the stitches evenly spaced, and be careful not to pull the thread too tight.

Fixing a Seam

Have you ever found a hole in your favorite pants or dress? Have you ever explored the "reduced for quick sale" rack in the best store in town, only to find the one thing you just love has a hole in it?

The first thing to do is to see what caused the hole. There are a few possibilities: a real tear in the fabric or a seam that has come undone.

If the fabric is actually torn, it might be difficult to fix. However, if the problem is that the seam has come undone, you're in luck.

Check to see how the seam came undone. There are two ways seams usually come undone. One is that the thread used to sew the seam broke or came unraveled. On mass-produced garments, it is often easy to undo a whole seam by pulling one thread just right. Another way a seam could come undone is from the material fraying because the edge wasn't finished properly.

If the seam is undone because the thread started to pull, you're in luck again. You can fix this seam quickly with a needle and thread:

1. Carefully cut off the thread that has come undone from the seam. Remember, the more you pull, the worse it gets.

2. With your needle and thread, start at least 1 inch to the right of where the opening occurred, if you are right-handed. Firmly secure your thread with a knot or several small back-tack stitches. Then backstitch in the seam over the stitches that are already there.

3. Continue backstitching across the opening. Use small stitches, and stay on the seam line. You will be able to see the seam line easily because of the holes left by the original thread.

4. Continue backstitching at least 1 inch past where the original stitches remain on the left side of the opening.

5. Secure the end of the thread.

If the material is badly frayed, you might not be able to fix the seam. If it is slightly frayed, you might be able to ease the frayed part into the seam allowance. However, if you pull the frayed part in too much, you will have a pucker at each end of the hole. On some garments, it will be easy to take out more of the seam or even all of the seam to ease the frayed section into the seam allowance.

If you can fix the frayed seam, drop a bit of fray preventer glue on the fabric where it was frayed, to keep the fabric from fraying further.

Sewing on Buttons, Snaps, Hooks and Eyes, and Hook and Loop Tape

Occasionally, buttons fall off or you need to move a button to make something tighter or looser. This is a relatively easy process.

> ### ✂ Cut It Out!
> Just be careful when you move a button or other closure that, when you snip the threads holding it on, you don't snip the fabric by mistake.

When you're making something new, you have several choices about what kind of closure to use, from buttons, snaps, hooks and eyes, to hook and loop tape. Sometimes you want the closing device to be invisible, and other times you might want something more decorative. The style of button, snap, and hooks and eyes you choose depends on the closure's purpose and whether you want it to be decorative, functional, or both.

For example, you can close the top of a zipper on a pair of pants with a button, which would show, or with a hook and eye, which wouldn't show. Sometimes buttons are used purely for decorative purposes and don't even have buttonholes to go through.

You can use very small snaps and hooks and eyes when they'll have almost no stress on them. For example, you might use a small snap for a wristband on a baby's dress. On the other hand, you would use bigger, stronger snaps on the under-seam of a pair of baby's pants that need

to be opened and closed many times a day to change the diaper.

You would probably use hooks and hand-made eyes, not snaps, to hold a train to a wedding dress.

You could use hook and loop tape when the hook edges do not have a chance to come into contact with other fabrics very often. The hooks of the hook and loop tape have a habit of catching on everything, often causing fraying or pulled threads.

Buttons

There are two basic kinds of buttons: those with holes and those with a shank or metal loop. The buttons with holes have either two holes or four holes.

Shank buttons have a metal loop on the back side.

When sewing on a button, you might want to use a larger needle and button thread. And you might think sewing buttons on with a double thread would go faster, but the chances of getting knots is very high and could slow you down.

> ### 🧵 Fringe Benefits
> If you are using a double thread, try knotting each end separately or using beeswax.

For a two-hole button, start with a knotted thread and pull the needle through the fabric, leaving the knot on the right side. Make one small stitch on the fabric where the button will be. Then slip the needle up through one of the button holes, and let the button slide down the needle and thread to the fabric. Pass the needle down through the opposite hole and through the fabric. Bring the needle up through the fabric and the first hole. Repeat this process several times.

If the button is primarily decorative and gets little use, secure the stitching on the wrong side. If the button is going to be primarily functional, place a toothpick between the holes and sew over the toothpick for several stitches. When you have several stitches in place, remove the toothpick. This leaves space between the button and the fabric. Wrap the thread several times around the threads between the fabric and the button to create a "shank." Then fasten off.

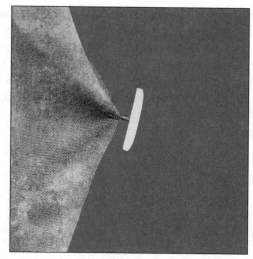

Be sure to wrap the thread around the thread shank for extra strength.

There are several ways to sew on a four-hole button, as shown in the following figure. Whatever you prefer, pick one and stick with it. Don't change your mind midbutton!

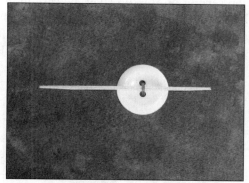

To make a flat button stronger, use a toothpick to create a shank.

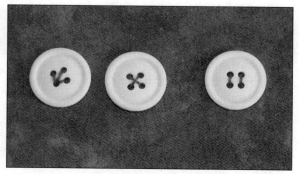

You can sew on a four-hole buttons in many ways.

When sewing on a button with a shank, start by taking a stitch through the fabric, pass the thread through the metal loop as you go, then fasten off.

If you decide to use buttons, you have to think about buttonholes, although there is nothing wrong with having the buttons be purely decorative and use snaps to do the actually work of fastening. It is possible to make button holes by hand, but I recommend using a sewing machine and following the directions that come with your specific machine.

Hooks and Eyes

There are several types of hooks and eyes: heavy-duty flat metal hooks with flat metal bars, hooks with straight eyes, and hooks with a U-shape eyes. For some fancy clothes, when you do not want the metal eye to show, you can make a handmade loop from thread the color of the fabric.

Hooks with the straight bars are used when the two sides of the closure overlap. Hooks with the U-shape eye are used when the two sides of the closure butt up against each other but do not overlap.

When sewing hooks, position the hook on the underside of the top layer. Stitch the hook into place with three or four stitches in each hole, being careful not to let the stitches show on the right side.

> ### Fringe Benefits
> If you're using regular hooks, take a few stitches over the post of the hook just below the curve. This keeps the hook from flopping around and gives it extra stability.

Pin the eye on the bottom layer with 2 pins. Check to be sure the eye matches up with the hook in the right place. Adjust accordingly. Attach the hook by making a few stitches in each hole, then fasten off.

For hooks and eyes with the U-shape eye, attach the hook so that the curve of the hook is at the edge of the fabric and the round part of the eye extends a tiny bit over the edge.

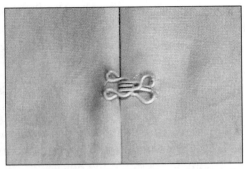

Be sure no stitching shows on the right side when attaching hooks and eyes.

Snaps

Snaps come in two halves, one with a small bulb that goes into the hole of the other half. When sewing on the top layer, be careful not to let the stitches show through to the right side of the material. Using a single strand of thread, make several overcast stitches in each hole. Fasten off.

Sewn-on snaps such as this are quick and easy.

Fringe Benefits

Some snaps come evenly spaced on fabric tape. It comes in different widths of tape and difference sizes of snaps and you buy it buy the yard. If you have a lot of snaps to sew on, especially in a straight line, you might want to consider using the tape. You can easily attach the tape to the fabric either by hand-stitching or machine-sewing. Snap tape is great for the under-seam in a baby or toddler's pants and for closures on pillows. The fabric tape doesn't come in many colors, though (usually just black or white), so you might not want to use it if there is any chance of the tape showing.

Hook and Loop Tape

There are many good uses for hook and loop tape, especially those that need a strong closure. Hook and loop tape comes in many colors, shapes, and sizes, from little dots to by the yard in a variety of widths. Some of the smaller shapes come with glued press-on backs, but you should still sew around the edge for security.

To attach hook and loop tape, you need a strong needle, a thimble, and strong thread. Sewing on hook and loop tape isn't always easy. If you are reinforcing the glued-on kind, you will have to change needles often and throw them out when you are finished because they get all gooed up from the glue. There is also a lightweight, flexible hook and loop tape on the market that the manufacturer claims is perfect for dressier fabrics. Test it out on a scrap of your fabric before you use it, to see how the hook half does.

The Least You Need to Know

- You need to learn only a few basic hand-sewing stitches.
- With only these few stitches, it is possible to sew almost anything.
- It is easy to fix a seam on a manufactured garment with the backstitch.
- The variety of buttons is seemingly endless, but there are only two basic types—those with holes and those with shanks.
- The variety of hooks and eyes makes them a good choice for closing most openings, such as waistbands and necklines.

In This Chapter

- ◆ Revitalizing stained tablecloths
- ◆ Creating a pillow
- ◆ Sewing a bib
- ◆ Making two aprons
- ◆ Fixing up an old blouse
- ◆ Hanging some curtains

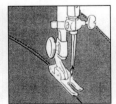

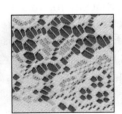
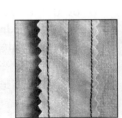

Chapter 5

Quick and Easy Hand-Sewn Projects

You have to start somewhere, so let's begin with some very simple projects, most of which can be made in less than an hour. Once you have the basic concepts in mind, sewing is intuitive. None of these projects requires perfect sewing. No home economics teacher is going to come by and judge your work or tell you to take out all your stitches and try again.

In some ideal universe, straight, even stitches might be a goal, but none of these projects requires pristine stitches. Don't worry if you make a mistake. You always have your handy seam ripper to "unsew" the seam.

The All-Purpose Lace Tablecloth

How many tablecloths do you have in your closet with stains in just the wrong places for the candles or flowers to hide? How many tablecloths sit in the laundry basket, waiting to be pressed? Here is an easy and elegant solution to both those problems. Buy a length of tablecloth lace that fits your table and is just a little—maybe 6 to 8 inches—longer than your regular tablecloth. This is not fancy dress lace. This lace is probably found near other tablecloth material in your local fabric store and is usually about 60 inches wide.

Hand-sew a narrow hem on each end of the lace. You don't even have to be too neat about your stitching because the stitches are lost in the lace and rarely, if ever, seen. You don't need to finish off the selvage edge, either. The selvage on most tablecloth lace is finished, sometimes in a nice, scalloped pattern.

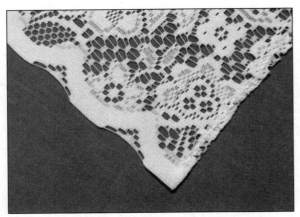

A lace tablecloth adds class to any table—and is easier to make than you might think.

Put your stained or unpressed tablecloth on the table, and spread the lace one over it. The lace adds class and covers a multitude of sins. Old tablecloths with designs, patterns, or color work well, as the color shows through the design in the lace.

I'll Be Darned

To get more use out of your lace tablecloth, change the tablecloths underneath for different occasions. One of my winter holiday tablecloths is very bright with red and green holly. It's almost too busy to use alone, and my dishes and other decorations get lost in the pattern. But with the white lace on top, it works perfectly.

Buying tablecloth lace by the yard saves money. Most tablecloth lace is very durable and washes easily. I have several different lengths that I use, depending on how many leaves I have in my table. I haven't pressed a tablecloth since I started my lace tablecloth collection about 20 years ago.

Fringe Benefits

For variation, make some white tablecloths of different sizes, as well as some ecru ones. At various seasons of the year, fabric stores carry lace in more colors, like red and green.

Spiffing Up an Old Blouse

Find an old blouse that you would like to spiff up a bit, and prepare to venture forth into fashion design. If you don't have any blouses in your closet you want to revamp, you can always find something in a recycled clothing store.

Cut off the blouse sleeves. Where is up to you and the new look you want to achieve. You don't even have to cut straight across, as slanted sleeves are in now. You might also want to cut the bottom of the blouse. Midriff blouses are also very popular.

Then, measure the perimeter of the cut-off sleeves and/or blouse bottom. Add 5 or 6 inches to that number.

Find some trim you like in the fabric store, such as lace or a ruffle, or beads, or fringe. Try to find something with one edge that is already finished.

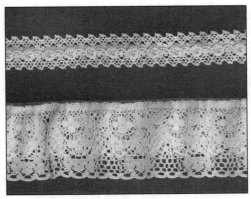

You can find many different trims in your local fabric or craft store.

If the trim has a nice finished edge, follow these steps:

1. After you've cut the sleeve to the desired length, fold the edge ¼ inch to the outside and press.

2. Lay the trim on top of the folded edge of the sleeve and pin.

3. Sew the trim to the sleeve with small running stitches or small overcast stitches. Use the stitch that works best for the trim you have.

Add trim with a finished edge to the right side of your blouse for a little something extra.

If the trim has a rough edge that you want to hide, follow these steps:

1. After you have cut the sleeve to the desired length, fold the edge ¼ inch to the inside and press.

2. Lay the trim edge on the inside of the sleeve and pin.

3. Sew the edge of the fold line to the trim with tiny stitches.

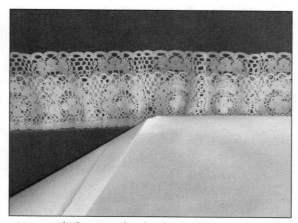

You can hide a rough edge by adding trim with an unfinished edge to the wrong side.

Pillow Talk

All you need to make a throw pillow in an hour is a hand towel, a 10-ounce bag of stuffing, a needle, some thread, and a thimble. The towel can be plain or fancy, solid color or multi-color. Plush towels make really nice pillows.

1. Fold the towel in half, with plush sides together if one side is plush.

2. Pin the edges together.

3. Backstitch around the hand towel with small stitches about ½ inch in from the edge. Some towels have nonpile selvages. Use the line where the nonpile meets the pile as your sewing guide.

4. Stitch around 2½ sides. Leave an opening on the third side.

5. Trim the corners (see Chapter 11).

6. Turn the towel right side out, pushing the corners out carefully from the inside.

✂ Cut It Out!

Small backstitches work best. Remember, no one is ever going to see your stitches, so don't panic if they're not even. However, when you turn the towel right side out, check around the seam. There should not be any gaping holes where a stitch might have been too big. Just turn the towel inside out and restitch over any places where there are holes.

7. Stuff to your desired fullness.

8. Sew the opening closed with small stitches, trying not to have stitches show. Because of the pile, most of the stitches will become invisible anyway.

With a few simple materials and techniques, you can make a lovely pillow in about an hour. Easy!

Drooly Bibs

Most babies drool, especially when they're teething, and some babies are droolier than others. You can make your favorite baby a drooly bib in just few minutes. All you need is a plain, square, really absorbent face fabric; 1½ yard grosgrain ribbon; a needle; some thread; and a thimble.

1. Cut 3 pieces of ribbon, each about 18 inches long.

2. Fold one corner of the washcloth down about 4 inches, and tack it down with a few stitches.

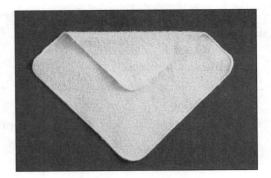

3. Slide 1 piece of ribbon through the slot made from folding over the corner. Find the middle of the ribbon and the middle of the slot. Sew the ribbon to the fabric in several places along the fold.

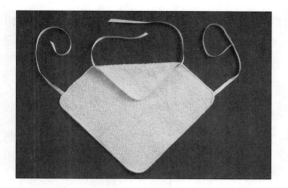

4. On the two side corners, sew the end of the ribbon in place. To make it look neater, fold the end of the ribbon over ½ inch before sewing.

Making a drooly bib for your favorite little one is a piece of cake.

Seasonal Apron

If you have a little time, make a variety of seasonal aprons. All you need is some nice seasonal fabric, a needle, thread to match, possibly embroidery thread if you want to top stitch for decoration, a thimble, and your scissors.

If your material does not have a nap or one-way design, you need about 1 yard. If is does have a nap or one-way design, you need about 1⅓ yards. There isn't a "right" size for an apron. Some people like them long; some people like them short. Some like big, deep pockets; some like small pockets. Your preferences and your creativity will determine your "right" size and style here. You will also need about 3 yards of cording, depending on the size of the apron wearer. Cording comes in all diameters and a variety of materials. Find a cord that will match or contrast your fabric and will withstand some wear. The apron is designed to slide up and down on the cord, and the cord gets tied in a bow.

The measurements in the following figure are the ones I used to suit me. You can adjust these accordingly to fit you better or to take advantage of the material you have. Because the St. Patrick's Day material I used was an even plaid, I cut the widths and lengths on the printed lines, not on inches.

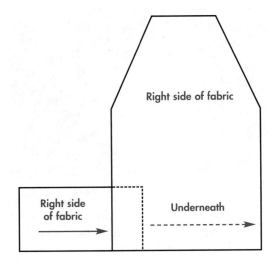

1. Cut the fabric to closely resemble the preceding figure. You will also need a pocket
piece. Cut the pocket the same width as
the bottom part of the apron and about
12 to 14 inches high.

2. Hem the top of the apron: Fold over the
edge ¼ inch and press. Then fold over the
edge again ½ inch and press. Pin the hem.
You are now ready to either blind stitch
or topstitch the hem.

Fringe Benefits

You can use the blind stitch for all
hems, or you can use small running
stitches with a contrasting-color embroidery
thread as a decorative topstitch, securing
the hem in place as you go.

3. Hem the top of the pocket.

4. *Important:* Usually directions instruct you
to put right sides together. This is one sit-
uation in which you do not that. Instead,
line up the bottom edges of the pocket
and the apron with the *right* side of the
pocket to the *wrong* side of the apron.

5. To check pocket placement, put in a few
pins near the bottom of the apron and parallel to the bottom edge. Fold the pocket to
the front, just to be sure the front of the
pocket and the front of the apron are facing you. If it is on the right way, put the
pocket back in place. Reset pins so they
are perpendicular to the bottom edge.

6. Backstitch a ½-inch seam across the bottom.

7. Fold pocket back to the front. Check that
there are no gaping holes in the seam, and
fix any as necessary. Press the seam open,
then press the pocket in place.

8. Pin the top of the pocket to the apron, to
keep things in place for the next steps.

9. On vertical sides of the apron, press under
¼ inch, fold again at ½ inch, and press
again. Be sure the pocket edge gets folded
into the hem. Pin in place.

10. Hem the vertical sides. Reinforce the place
where the top of the pocket meets the
apron with a few stitches on top of one
another. If you have topstitched the seam,
reinforce this point invisibly with regular
thread.

11. Fold under ¼ inch on the vertical edges of apron and press. Fold under another inch and press. Pin in place. Depending on what size cord you have for the ties, this hem could be smaller.

12. To fix the pocket so it won't keep falling open, section it off into 2, 3, or 4 smaller pockets. Use a decorative running stitch to make the smaller pockets.

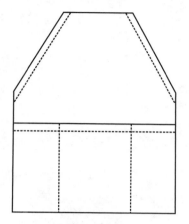

13. Run the cord up through the casing on one side of apron, leaving enough cord to get your head through the top, and then run the cord down the other side. The apron is designed so you can slide the apron up and down the cords to fit various sizes. Then tie in back.

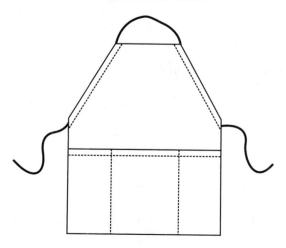

14. After the cord is threaded through the apron facings, put a figure-8 knot on the ends of the cord to keep it from fraying.

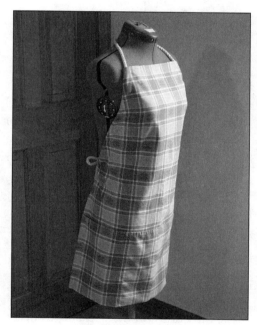

You can create an apron in little time with a few simple steps.

No-Sew Café Curtains

With two rectangles of fabric and some iron-on adhesive hem, you can make a pair of no-sew café curtains. (For more curtain designs, see Chapter 14.)

For these curtains, you will need 2 yards of fabric, iron-on adhesive, 1 curtain rod, and some clip-on rings. Here's how to start:

1. Cut 2 rectangles 30 inches wide by 32 inches long. The length is up to you, but usually these curtains hang from the top of the bottom window to the top of the bottom window sill or halfway up the side of the window. The width is also up to you. These dimensions are for a 36×58-inch window, to the edge of the frame, and the top of the bottom window at 27 inches on the inside of the frame.

Cut It Out!

Be sure you cut the material on the grain, the length of the curtain parallel to the selvage and the grain of material.

2. If there is a nap or a right end up, mark the top of both rectangles with a pin or chalk mark.

3. If the fabric has a border design, be sure you mark where the top of the curtain is going to be.

4. Trim the edge all the way around with pinking shears, if you have them. Otherwise, be sure the edge is straight and smooth.

5. On the side edges, press under the edge the width of the iron-on tape, following the directions on the package, to make side hems.

6. On the top edge, fold under 1½ inches and press. Attach iron-on tape.

7. On the bottom edge, fold under 3 inches and press. Attach iron-on tape.

8. Attach clip-on hooks at even increments. Slide rings on curtain rod, and hang curtains.

These curtains couldn't be easier to make! (But you don't have to tell anyone!)

No-Sew Table Runner

Create a no-sew table runner in an hour for your upcoming dinner party or to add seasonal color to your table. Table runners or table toppers can be any size or shape. (See Chapter 11 for more choices.)

For a no-sew runner, be as creative as you want to be. Decorate a plain piece of fabric with designs and trim. For this project, you will need a piece of plain fabric, several designs or pictures to appliqué, trim, iron-on hem tape, and iron-on fusible web:

1. Choose a plain piece of fabric that is heavy and smooth, like Trigger fabric.

2. For the design, create your own, download a design from a favorite website, trace cookie cutters, or cut out pictures from some other fabric. In the runner shown in the following figure, I found some butterfly material and cut out a few butterflies. (*Important:* See step 5 before you cut out your designs.)

3. Cut your fabric on the grain to fit the top of your table.

4. If you are going to trim the edge, hem the edge of the fabric to the right side, following the no-sew hem material instructions. If you are not going to trim the edge, hem the edge to the underside of the fabric. If you make the hem on the right side, be sure the trim will cover the raw edge.

5. Following the directions on the fusible web, fuse the web onto your design fabric, then cut out your designs. Press your designs onto the runner. *Important:* Be sure you press your designs onto the web before you cut them cut. They are easier to cut, especially in little corners, and they won't fray.

6. Use the iron-on trim to attach the trim to the edge of the runner. Be sure to cover the raw edge.

Fringe Benefits

If you keep a supply of iron-on materials on hand, you will always be able to whip up a new runner in a matter of minutes.

You can easily use your iron to whip up a fun runner—without threading a single needle.

No-Sew Blanket

If you have or find a nice piece of wool (any size), you can make a lap blanket or a blanket to put on the back of your couch, ready for your next nap. It helps if the wool has a smooth finish and clean selvages. Use heavy-duty iron-on tape to make a quick hem on the cut edges. On the blanket in the following figure, I found a nice piece of wool that was different on each side—but it was difficult to decide which was the right side! I iron-on hemmed one hem on one side and one hem on the other. With the iron-on tape, no stitches show, so the hem became decorative as well as functional. Fleece also works well for a blanket (see Chapter 25).

The Least You Need to Know

- You can make many simple projects in less than an hour.

- Making projects from certain fabrics like terrycloth and lace is easy even if your stitches aren't perfect.

- Using already-finished articles such as towels or bandanas will speed up your project time.

- Iron-on adhesive saves time when making hems.

In This Chapter

- ◆ Learning about sewing machines
- ◆ Using a sewing machine
- ◆ Threading a machine correctly

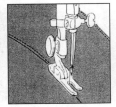

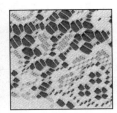

Chapter 6

Sewing Machines

One hundred years ago, sewers didn't have many choices about what kind of a sewing machine they could buy. Most sewing machines were not powered by electricity. Instead, sewers moved their feet in a back-and-forth motion on a treadle. This moved the needle up and down, and there was only one stitch, the straight stitch. There was some choice about the length of the stitch, but that was it.

With the introduction of electricity, sewing machines became more sophisticated. By the middle of the twentieth century, sewing machines could zigzag, blind-stitch a hem, and make button holes. Some had a stretch stitch specifically designed to sew knits. Most sewing machines were portable, and a pedal on the floor controlled the power to the machine.

Toward the end of the twentieth century, with the introduction of computers as a way of life, sewing machines took on a whole new look. Some were designed for specific tasks, like embroidery. With the embroidery machines, you slip in a disc with the picture of choice into the machine, put the fabric under the needle, push a button, go get some tea, put your feet up, and read a book while your machine sews away.

Where to Start?

Whether the machine is five decades old or brand new out of the box, sewing machines still more or less have the same basic shape with the same basic parts. You don't have to know everything there is to know about every machine on the market. There are just too many. It does help, though, to know the big picture about how it all works. In some ways, it's like owning a car. You don't need to be a mechanic, but it helps to know how to drive it.

If you don't own a sewing machine and are thinking of buying one, my advice is to start simply. Find a basic machine that sews basic stitches, including the stretch stitch for sewing knits. Choose a machine that has a free arm option. Having a free arm option makes sewing sleeves and pant legs easier.

You can buy a sewing machine in all the major chain stores, such as Wal-Mart, Target, and Sears. However, if you are really new to sewing, you might want to try a small independent sewing machine store. The machine might cost a little more, but the store will probably offer lessons on how to use your new machine. The staff of these small stores are knowledgeable and, in my experience, extremely helpful. If you are having problems with your machine or don't understand how something works, these folks are there to help you. If you can take the classes that are offered, do it.

The Basic Machine

All sewing machines have the same basic parts and are designed in the same general way, though some of the new computerized machines have most of the parts hidden. Your machine might not look exactly like the one in the following figure, but you should still be able to identify the main parts when comparing the two. (The instruction manual that came with your sewing machine should be able to answer any questions you might have.)

Cut It Out!

Don't lose the instruction manual that comes with your sewing machine. Keep it in a safe but handy place so you can refer to it whenever you need to. If you're thinking of buying your machine from an online source such as eBay, find out if the instruction manual comes with the machine. Try not to buy a machine without a book! If you have lost yours, you might be able to find one online that goes with your machine.

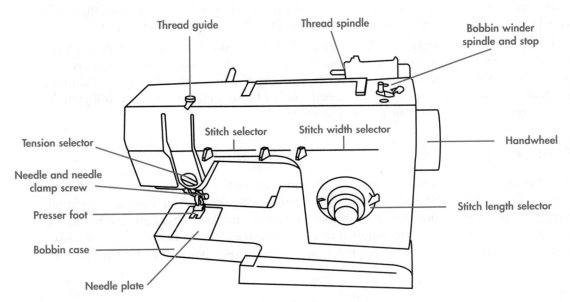

All sewing machines are basically the same.

Get out your machine, and let's start identifying its basic parts. First, be sure the power cord is plugged into the machine and into the wall. Put the speed controller on the floor in a convenient place for your foot. The underside of the speed controller should have some type of nonskid surface. If it slides away when you gently push against it with your foot, glue some type of nonskid material onto it. You will be amazed at how easily the speed controller seems to slide away and hide.

Next, find the on/off switch and turn on your machine. On some machines, the light above the needle will come on when the power switch is turned on, but on other models, you have to turn on the light with another switch.

Cut It Out!

Don't try to sew without the light, even if you have the best eyesight in the world. Replace the bulb if it isn't working. When changing the bulb, be sure the power is off and you have disconnected the power plug from the wall. Use the size bulb recommended by your sewing machine manufacturer, not something you just happen to have handy.

Now that your machine is up and running, let's go over some skills you should eventually be able to do without having to look them up every time. The best way to become familiar with these skills is to keep sewing. Don't get discouraged. If you use your machine once every year, you will forget some of the details. Use your manual to refresh your memory.

Using the Correct Needle

Some machines use needles unique to that specific machine, so be sure to read your instruction book to find out what needles fit your machine if you're not sure. The needle packages will also tell you what machines the needles will fit. Be sure to have a supply of needles on hand in a variety of sizes.

The top of sewing machine needles has one flat side and one rounded side. This is to help you position the needle correctly. The flat side of the needle fits against the flat side of the hole.

When you're putting the needle in the hole, be sure the needle clamp is hand tight.

If you've been sewing for a while with the same needle, check the tightness on the needle clamp occasionally. Sometimes needles become loose. If you are sewing heavy material and the needle is loose, the needle might pull out of the machine and get stuck in the fabric. Also, if you are sewing for hours, change the needle often and throw out the old ones! A dull or burred needle will make holes in the fabric or split the fibers in synthetic materials.

Filling the Bobbin

Before you thread your machine, you need to fill the bobbin. Some machines have removable bobbins, and some are fixed. If your bobbin is removable, follow these steps:

◆ Locate the bobbin winder spindle, usually on top of the machine. In some models, this might be on the right end or the right front of the machine.

◆ Find the place where the spool of thread goes while you're filling the bobbin. In some cases, the thread stays where it is for regular sewing. In older models, you might have to move it, especially if the bobbin spindle is on the right end of the machine.

Fringe Benefits

With many machines, it is necessary to unthread the machine before you can fill the bobbin. If you think you are going to need more than one bobbin's worth of thread for your project, fill several bobbins at once. It is very frustrating to get halfway down a seam and have to stop and unthread the machine to fill a bobbin. It is much nicer if you have a stash of filled bobbins so you can just pop one in when you need it.

◆ With the help of your machine's instruction book, identify the path the thread takes from the spool spindle to the bobbin spindle. Usually, the thread has to go through a bobbin winder tension disc. This helps keep the thread on the bobbin at an even tension. Don't take any shortcuts, and follow the path exactly.

Cut It Out!

Most thread spools come with a little nick in the top of the spool. This is the place to slip the end of the thread when it is not in use. Securing the end of your thread keeps the spools from unwinding and getting all tangled up. However, especially with the plastic spools, the thread sometimes gets caught in the slit as you are sewing or filling a bobbin. To prevent this from happening, put the spool on the spool pin so the thread is feeding off the end that does not have the nick.

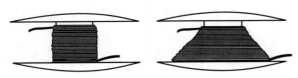

Be sure to fill your bobbin evenly, like the one on the left.

Fringe Benefits

As the bobbin fills, the thread should move up and down evenly. Once in a while the thread seems to favor one side of the bobbin. If this happens, just put your finger under the thread and gently move your finger and the thread up and down. This helps distribute the thread evenly on the bobbin.

◆ Disengage the needle. This doesn't mean you have to turn off the machine. Somewhere on your machine, there is a button or switch that will disengage the needle from the motor. You do not want the needle going up and down while you are filling the bobbin. On some machines, you'll have to turn the inner part of the handwheel backward while holding onto the outer part. Your manual will tell you how to do this for your specific machine.

◆ Thread the bobbin by inserting the thread from the inside to the outside through one of the small holes on the bobbin. Hold on to the end of the thread as you place the bobbin on the spindle. On some machines, you might also have to move the bobbin winder spindle for the bobbin to spin. Continue to hold the end of the thread as you step on the speed controller. Sometimes the thread you're holding will break off as the bobbin winds, and that's fine. If it doesn't break on its own, cut it off when the bobbin is filled.

◆ When the bobbin is full, many machines will stop winding automatically. If yours does not, watch the bobbin to be sure you don't fill it too full.

◆ Re-engage the needle when you are finished winding the bobbin!

Follow your manufacturer's instructions to place the filled bobbin in your machine. Some machines feed the bobbin into the top of the machine; some feed it from the front. The ones that drop in from the top tend to be easier. If the casing is a separate piece, be sure to set it into the machine correctly, and in all cases, be sure the bobbin thread goes through the parts of the casings in the right direction.

Cut It Out!

If you are buying a new machine, be sure you know how the bobbin casing works. In some models, getting the casing in can be a trial even in the best of times, and you don't need to be spending 10 to 15 minutes trying to get the bobbin into the machine correctly. This step has to be easy, and is on most machines.

Also check out how the extension for the free arm attaches. You don't want to have to remove it every time you need to change the bobbin. Machines with bobbin casings that go in from the front might have this problem.

Threading the Machine

Threading your machine is one time when you *must* read your manual. The task is to get the thread from the spool pin to the needle. The trick is to do it in the right order. Most likely, you will have to start by going through a thread guide. You definitely will have to go through the tension discs and the take-up lever (be sure to start with the take-up lever in its top position). Then you will probably have to go through one or more thread guides before you get to the needle.

Follow the directions exactly. Many problems, like uneven stitches or the upper thread breaking constantly, occur when the machine is not threaded properly. Sometimes you can be happily sewing along, only to discover that the bobbin thread is in a tangle.

If the underside of the project is a tangle of threads, your machine is probably not threaded correctly.

Starting Out on the Right Foot

You'll use two basic presser feet in most of your sewing: the one for straight stitching and the one for zigzag. Many other feet are available for specific tasks (some are described in the later "More Foot Options" section). Except for the zipper foot, you do not need most of these when you're just starting sewing.

Fringe Benefits

When changing the presser foot, you need a short screwdriver because it is difficult to get the attachment clamp tight enough by hand. If you sew a lot, periodically check to be sure the foot is not loose on the shank.

Look at the needle plates that come with your machine. You might have two or more. When using the all-purpose foot, use the plate with the small hole. The small hole keeps the fabric from sliding around in the hole. It is also good when sewing on sheers or very fine material because sometimes the lighter fabrics get caught in the wider hole.

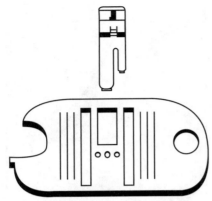

You can use a straight foot and plate for most sewing projects.

When using the zigzag foot, use the plate with the wider hole.

It is better to always use the right plate with the right foot, but it is possible to use the zigzag plate with the straight foot. The reverse is not true. If you have been using the plate with the small hole and switch to zigzag without changing the plate, you will bend or break your needle.

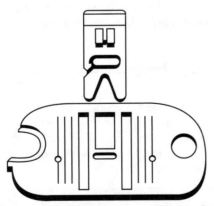

When you're zigzagging, use a zigzag plate.

You can raise and lower the presser foot using the presser foot lifter. On most machines, this lever is located behind the needle, and you usually move it up and down with your right hand. Every time you sew, you need to lower the presser foot to press the fabric between the foot and the *feed dogs*. The fabric will not feed if the presser foot is up when you try to sew,

and it will make a big mess. When you have finished sewing, lift the presser foot before removing the fabric.

Sew You Say

Feed dogs are the jagged teeth below the needle that move the fabric along as you sew.

Tension Headaches

Most machines have settings that need to be regulated each time you change fabric. Heavier fabrics might require different settings than finer, lighter-weight fabrics. You will also change the stitch length often.

Stitch Length

The stitch length regulator is usually on the right front of the machine. Some are marked in stitches per inch, and some are marked in whole numbers between 0 and 5, for example.

A 0 setting means the stitches will be on top of one another and the fabric will not move as you sew. Zero stitch length is used to sew on buttons or to tack the end of a seam. If the dial is in stitches per inch, the larger number means more stitches per inch. However, if the dial goes from 0 to 5, the larger number indicates wide stitches or fewer stitches per inch. The widest stitch is used for basting.

The average stitch length will be about halfway between 0 and the highest number on your dial, or 10 to 12 stitches per inch. This is probably where you will do most of your stitching, and some machines even have the average labeled. Except in rare cases, you should keep the dial between the marks.

Your machine's stitch regulator changes the length or size of the stitch.

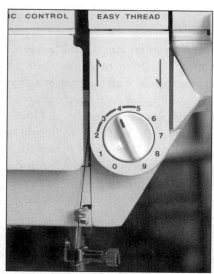

Your machine's tension regulator changes the top thread tension.

Tension Control

If you can, look behind the tension dial knob. You should see two metal discs. When you're threading the machine, you want the thread to go between those two plates. The tension control regulates how much tension is placed on the thread as it passes between these two discs.

The goal is to have the top thread and the bobbin thread meet exactly in the middle of the thickness of the fabric. In most cases, the fabric is not very thick, so there isn't much space for the top thread and bobbin thread to meet.

If you can see the bobbin thread when you look down at the top of the fabric and the fabric is slightly puckered, or you see little loops on the top of the fabric, the tension is too tight. The top and bobbin thread are meeting on the top of the fabric because the tension on the top thread pulled the bobbin thread all the way through the fabric instead of meeting it halfway. If you can see the top thread when you look at the underside of the fabric, the tension is too loose.

When you're using the zigzag stitch, if the fabric creases between the stitches, the tension is too tight.

Keep testing by changing the tension dial until you get it just right.

Fringe Benefits

Save your scrap tests. Write on the scrap with a permanent marker, recording the kind of thread used, the tension that worked, and any other pertinent information. File the scraps in a folder, so when you come back to the project you won't have to figure out the tension again. Some of the new computerized sewing machines remember all this for you.

Pressure Regulator

Most machines have a pressure regulator that enables you to change the pressure between the presser foot and the feed dogs. Other machines allow you to lower the feed dogs totally, which is convenient if you choose to sew on buttons or do freehand quilting and darning. Some machines come with a darning plate, too. This plate covers the feed dogs for these tasks instead of lowering the feed dogs.

Zigzagging

In addition to stitch length and tension, the zigzag stitch has a few more regulators. First, you have to decide which zigzag stitch you want. Depending on your machine, you might have 5 or 50 plus to choose from. Once you've chosen your stitch, you have to decide how wide you want it. When you're working with the zigzag stitch, keep adjusting both the width and the stitch length to get the look you want.

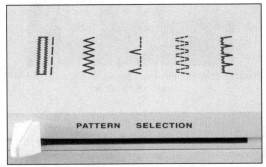

Many machines have a variety of zigzag stitch styles …

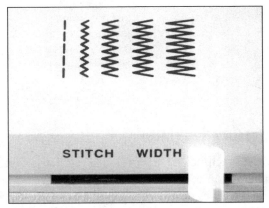

… as well as a variety of zigzag stitch widths.

More Foot Options

When you bought your sewing machine, it might have come with a few different feet. If it didn't, you can buy them in your local sewing machine store or online. The kinds of presser feet you will need depends on the type of

sewing you will be doing. Most machines come with a zipper foot for regular zippers.

Before you acquire any specialty presser feet, you need to know whether your machine has a long, short, or slanted *shank*. The shank is measured from the bottom of the presser foot to the attachment screw. All presser feet fit one of these three sizes. Some feet snap on rather than screw.

There are so many presser feet options available today, it is impossible to describe them all, and some new machines do things that you needed a special attachment for on the old machines. Here are a few of the basics and ones you might want to get started with.

Zipper Feet

Zipper feet are designed so you can sew right next to the zipper teeth. The main part of the foot slides from side to side, which enables you to sew down both sides of the zipper without having to turn the zipper and fabric around. You also use the zipper foot when you are sewing next to cording or other kinds of trim, such as beading.

For invisible zippers (zippers that leave no stitching showing on the right side of the garment), you need a special zipper foot. It is much wider than the regular foot and has a grove that guides the foot along the teeth or coil of the zipper.

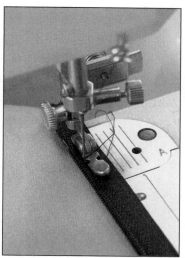

Zipper feet are narrow and slide back and forth to make it possible for you to sew down both sides of a zipper.

Invisible zippers are sewn in with a special zipper foot.

Walking Foot or Even Feed Foot

The walking foot helps feed all the layers of fabric through at the same time. Sometimes, especially when you're sewing long seams, the top and bottom pieces do not come out even at the end. Because the bottom layer is pulled along by the feed dogs and the top layer is pulled along by the friction of the bottom layer, even if you've pinned the layers together, bubbles can start to form just before the pin. If you continue, you'll get a little tuck in the seam. This is not desirable! If you haven't pinned, the top layer comes out longer than the bottom layer! The walking foot helps to prevent this by having feed dogs on both the top and bottom.

What to Do If ...

In the back of your instruction manual, you should find a troubleshooting chart to tell you what to do if .... (I also give you one in Appendix C.) This chart might become your best friend. Cut out one of these charts and attach it to the wall just above your sewing machine.

Also in the back of your manual you will find instructions for caring for and cleaning your machine. Do what it says, because sometimes the problem can be solved with just a good cleaning. Your machine needs to be lubricated and cleaned routinely. If you never change the oil in your car or you never add oil, the motor will lock up and your car will die. The same is true for the sewing machine; it needs lubrication to keep it going.

Lint buildup in parts of the machine you didn't even know existed can cause the machine to not work at its best. Get in the habit of delinting your machine before each project, particularly in the bobbin area. If you pull out a handful of lint when you clean your machine, you know you are not doing it often enough!

If you've tried everything and you're still having troubles, you might need to take your machine to a repair person.

The Least You Need to Know

- ◆ With the many sewing machines on the market, the choices can be overwhelming. Start with a simple model.
- ◆ Use the instruction manual that comes with your sewing machine to learn how to thread it, troubleshoot any problems, and keep it running in good form.
- ◆ A variety of presser feet are available for different stitches.
- ◆ Take care of your machine by cleaning it regularly.

In This Chapter

◆ Knowing when to sew what seam

◆ Sewing nicely finished seams

◆ Making gathers, darts, and pleats

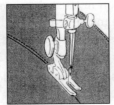

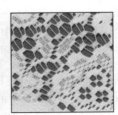

Chapter **7**

Variations on a Seam

When joining any pieces of fabric, to make the fabric conform to a shape, you must start with a seam. All our clothes and most of our soft home furnishings are put together with seams.

Seams are primarily functional, but some are decorative. Some are designed never to be seen, and some proudly show their stitches. You can choose from several basic seams, depending on the fabric you are using and the purpose of the seam.

Practice Makes Perfect

If you were learning how to play the piano, you would practice. Even great pianists practice every day for hours. You also wouldn't try the most difficult ski trail the first day you put on skis. So it is with sewing. Don't expect to be an expert the first time you try to make something. Also, don't get discouraged if your seams are wiggly at first.

In some ways, sewing is like driving a car. You have to learn how each car behaves when you step on the gas. Likewise, you have to learn how the sewing machine works when you step on the pedal. Some cars steer easy, some hard. Some fabrics steer easy, some hard. Driving on twisty-turny mountain roads means slowing down. Sewing around curves also means slowing down. The car wants to naturally go in a straight line, and so does the fabric—although sewing some fabrics is more like driving on ice: they always want to slip into the ditch!

All you need is practice. Here are a few starter tips:

1. Unthread your machine and take out the bobbin. Make copies of the practice sheets provided in Appendix B, and practice sewing straight lines and then some curves. Sewing on paper is different than on fabric, but it will help get you started.

2. When you feel you can sew a straight line on the paper, draw a straight line on some cotton or broadcloth. Rethread your machine, put in the bobbin, and try sewing on the line.

3. Then try sewing a straight line without drawing a line on the fabric. Use the markings on the plate instead. Keep the right edge of the fabric on the ⅝-inch mark.

4. Cut out a circle of material. Put the right edge of the material at the ½-inch mark. Practice sewing around the edge.

As you're practicing, move your hands around and try different positions on the fabric and around the machine. Find what feels most comfortable on straight lines and what works best on curves. Practice on different materials, too. You wouldn't want to get comfortable sewing on a cotton, then slide into the ditch on a more slippery fabric.

Straight Seams

The most common seam is the straight seam. A straight seam is a row of stitching a certain distance from the edge of two or more pieces of fabric you want to sew together. For most clothes, the seam allowance, or the distance from the edge of the fabric to the stitching, is ⅝ inch. For quilts, the standard seam allowance is ¼ inch. If you are using a pattern for your project, the directions will tell you what seam allowance to use.

Most needle plates (see Chapter 6) have guidelines marked at ⅛-inch intervals. Check out the plate on your machine. With the needle in its middle position, use a ruler to measure from the needle to each line. On some machines, the measures are already etched onto the plate. With or without the numbers, the ⅝-inch mark might already be highlighted in some way. On my machine, it is longer than the others.

If your plate is not marked, you might want to put a piece of tape at the ⅝ inch position. Or you can buy a variety of guides that screw into the machine. These are very helpful, especially if you plan to sew many long seams.

If you plan to do mostly piece quilting, you will need the presser foot that is exactly ¼ inch wide on the right side. You can't put a tape at ¼ inch because it will probably cover the feed dogs.

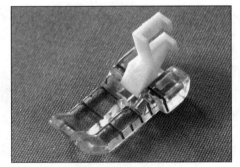

The ¼-inch presser foot is specifically designed for quilters who use quarter-inch seam allowances.

Plain Seam

All seams have a few steps in common. Practice making a plain seam by following the directions in this section. Find two pieces of fabric that have a straight edge. Put right sides together, and line up the straight edges.

> **Fringe Benefits**
>
> Regardless of what you are creating, you will probably make a seam by putting the right sides of the material together. There are a few cases when this isn't true, however. The directions for what you're making will tell you what to do. If the directions don't tell you, assume right sides together.

1. Pin the fabric together with the pins perpendicular to the edge and the head of the pin to the right and just off the edge of the material.

2. Select the stitch length.

3. Raise the take-up lever to its highest position by hand.

✂ Cut It Out!

If the take-up lever is not in its highest position and you step on the power, the thread will likely slip out of the needle. To prevent the needle from unthreading every time you start a seam and press on the pedal, you have three choices:

1. Make the tail of the top thread long enough so when the machine starts and the lever pulls on it, it is long enough to stay in the needle.

2. Hold on to the top thread tightly when you step on the pedal so the lever pulls from the bobbin, not from the tail.

3. The best solution: Start with the take-up lever in its highest position.

4. Slide the top and bottom threads toward the back and under the presser foot.

5. Position the fabric so the needle will go into the fabric at the desired seam allowance.

6. Lower the presser foot.

7. *Back-tack.* To back-tack, push the reverse button or lever to reverse and make a few stitches backward. Let go of the reverse button and sew forward over the reverse stitches to secure the end of the seam.

Sew You Say

To **back-tack** or backstitch, sew a few stitches backward, then sew over the backward stitches when you sew forward (when the fabric is going away from you). This locks the stitches in place.

8. Sew along the desired seam allowance, and take out the pins as you sew, even if your machine is designed to sew over the pins. Sewing over the pins increases the risk of the needle hitting one. When you hit a pin, the pin or needle might bend or even break. At the very least, you will dull your needle.

9. When you finish the seam, back-tack again.

10. Raise the take-up lever to the highest point by hand.

11. Raise the presser foot. As you remove the fabric, you will pull both the bobbin and top threads. Cut these threads with the thread cutter found on the back of the presser bar or with scissors.

12. Press the seam open or to one side, as directed by the pattern instructions.

Different fabrics require different amounts and types of guidance in front of the presser foot. A common position is to use your right hand to guide the fabric just in front of the needle—but watch your fingers! Place your left hand lightly on the fabric to the left of the needle.

To guide most fabric, put your left hand lightly on the fabric to the left of the needle and your right hand in front of the needle.

On very lightweight fabrics and filmy sheers, hold the fabric with your right hand in front of the needle and your left hand behind the needle, and gently hold tension on the fabric.

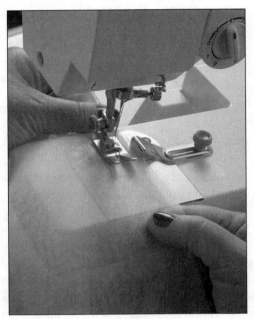

When guiding very lightweight fabric, put your left hand behind the needle.

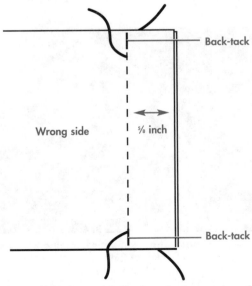

Most straight seams are back-tacked at each end with a ⅝-inch seam allowance.

Flat-Fell Seam

Use flat-fell seams when extra strength is required. Most men's shirts are sewn with flat-fell seams, as are work pants and jeans. On flat-fell seams, two rows of stitching show on the right side of the garment. No raw edges show on the wrong side.

To sew a flat fell, follow these steps:

1. Pin together the *wrong* sides of the fabric.
2. Sew the seam at ⅝ inch.

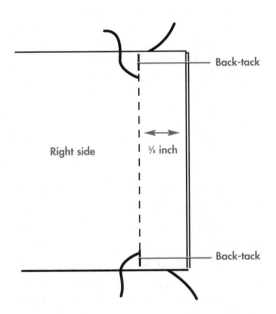

3. Trim one seam allowance to ⅛ inch.

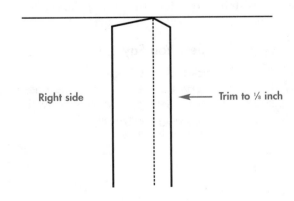

4. Fold the other seam allowance to ¼ inch, and press.

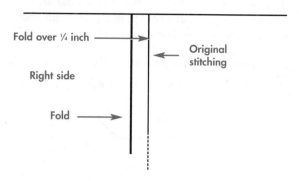

5. Pin the folded seam allowance to the article, hiding the raw edges in the fold.
6. Edge stitch on the fold.

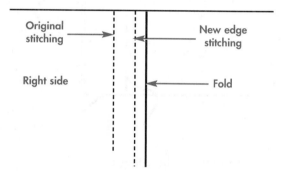

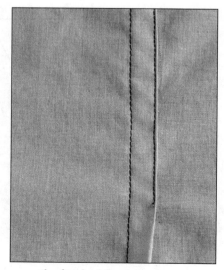

The finished flat-fell seam.

French Seam

For long, straight seams, particularly on fabric that has a tendency to fray, such as sheer, the French seam works best. It does not work well on curved seams.

1. Pin together the *wrong* sides of the fabric.
2. Sew a ⅜-inch seam.

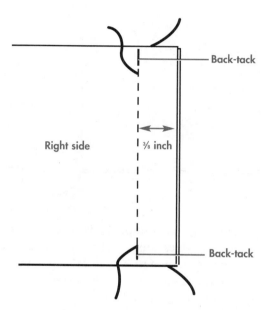

3. Trim seam allowance to ⅛ inch. Press open to set.

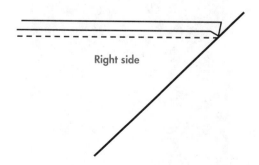

4. Fold together the right sides at the fold, and pin. Be careful that the previous stitching line is exactly on the fold.

5. Sew ¼ inch from the folded edge. The raw edges are now inside the two seams. Press to one side.

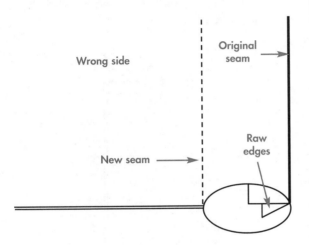

6. Check seam from the right side to be sure no raw edges show, and trim if necessary. If you trimmed to ⅛ inch in step 3 and sewed the seam at ¼ inch in step 5, this shouldn't be a problem.

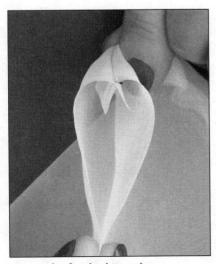

The finished French seam.

Self-Bound Seams

The finished self-bound seam is similar to the French seam, except that it is all done on the wrong side of the fabric.

1. Pin together *right* sides of the fabric.

2. Stitch a plain seam at ⅝ inch.

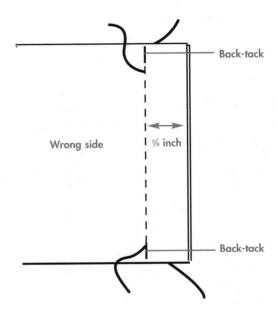

3. Trim one of the edges to ⅛ inch.

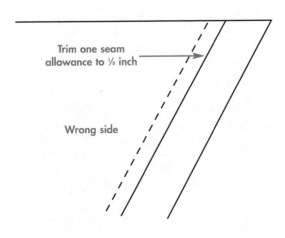

4. Fold and press the other edge at ⅛ inch.

5. Fold the edge again, enclosing the trimmed edge, and press and pin.

6. Sew on the folded edge as close to the original stitching as possible.

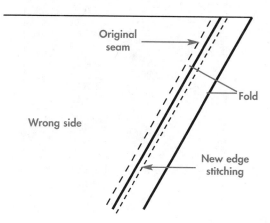

7. Press to one side.

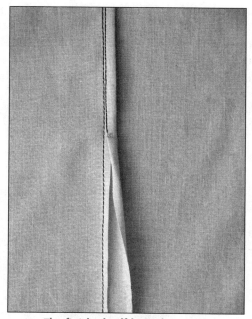

The finished self-bound seam.

Curved Seams

Sewing a curved seam requires two extra important steps. First, you need to reinforce the seam with an extra line of stitching called *stay stitching*. Second, when you've finished the seam, you need to clip the seam allowance so the finished piece lays flat.

Sew You Say

Stay stitches are machine stitches sewn just inside the seam allowance to prevent tearing when the seam allowance is clipped. If the material frays easily, you might also want to seal to the clipped edges.

Here's how to do it:

1. Stay-stitch each curve just inside the seam line before putting the pieces together. Clip the curve in the seam allowance at several intervals.

2. With right sides together, pin together the curved pieces, matching any markings. If you are using a pattern, there will be marks (see Chapter 19) on the pieces you're put-ting together. The pattern directions will tell you which marks have to match up.

3. If, for example, you're sewing a sleeve onto a bodice and one piece is straight and one is curved, pin the curved piece so it is on top when you're sewing. Sew the pieces together on the seam line, being careful to keep the straight piece flat as you sew.

4. Cut small notches in the seam allowance of the curved section of the seam.

5. Press the unopened seam together on both sides to set the stitches.

6. Press the seam open. If you have one, this is where a ham is very helpful.

Finishing a Seam

I can still hear my grandmother and mother saying, "The inside should look as neat as the outside." You never know who's going to be looking at the underside of your garments and inspecting your seams, so always tidy up your seams with a nice finish.

You won't have to finish French seams, flat-fell seams, or self-bound seams because they are already finished. On straight seams, choose one of the finishes in the following sections. Some finishes work better on different fabrics. For example, the zigzag finish doesn't work well on sheer fabrics, and a turned and finished edge might be too bulky for heavier fabric.

Selvage Finish

If the material you're using has a very finished selvage (like broadcloth, cotton, and wool) and there are pattern pieces that have long, straight edges on the grain (like curtains or the backs of some skirts), arrange the pattern so the selvage can be used in the seam allowance.

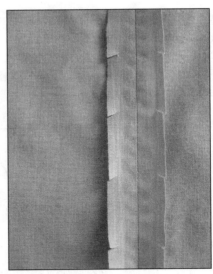

Clip the edge on a diagonal about every 3 to 4 inches for a selvage finish.

Pinked Finish

If you have pinking shears, pinked finishes are easy to do. Stitch ¼ inch from the edge of each seam allowance. Then, using pinking shears, trim the edge next to the stitching. This prevents fraying on almost all fabrics. However, this is probably not a good finish for fine sheer fabric.

> **Cut It Out!**
>
> Some selvages are very wide and might be wider than the seam allowance called for in the pattern. If you choose to use this method, be sure to adjust the seam allowance so the seam line is not in the selvage width. If you do this, also remember that the seam allowance will be different in seams that use the selvage than what the pattern suggests.

When the selvage is going to be the finished edge of your seam, clip the edge on a diagonal about every 3 to 4 inches to keep the selvage from shrinking and puckering.

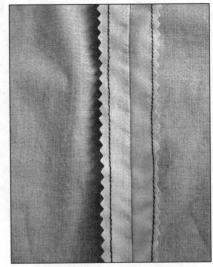

For a pinked edge, simply trim the edge with pinking shears.

Turned and Stitched Finish

This finish works best on medium-weight woven fabrics.

1. On each seam allowance edge, make a line of stitching ⅛ inch in from the edge. Use this stitching for your fold line.

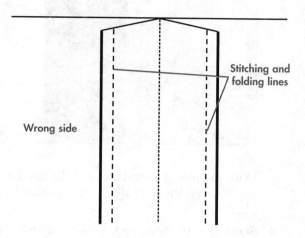

2. Fold on the stitching line.
3. Stitch close to the fold.

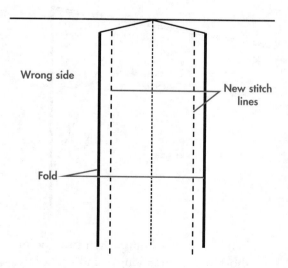

Zigzag

There are two ways to zigzag a finish. One is to zigzag near but not over the edge and then trim off the excess. The other is to zigzag over the edge. Use a wide zigzag width and a long stitch length for both.

When you sew a zigzag stitch down the edge of a seam allowance, some fabrics will pucker. If this happens, loosen the tension.

Topstitching

Topstitching is decorative, and the stitches purposefully show. When topstitching, choose a thread to match or contrast with the fabric. Test both threads to see which one you like best. Set the stitch length to about 8 stitches per inch, and use a seam guide to keep the stitches the same distance from the edge. If you want two rows of topstitching, try using a double needle.

Cut It Out!

If you haven't perfected the art of a perfectly straight line of stitches, don't try topstitching. It's better to have no topstitching than a really crooked, irregular line of stitches everyone can see.

Darts

All fabric is flat, and all human beings are curvy—hence the invention of the dart. Darts make flat fabric curvy. Darts are sometimes found in loose, flowing garments, but you'll find a dart or two somewhere in most fitted clothes. Darts can be used in pants and skirts to shape the material from waist to hip, and they also shape the fabric over breasts in blouses and tops.

There are two basic darts, single pointed and shaped. Single-pointed darts are made in skirts, pants, and tops, and shaped darts are primarily used in fitted dresses made of a single piece of fabric from neckline to hem. Some long, fitted jackets also have shaped darts at the waistline.

Single-Pointed Dart

The single-pointed dart is shaped like a triangle; some are long and narrow, and some are short and wide. Skirt and pants darts tend to be long and narrow, while bust darts tend to be wider. The size of the darts depends on the size and curviness of the person for whom the garment is intended.

1. Mark the dart. (See Chapter 19 for different ways to mark darts.)

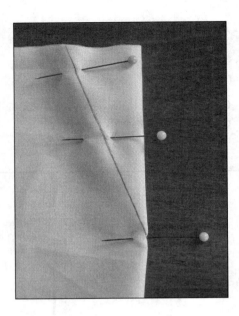

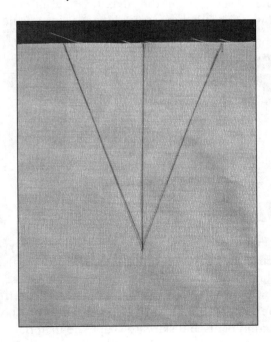

2. Fold the dart on the fold line.

3. With the pins perpendicular to the stitching line, pin the dart along the stitching line.

4. Starting at the wide end, back-tack, and then sew to the point, removing pins as you go.

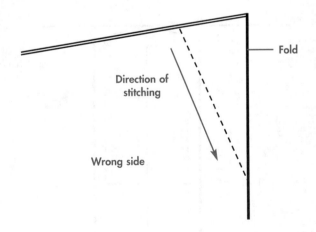

5. When you are about ½ inch from point, shorten the stitch length and sew a few stitches. Do not back-tack. Stitch off the edge of the point.

6. Lift the presser foot, and pull the threads out about 1 inch. About 1 inch up from the point of the dart, take a few stitches near the fold to anchor the thread ends.

7. Press the dart to one side, following the pattern suggestions. Darts are usually not trimmed, except in the case of really wide darts or darts in bulky fabric.

Wide Darts

If you need to make a wide dart, follow the preceding directions for single-pointed darts until step 7:

7. Cut the dart on the fold line to ½ inch from the point. Trim the edges to ⅝ inch.

8. Press the dart flat like a regular seam, and press the point flat.

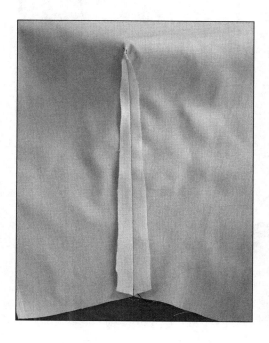

Shaped Dart

Shaped darts have a point at each end and are wide in the middle.

1. Mark and pin the dart.

2. Starting in the middle, sew to one point as if you were making a single-pointed dart.

3. Turn over the fabric and sew to the other point. Overlap the stitching in the middle.

4. Clip the dart in several places.

Cut It Out!

If you start sewing a dart from the points, you'll get a big lump. Always start at the widest part of the dart and sew to the points, shortening the length of the stitch near the point to prevent the dart from coming undone.

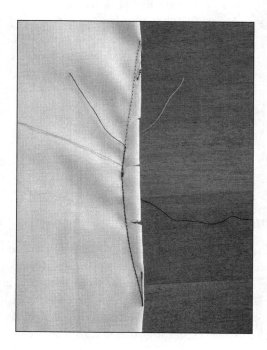

Gathers

In addition to being decorative, gathers serve two purposes: They allow you to put a lot of fabric in a small space, and in some cases they function much like darts. For example, instead of putting in one or two darts in a blouse to fit around the bust, you can use gathers to create a more flowing look.

You can create gathers in many different ways, some of which work better on different fabrics than on others. For example, using elastic without a casing doesn't work as well on heavy materials (see the following "Elastic Not in Casing" section). If the bottom of a sleeve or pant leg ends with gathers, elastic is preferable because it has give. However, if you choose to put a cuff on the same sleeve or pants, then elastic wouldn't work and the two stitching line method would be better. If you're using a pattern, follow your its suggestions.

> **Fringe Benefits**
>
> Before stitching, be sure to mark both the piece to be gathered and the piece to which the gathers will be attached. If the distance is less than 2 inches (for example, a shoulder seam), follow the markings on the pattern. If the distance is large (for example, a full skirt or a pillow), mark both pieces at the ½, ¼, and ⅛ points. This will make it easier to evenly distribute the gathers across the ungathered piece.

Two Stitching Line

The most basic way to make gathers is to use the two stitching line method. If the fabric is light-weight and the amount to be gathered is small—less 4 inches—you can get by with only one line of gathering stitches. However, to be safe, use two stitching lines for almost everything else.

1. Using the widest stitch length possible, make two rows of parallel stitching about ¼ inch apart. Be sure one line is on the seam line and one line is in the seam allowance.

2. Put a pin perpendicular to the edge at one end of the stitching. Tie the ends of the thread around the pin in a figure-eight fashion.

3. Pin the gathered piece to the straight piece at all the points you marked earlier.

4. *Gently* pull on both bobbin threads, creating gathers as you go. Keep pulling until the gathered piece is the same size as the straight piece. Tie off the thread in a figure-8 fashion on another pin.

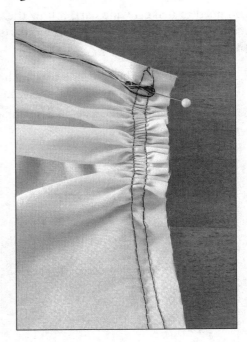

> **Cut It Out!**
>
> Pulling *gently* is important, particularly if you have a great deal of material to gather. If you don't pull gently, one of the gathering threads will most likely break. You will not be happy when this happens!

5. Evenly adjust the gathers. When you're satisfied that the gathers are where you want them, pin the gathered piece to the straight piece in many places.

6. Reset the stitch length to its normal setting.

7. With the gathered side up, stitch along the thread that was on the seam line.

8. With your hands on either side of the needle, hold the fabric taut. The under piece must stay flat. If it doesn't, you might accidentally sew tucks into it.

9. Trim according to the pattern directions, then press.

Zigzag

With the zigzag method, you make a zigzag casing over a cord. Find a cord that is very small in diameter but very strong. Carpet thread or heavy button thread will work, as will crochet thread. Test to be sure whatever you choose will not break, and find a color that matches what you are doing.

1. Lay the cord on the fabric close to the seam line.

2. Using the widest zigzag stitch, zigzag over the cord.

3. Be sure not to stitch the cord. The cord should move freely under the zigzag stitches.

4. Secure one end of the cord around a pin in a figure-8. Pull the gathers along the cord, and to finish, follow the "Two Stitching Line" section directions starting at step 5.

Fringe Benefits

You can also make the gathers by securing the cord in the center by stitching over it. Then push the gathers toward the center of the cord from both ends.

Elastic in Casing

Elastic comes in many widths, with a variety of stretch abilities, and in a host of different styles. Sometimes the elastic is threaded through a casing, and sometimes it is used without a casing. Purpose and taste will dictate whether you use a casing.

For the casing, use some form of bias strip that is ¼ wider than the elastic on the inside measure. The elastic needs to easily slide through the casing and not be forced to fold over because the casing is too narrow.

1. Select appropriate casing.

2. Mark a line on the garment for the casing.

3. Pin the casing to the wrong side of the garment, starting at a seam.

4. Fold under ½ inch on both ends of the casing.

5. Carefully stitch both edges of the casing close to the edge.

6. Pin a safety pin to the end of a piece of elastic that has been cut to the correct length. (You can also pin a safety pin to the other end of the elastic to keep it from slipping into the casing.)

7. Thread the safety pin through the casing.

8. Overlap ends of elastic at least ½ inch. Sew the ends together with a straight or zigzag stitch.

9. Thread the seam of the elastic into the casing.

10. Slip stitch the ends of the casing together.

Elastic Not in Casing

Putting elastic on without a casing saves a few steps, but it doesn't seem to gather as evenly or as fully as it does in a casing. Also, if you choose not to use a casing, be sure to find an elastic that is strong and comfortable to have against your skin if you'll be using it in cuffs.

1. Mark a line on the garment for the elastic.

2. Place a pin on both the elastic and the garment at ½, ¼, and ⅛ points.

3. Pin the elastic to the wrong side of the garment, matching the marking points.

4. Stitch the elastic to the fabric by placing one hand at a pin in front of the needle and the other hand at a pin behind the needle, stretching the elastic to the size of the fabric between each set of pins.

5. For narrow elastic, try a zigzag stitch. For wide elastic, sew both edges with a straight stitch.

6. Be sure at least ½ inch of elastic is in the seam allowance on both ends.

Pleats

Pleats, most often found in skirts and draperies, are another way to fit a great deal of fabric into a small space. Pleats accomplish the same task as gathers, but the look is entirely different. Gathers tend to give a casual look, and pleats tend to look more formal. Think of the pleat as a dart without a point.

Pleats require measuring and marking. If the pattern has pleats, they will be marked, so be sure to transfer every mark. Follow the instructions given in your particular pattern for folding directions and pressing directions.

The Least You Need to Know

- Practice makes perfect.
- There are several different ways to sew a straight seam.
- Finishing a seam makes the inside of the garment as neat as the outside.

- It is important to know which side of the material is the right side.
- Pleats are just darts without points.
- When sewing on material that frays easily, it is best to use a French seam.

In This Chapter

- ◆ Choosing the right hem
- ◆ Finishing a hem
- ◆ Putting up a hem and decorating at the same time

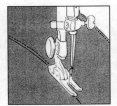
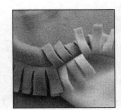

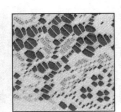
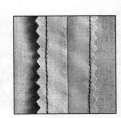

Chapter 8

Getting to the Bottom Line: Hems

Often the last thing you do before finishing a project (except possibly adding fasteners, such as buttons), hems are the bottom line of your home decorating project or your new wardrobe item.

We have hems for two main reasons: to prevent fraying and be tidy. Many materials fray if they are left unfinished, and hemming reduces the amount a material might fray. Being tidy, of course, is a matter of taste.

Since the introduction of woven materials centuries ago, some people have considered it untidy or gauche not to have their hems finished in an aesthetic fashion. Hem length and style were controlled by the fashion industry: They were a certain distance from the floor, a certain width, and done in a certain way. It wasn't uncommon for everyone to know that hems were "6 inches" from the floor that year, and no one would consider having a hem at the wrong length. It was also considered inappropriate to have any hem stitches show, and almost every hem was sewn by hand. There were sewing standards, and one was considered a terrible seamstress if he or she didn't adhere to the standards.

Fortunately, all that has changed. Today, there is no set standard, and you can put a hem anywhere you want to. Hems can be machine-sewn, they can be any height off the floor, and they don't even have to go straight across. Although it is still important to know the basics about different kinds of hems, it's also possible to be more creative with your hem styles.

On Straight Edges

The easiest hems, of course, are on straight edges: straight pants, straight skirts, plain draperies, and curtains. If you are following a pattern, it will give you suggestions for the type and width of hem to make, but in many cases, you can do your own thing. Most projects still will have a turned hem.

Turned Hems

The width of a turned hem is somewhat determined by the fabric you're working with. Turned hems work well on light- to medium-weight woven fabrics when the hemline is straight. The hem itself can be up to 3 inches wide if the hemline is straight; on flared skirts, a 1½- to 2-inch hem works best.

Decide on the length and the width of hem you want, then follow these steps:

1. Straighten the bottom edge where you want the hem. Be sure the places where the seams meet are trimmed even. Trim any frayed threads.

2. Fold the raw edge over ¼ inch to the inside, press, and machine-stitch next to the folded edge.

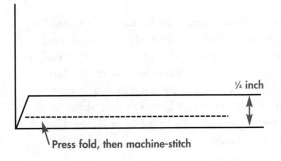

¼ inch

Press fold, then machine-stitch

3. Fold the hem to the desired width, press, and pin.

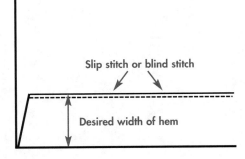

Slip stitch or blind stitch

Desired width of hem

4. Hand-hem using the slip stitch or blind stitch, picking up only one or two threads from the main fabric so your stitches don't show through.

Cut It Out!

Do not pull the thread too tightly when hand-hemming because it can cause puckers.

Double Turned Hems

Double turned or double folded hems are used primarily on draperies and curtains. Double hems are usually 1 inch wide on the sides of a drapery panel and usually about 4 inches on the bottom hem. On sheer or lightweight fabrics, the bottom hem can be as much as 6 inches; on short curtains or valances, the bottom hem can be as small as 1 inch.

Decide on the length and the width of hem you want, then follow these steps:

1. Be sure the raw edges are straight, especially at the seams. Trim any loose and frayed threads.

2. Fold the hem to the inside to the desired with—for example, 4 inches—and press.

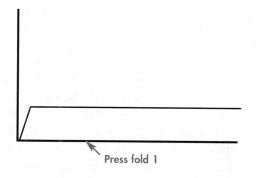

Press fold 1

3. Fold over again the same amount as before (in this case, 4 inches) and press.

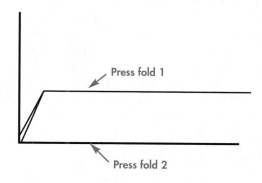

Press fold 1

Press fold 2

4. Machine-stitch close to the top folded edge.

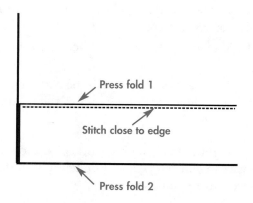

Press fold 1

Stitch close to edge

Press fold 2

Fringe Benefits

When machine-sewing hems, be sure the thread matches the material because it will show on the right side. If you can't find the exact match, choose the next closest darker shade.

On Curved Edges

It is possible to make a turned hem on a curved edge, but it is difficult to make the ¼-inch fold without getting creases in it. Curved edges have extra fullness that has to be eased in.

Decide on the length and the width of hem you want, then follow these steps:

1. Do not fold over the raw edge. Lessen the tension on your machine, and sew ¼ inch in from the raw edge.

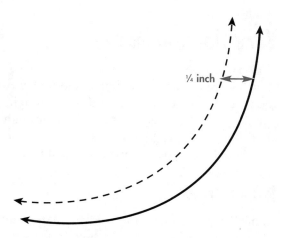

¼ inch

2. Fold the hem at the desired length. Hand-baste with large stitches near the fold.

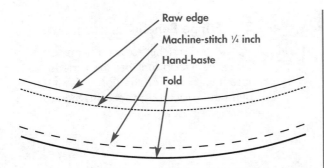

Raw edge

Machine-stitch ¼ inch

Hand-baste

Fold

3. Gently pull up on the bobbin thread at evenly spaced intervals around the edge, and ease in the fullness.

4. Press the hem to shrink and ease out fullness.

5. Finish the raw edge with pinking or zigzag.

6. Pin the hem in place, matching the seam lines.

7. Hand-hem using a slip stitch.

8. Remove the basting thread.

Very Narrow Hems

Very narrow hems—hems that are less than a ¼ inch—are used on table linens and fine evening wear. If the fabric is sheer or see-through, you might not want any hem to show through at all, but the raw edge still needs to be finished. For these hems, you can use the rolled hem.

Rolled Hems

Rolled hems are found on handkerchiefs, some table linens, and sheer fabrics used in formal dresses. Rolled hems take some practice. The goal is to get the tiniest hem possible without folding.

One technique is to roll the edge between your thumb and index finger. Then, with extraordinarily small stitches, slip stitch the rolled

edge to the fabric, being sure your stitches don't show on the right side. The stitches need to be the right tension. If they're too tight, they'll cause the article to pucker; if they're too loose, the loops of the stitches will show on the back.

On garments where it would be rare to see the inside, nobody will notice if little loops show up occasionally. On items such as handkerchiefs and napkins though, the right side and the wrong side should be equally neat and tidy, especially around the hem.

I'll Be Darned

On very fine fabric such as sheer or organdy, you can roll the edge without sewing. This works very well especially when you're working with a bias. Wash your hands thoroughly. Lightly dampen your thumb and index finger, and tightly roll the edge, working about an inch at a time. You do not need to sew it, but keep in mind it will not last through a washing or dry cleaning, and you will have to do it again.

Variation on a Rolled Hem

You can also make a very narrow hem that isn't rolled but is still quite narrow:

1. Machine-stitch about ⅛ inch from the raw edge.

2. Then, as you hand-stitch the hem, turn the edge under with the point of the needle as you go.

It might help to pin the worked end to a surface so you can keep a little tension on the fabric while you're sewing.

Fused

Thanks to modern technology, you can put up many hems without sewing a stitch. You can use any of the various weights and widths of fusible webbing. Or if what you are making has a right side and a wrong side no one will see, stitch ¼ inch from raw edge, pink the raw edge, press the hem to the desired width, and fuse with iron-on webbing (follow the manufacturer's directions on the package).

Machine Blind Stitched

Many sewing machines have a blind hem stitch setting. Some also have a blind hem presser foot. You do not need the blind hem presser foot; the zigzag foot also works. Check your machine's instruction book to see if using the zigzag foot is an option.

Making a blind hem with a sewing machine is terrific for long, straight edges such as draperies and curtains:

1. Finish the raw edges.
2. Fold and press the hem at the desired length and width.
3. Hand-baste the hem to the article with long stitches ¼ inch from the finished edge.
4. Place the hem allowance right side down under the needle.
5. Fold the rest of the garment back to the basting line.
6. Select the blind stitch from your machine's zigzag choices.
7. Stitch along the hem close to the fold. Be sure the zigzag stitch catches the fold.

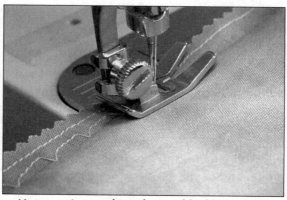

Many sewing machines have a blind hem stitch.

8. When you're finished, open the hem and press it flat.

Cut It Out!

Machine blind stitching takes some practice. The width of the zigzag should be just wide enough to catch the folded-back part of the material, but not so wide that gigantic stitches show on the right side of the article. Some materials slip around, and the zigzag stitch misses entirely.

Practice on some scraps first. Go slowly and be patient. The stitches will show on the right side, be placed fairly far apart, and with luck and skill, be the same size. It is important, however, to use the same color of thread as the material. If you cannot find the exact color, use the next darker shade. This is not a decorative stitch, and you really do not want the stitches to be too obvious!

If you have trouble, you can always hand-hem.

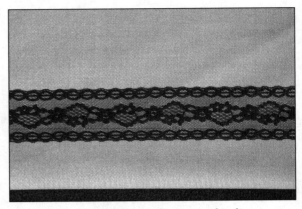
For a nice finish, use lace seam binding.

Hem Finishes

Just as with seams, if you want the inside of your project to be as neat as the outside, and if you want to prevent the raw edge from fraying, you can select from a variety of hem finishes. With the simple turned hem, your hem is already finished. For most lightweight woven fabric, this is all you need. If you want another finish, though, following are a few options.

Seam Binding

If you're using a heavier-weight fabric, you can eliminate some of the bulk by using seam binding. Match the color of the seam binding to the color of the garment. If you want something more decorative, choose a lace seam binding.

1. Sew the binding to the right side of the hem at the raw edge.

2. Press and pin the hem to the appropriate length, then hand-sew the seam binding to the garment using a slip stitch.

Pinked

For heavier-weight materials, stitch ¼ inch from the raw edge, pink the raw edge, press, and pin the hem. Instead of catching the fabric of the hem when you hand-stitch, pick up the bobbin thread on the underside of the hem.

Bound

On heavy material, especially if there is a tendency for it to fray easily, you might want to try a bound hem. Encase the raw edge in double-fold bias tape, fold the tape, press, pin, and slip stitch.

Zigzag

Zigzagging the raw edge works particularly well on knits where you need the extra stretch of the zigzag stitch. It is usually easier to sew the stitch in from the edge and then trim the edge later.

Decorative Hem Stitches

With all the decorative stitches available on today's sewing machines, there has been a trend away from hiding the hem stitches. Today they're not only visible, but they're also often part of the decoration.

The simplest decorative hem stitch is the topstitch. Use two or more parallel lines of stitching, one of which is the actual sewing of the garment's hem.

Fringe Benefits

If you have trouble keeping your stitch lines evenly spaced, this might not be the best hem choice for you. You can accomplish the same hem stitch with the twin needle, though. Place one of the needles at the fold and the other needle on the hem.

Depending on your sewing machine, you might be able to use other decorative stitches to attach your hem and decorate your project at the same time. Remember that, in most cases, you will be turning the hem to the underside and stitching from that side, making the bobbin threads the ones that will show on the right side of the garment. On a scrap of fabric, check to see if you like what that looks like. It might or might not be similar on both sides.

In Chapter 5, I give you directions for a no-sew table runner. You can also make this table runner by sewing the hems rather than gluing them. If you put the trim on top, you only need to sew a single hem turned to the right side, in this case the top. If you put the trim lace underneath, you only need to turn a single hem to the wrong side, the bottom. Because the lace trim is going to cover the hem on either the top or the bottom, you don't need to turn the hem twice. The raw edge will be under the trim.

The Least You Need to Know

- Turning a hem is easy on projects with straight hems.
- Fusible hems are quick and easy and great for emergencies.
- Finished hems make the garment look nice, even on the inside.
- Bound hems are used on heavy-weight materials that fray easily.
- Double hems are used primarily for draperies and curtains.
- You can hem and decorate at the same time.

In This Chapter

- ◆ Letting down a hem
- ◆ Putting up a hem on a dress or a skirt
- ◆ Putting up a hem on pants
- ◆ Fixing an emergency hem

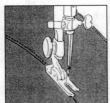

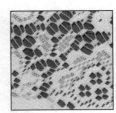

Chapter 9

Up and Down: Changing a Hem

Children grow. Styles change. Manufactured clothes don't always come in the right length, in spite of the labels marked short, medium, and tall. When your favorite clothes are too short or too long, you don't have to give them away. When you find a great bargain, you don't have to pass it up because the length is too long or too short. Changing a hem is relatively easy (with a few exceptions).

The easiest garments to shorten are straight skirts and straight-leg pants. The next easiest are lined straight-leg pants, lined straight skirts, slightly flared pants, and A-line skirts. The harder hems to change are tapered pants with or without a lining, pants with cuffs, flared skirts, and skirts with kick pleats.

By the end of this chapter, you'll be able to let down or raise a hem in nearly anything in your closet.

Letting Down a Hem

When you're thinking of letting down a hem, first check to see if there's enough hem to let down. If there is, the job will be easier. If there isn't, it's still possible to lengthen the garment, but you need to be a little more creative.

On a Hem with Enough Fabric to Let Down

First, undo the old hem. On manufactured garments, you can sometimes find the one lucky thread to pull that will release the hem in a flash. It pulls out all the way around, and you don't have to cut anything. If you can't find that lucky thread, you'll have to cut the threads carefully with your seam ripper, then pull out all the loose ends.

Next, press out the crease. One major problem with letting down a hem is that the crease line of the old hem might be difficult to get out. In some fabrics, it will press out immediately. If this doesn't work, try a damp pressing cloth. If that doesn't work, try a little vinegar-and-water mist. If this still doesn't work, and if the raw edge of the hem is finished and the material is washable, try putting the garment through a wash cycle, and taking it out of the dryer while it is still slightly damp, and press again.

Sometimes, if the garment has been washed several times, the old hem line will show because of discoloration or fading. This is the time to get creative. You could put some trim on top of the old crease line, or you might want to sew a decorative machine stitch or hand-embroider a stitch to hide the line.

Then redo the hem with one of the methods suggested in Chapter 8.

On a Hem Without Enough Fabric to Let Down

This is another opportunity to be creative. The following are only a few of the possibilities of many creative solutions. Use your imagination. I'm sure you can think up more.

- On pants and skirts, sew a ruffle to the bottom of the existing hem.
- On pants and skirts, add a strip of similar-weight fabric in a contrasting color to the bottom of the existing hem.

To lengthen a pair of pants, add a fun ruffle.

To lengthen a skirt, add a piece of contrasting fabric.

- Cut off a strip of the bottom edge, add a piece of contrasting-color fabric, and reattach the cut-off edge.

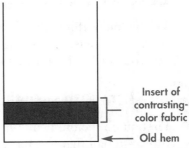

To lengthen a skirt, cut a strip off the bottom edge, add a piece of contrasting-color fabric, and reattach the cut-off edge.

- Cut off the bottom edge entirely and make a mini-skirt, shorts, or capri pants.

Raising a Hem on Skirts and Dresses

Putting up the hem on a skirt is generally easy. You just take down the old one and put up the new one using one of the methods suggested in Chapter 8. Depending on the material and the design of the skirt, however, there are some things to keep in mind.

The following steps are the same for putting up the hem on all kinds and fabrics of skirts:

1. Carefully take out the stitching that's holding the hem in place.

2. Put on the garment, and have a friend pin up the hem—be sure to stand up straight!

   If you don't have anyone to help you, you will have to do it by trial and error. Put on the garment, put a pin where you think you want the hem, take off the garment, pin it all the way around, and try it on again to see if the hem is where you want it.

Proceed with one of the following sections, depending on the style of skirt you have. In general, it is a good idea to replicate what was there already, if you have the tools and supplies available. For example, if the hem was finished with seam binding, put new seam binding on the new hem. If you don't have the tools or supplies to match what was there, it doesn't matter, as long as the hem is neat and doesn't cause lumps or puckers, and that the finish is appropriate to the weight of the fabric.

On Straight Skirts

If the skirt does not have a kick pleat:

3. Press the hem, remembering to remove the pins so you won't scratch your iron.

4. Cut the new hem to the same width as the old hem.

5. Finish and attach the hem, either copying what was there or by using one of the methods suggested in Chapter 8.

If the skirt has a kick pleat and the pleat is long enough to be shortened without looking odd, just copy what is there.

If the skirt has a kick pleat and the pleat is too short to be made any smaller, you might decide that it's not worth the trouble to hem the skirt. Remaking and raising a kick pleat in a seam might not be worth the time and energy. However, if you are shortening the skirt enough, you might not need the kick pleat at all. Sew the kick pleat together like a regular seam, trim off the facings, and hem as described earlier for skirts with no kick pleat.

On Skirts with Curved Hems

If the skirt has a curved hem, be sure to keep the shape and width of the original hem's curve when cutting off the excess fabric. If it's impossible to ease in the fullness with the method suggested in Chapter 8, remove some stitching on the seams from the raw edge to the new fold line. Replace the seam stitches, taking in some of the fullness. Then just trim the seam and finish the hem.

Raising a Hem on Pants

Pants come in many styles of pant legs and in a wide variety of fabrics. Each style and each material needs special consideration. Of course, pants with straight legs are the easiest, particularly if they are not lined.

The following three steps are the same for putting up the hem on all pants, except jeans:

1. Carefully take out the stitching that's holding the hem in place.

2. Have a friend pin the hem where you want it. If you don't have anyone to help you, you will have to do it by trial and

error, or you can use another pair of pants that are the right length for a measure.

3. Pin up the hem on each leg. Check to be sure the inside seams are the same length.

> ### ✂ Cut It Out!
>
> Don't just fold up the original hem and sew it down. This usually causes too much bulk at the pant hem line.

On Straight Pants

If you're hemming straight pants:

4. Press the hem, remembering to remove the pins so you won't scratch your iron.

5. Trim the hem to 1 to 1½ inches.

6. Finish the hem, copying what was there before or using one of the suggested methods in Chapter 8.

> ### Fringe Benefits
>
> Always try on the pants after you've pinned them to be sure they are the length you want. If you have used a pair of your other pants as a measure, this step is particularly important. Different fabrics sometimes hang differently. To be on the safe side, always try on the pinned-up pants with the shoes you think you will wear with those pants.

On Flared Pants

When putting up a hem on pants with a flared leg, you'll notice that you have more fabric in the hem than in the leg. If there's only a slight flair, follow the directions in Chapter 8 for putting up a curved hem, easing in the fullness as suggested.

If there is too much fabric to ease in without it becoming bulky, you have two options:

◆ If the fabric is soft and lightweight, consider a narrower hem. If the pants already had a narrow hem, this is a good option. Cut off the excess material, and replicate the original hem, substituting hand-hemming for the machine-hemming, if you want to.

◆ If you want a wider hem, undo the seams from the raw edge to the fold of the hem. Restitch the seam line so it takes in some of the fullness.

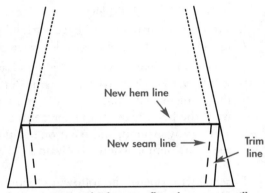

When putting up the hem on flared pants, you'll have to eliminate some of the extra fabric.

On Tapered Pants

Tapered pants have the opposite problem as flared pants—the hem edge is smaller in circumference than the pant leg. To hem, undo stitching on the seams from the raw edge to the fold line, and restitch the seam line.

Once in a while, even opening the seam allowance isn't enough to make the hem as wide as the pant leg. In this case, you might have to live with the gap. Secure the seam close to the hem's fold line so it will not come undone. Pin the hem, starting at the center front and back, leaving the gap evenly spaced over the side seams.

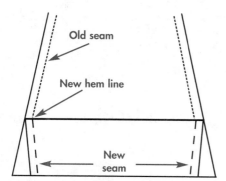

When putting up the hem on tapered pants, you'll have to let out some of the seam allowance.

On Jeans

Jeans are different only in that the hem is almost always machine-sewn, topstitched, and narrow. This shouldn't present any problems, though.

Just cut off what is there to the right length and make a narrow hem. The outside seams on jeans are usually flat-fell seams (see Chapter 7) and might be difficult to stitch over. The good news is that you will not have to take out much of the seam because the hems are usually narrow.

> **Fringe Benefits**
>
> Raw, frayed edges are in style in certain areas, particularly in garments made of denim. Just cut the jeans to the desired length, forget the hem, and let them fray. You might want to put one line of stitching about ½ inch from the raw edge just to put some control on how much fraying the jeans will do, but that's it.
>
> And be sure to save any cut-off denim pieces for use in other projects. See Chapter 26 for a pillow made entirely from cut-off jean legs.

Putting Up Hems on Lined Pants and Skirts

To put up the hem on a pair of pants or a skirt with a lining, you generally do whatever you

did to put up the hem on the garment. The differences are that linings almost always have a very narrow hem and are usually machine-sewn. If you don't have a machine, just hand-sew a narrow hem. Here's how:

1. Hem the pants or skirt first.
2. Adjust the lining so it doesn't hang below the bottom of the garment hem. Cut the lining so that after it's been hemmed, it hangs about 1 inch above the garment hem.

If there's a flare or taper to the lining, you might have to fix the seams just as you did on the garment.

In Case of Emergency

If you are in a hurry and just have to have those pants hemmed *right now*, use fusible web. Without undoing anything, turn up the hem and tack it up with the iron-on webbing. You don't have to go all the way around the hem, but you do need to do enough to keep the hem from sagging. You don't want to get your foot stuck in the hem and pull it down while you are out on the town! A fused hem won't be perfect, but remember that it is temporary and that you are going to fix it when you have time.

The Least You Need to Know

◆ When letting down a hem, you might have to add trim to cover an old hem fold line.

◆ When rehemming a skirt with a curved bottom, keep the shape of the new curve the same as the old one.

◆ When putting up a hem on pants with tapered legs, you might need to let out the seams first.

◆ In case of emergency, you can always put up a hem with fusible tape.

In This Chapter

- ◆ Selecting zippers
- ◆ Sewing in zippers

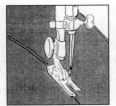

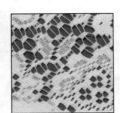
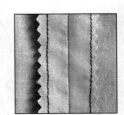

No-Stress Zippers

Zippers have a bad rap. I still feel some old shudder when it comes time to put in the zipper. I don't know who instilled that fear in me, but I wish they hadn't done it.

Putting in a zipper is easy and no more difficult than sewing any seam. I guess there might be some angst that the stitching that shows might be crooked or something. You can solve this problem in many projects by using an invisible zipper. (Those are really easy to put in, too.)

The Right Zipper for the Job

You have a few zipper choices available, depending on what kind of use the zipper will have and whether you want the zipper to be visible or not. Along with the kind of zipper, you also have options when it comes to sewing in the zipper. You have four basic options for sewing in regular zippers and one for invisible zippers. In most dresses, skirts, blouses, and pillows, regular zippers are centered or lapped. Pants might have a centered, lapped, or fly zipper, depending on whether it is in the front, the back, or the side. Jackets have separating zippers. You can use invisible zippers on most clothing that calls for a centered or lapped zipper. Invisible zippers are also good for fancy clothes and wedding dresses.

Zippers come in a variety of sizes and colors. If you're following a pattern, it will tell you what size to buy. Try to match the weight of the zipper to the weight of the material. You don't want a heavy metal zipper in a silk blouse, just as you don't want a lightweight nylon zipper in a pair of tight jeans.

Regular Zippers

You probably know what a zipper looks like: two rows of individual metal or plastic teeth that zip together. These regular zippers are good for medium-weight fabrics. Other zippers are made with polyester or nylon coils rather than teeth and are more appropriate for lighter-weight fabrics.

Both teeth and coil zippers are held together at the bottom with a bottom stop. They also have a top stop on each side of the zipper that keeps the slider from falling off when the zipper is zipped up.

I'll Be Darned

Some zippers are closed at both ends. These zippers were originally used during the mid-1900s in the left side seam of women's dresses, and you can sometimes find them in some clothes today. These zippers can be hard to find in some notions departments, but if you can find them, you can use them in pillow openings or any other applications where both ends of the seam, above and below the zipper, are stitched together.

Separating zippers have metal or plastic teeth and are usually more heavy duty because they are used in jackets and get lots of use. The zipper separates at the bottom, but it still has bottom and top stops to keep the slider from falling off.

Fringe Benefits

Every sewing book and every home economics teacher has the perfect way to put in a zipper. The zipper package should have installation directions. Your sewing machine instruction manual might also have directions. If you have more than one set of directions, read them all and find one that works easily for you, and stick with it.

Centered Zippers

With the zipper teeth on the seam line and two lines of stitching equidistant from the seam line that holds the zipper in, centered zippers are just that—centered. Centered zippers are mostly found in the back of dresses or in skirts with a back zipper. They are also used in some pillow covers.

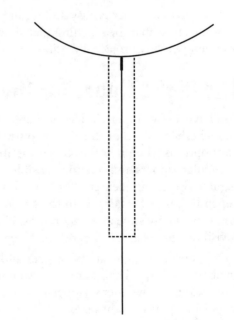

Don't be intimidated by the thought of putting in a zipper. It's not as hard as you might think.

Here are the basic steps for putting in a centered zipper:

1. Mark the seam allowance where the bottom of the zipper will be. The length of the seam opening is generally the length of the zipper coil plus 1 inch.

2. Stitch the seam with a regular stitch length from the bottom hem edge to the marking for the bottom of the zipper. Back-tack.

3. Change the stitch length to a basting stitch. Baste the seam where the zipper will go.

4. Clip the basting stitch every 2 inches to make it easier to remove later.

5. Press open the seam.

6. Apply fabric glue or a glue stick to the right side of the zipper facing. This will help hold the zipper in place while you sew.

7. With the zipper zipped, carefully glue the zipper to the seam allowance with the teeth directly over the seam line, making the top stop 1 inch below the top edge of the garment. Let the glue dry.

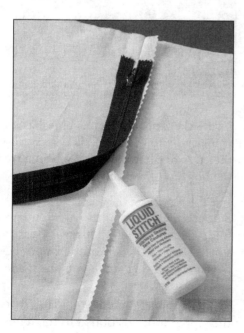

8. When the glue is dry, lay the garment flat, right side up. Using ½-inch-wide tape the same length as the zipper, place the tape over the seam where the zipper is, being sure the tape reaches just below the bottom zipper stop.

Cut It Out!

Do not use tape on fabrics that have nap or that might be sensitive to the tape adhesive.

9. Using a zipper foot and starting at the bottom of the zipper at the seam, topstitch across the bottom of the tape, leave the needle in when you turn the corner of the tape, and stitch up the other side of the tape. Slide the zipper foot to the other side and repeat on the other side of the tape.

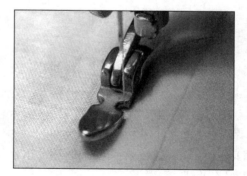

10. Pull all threads at the bottom of the zipper to the wrong side, and knot.

11. Remove the basting threads from step 3.

Lapped Zippers

With a lapped zipper, the stitching is close to the teeth on one side of the zipper, and on the other side, the teeth are sewn in such a way that an overlap is formed. Only one line of stitching shows on the right side of the garment. Lapped zippers are used on dresses and skirts with back zippers, as well as on some garments with side zippers.

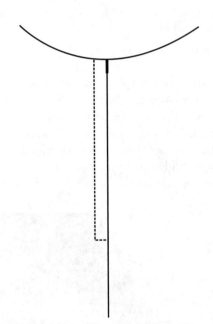

Putting in a lapped zipper isn't tough, either.

Here are the basic steps for putting in a lapped zipper:

1. Mark the seam allowance where the bottom of the zipper will be. The length of the seam opening is generally the length of the zipper coil plus 1 inch.

2. Stitch the seam with a regular stitch length from the bottom hem to the marking for the bottom of the zipper. Back-tack.

3. Change the stitch length to a basting stitch. Baste the seam where the zipper will go.

4. Clip the basting stitch every 2 inches, to make it easier to remove later.

5. Press open the seam.

6. Open the zipper.

7. Put the zipper face down on the wrong side of the seam. Glue, pin, or baste one side of the zipper to one seam allowance, being sure the teeth are snug up against the seam. The top stop should be 1 inch below the top edge of the garment.

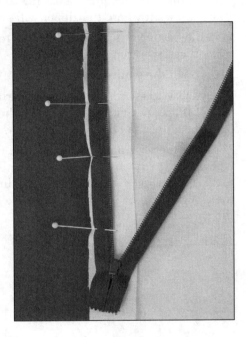

8. Using the zipper foot, machine-baste the zipper tape to the seam allowance close to the edge of the coil or teeth. Stitch from the bottom of the zipper to the top.

9. Close the zipper.

10. Smooth the zipper to the right and everything else to the left. This will create a small space to the left of the zipper between the basting stitch you just made and the seam.

11. Using a regular stitch length, and with the zipper foot positioned to the left and the needle near the teeth but on the fabric, stitch from the bottom to the top.

12. Put the garment face down and with the zipper opened. Glue or pin the other zipper tape to the other seam allowance.

13. If you have pinned the zipper to the garment, machine-baste through this zipper tape and this seam allowance only. If you have glued the zipper to the seam allowance, you can skip this step.

14. Turn the garment to the right side. Place ½-inch-wide tape on the seam line with one edge of the tape on the seam line and the bottom of the tape just below the bottom zipper stop.

15. Using a zipper foot, and starting at the seam at the bottom of the zipper, topstitch across the bottom of the tape, leave the needle in when you turn the corner of the tape, and stitch up the other side of the tape.

16. Pull all threads at the bottom of the zipper to the wrong side, and knot.

17. Remove the basing threads from step 3.

Fly Zippers

Fly zippers go in pants. Jeans and other heavy-weight pants usually need a metal or a heavy plastic zipper.

Patterns calling for fly zippers will have a fly facing as part of the pattern and lines indicating where the stitching line should be placed. Mark the stitching line on the fabric with hand-basting. Also mark the bottom of the zipper (see Chapter 20 for more information on marking a pattern). Follow the directions on the package or on your pattern for putting in a fly zipper.

Separating Zippers

Separating zippers are primarily used for jacket openings and are usually heavy duty. You can either sew them in with the teeth showing or not. Some even have colored plastic teeth for decoration.

Here are the basic steps for putting in a separating zipper:

1. Close the zipper.

2. Press the garment's seam allowance.

3. Place the zipper face up on a surface, then glue the garment to the zipper tape. For a covered separating zipper, the garment's folded edges should meet over the center of the teeth. For an uncovered zipper, the garment's folded edge should be close to teeth but not covering them. Be sure the top and bottom edges of the garment are aligned before gluing them to the zipper. Follow the pattern instructions for the amount of fabric to leave above and below zipper.

4. For a covered zipper, topstitch the zipper in place ⅜ inch from the edge or the distance suggested in the pattern.

   For an uncovered zipper, topstitch close to the zipper and again ¼ inch from the first stitch line.

   Stitch from the bottom to the top on both sides.

Invisible Zippers

You need an invisible zipper foot to attach an invisible zipper. These feet are readily available wherever invisible zippers are sold, and the directions on the invisible zipper package are easy to follow.

There are a few major differences between putting in a regular zipper and putting in an invisible zipper that you should be aware of. When sewing in a regular zipper, you first sew the seam with the place for the zipper basted close. With an invisible zipper, you put the zipper in first, and then you finish the seam.

Also, with regular zippers, you generally sew from bottom to top. With invisible zippers, you sew from top to bottom.

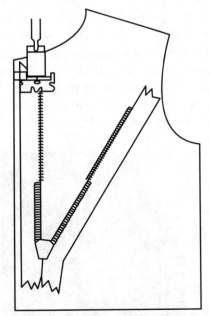

Leave the seam open before putting in an invisible zipper.

Fringe Benefits

When sewing in an invisible zipper, know which side of the fabric is the right side and which is the wrong side, and follow the directions on the package exactly. You will probably have moments when you're putting one piece to another that it seems like it will never work out right, but have faith. Keep following the directions. It is really very easy, as long as you follow the directions and don't try to second-guess them.

The Least You Need to Know

◆ Most zippers are easy to attach.

◆ You can sew in zippers in many different ways, depending on what you want the finished product to look like.

◆ Match the weight of the zipper to the weight of the fabric for best results.

In This Part

Easy Home Projects

Almost all home projects start with basic shapes[md]squares, rectangles, and occasionally circles. With these shapes and a few simple seams and hems, you'll be able to create an infinite variety of pillows, curtains, drapes, tablecloths, place mats, table runners, and napkins.

Part 3 gives easy-to-follow directions for the basics. You can take it a step further and add all the frills and adornments you like. This is an opportunity to let your imagination run wild and add color and pizzazz to every room of your home!

In This Chapter

- ◆ Choosing pillow styles
- ◆ Picking stuffings
- ◆ Choosing closures
- ◆ Sewing pillows

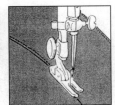

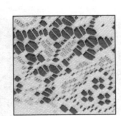
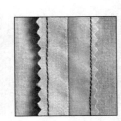

Chapter 11

Pick a Peck of Pillows

One of the quickest and easiest ways to add color and pizzazz to a room is to make a few pillows. All sewing projects give you the opportunity to use your creative talents, but you can really let your imagination go wild when you're making accent pillows. Plus, if you don't like what you've made, you can easily change it without too much waste of time or money.

Unlike other projects, such as a room's worth of draperies, the materials for pillows cost next to nothing, and some pillow covers don't even require sewing! You can make a bevy of removable pillow covers and change them regularly or seasonally. The more you allow yourself to be creative, the more fun you will have making pillows.

Personalizing Your Pillows

Pillows come in all shapes and sizes, and can be covered with almost any type of material. They can be plain or highly decorated. They can be made to look formal or informal. They can be stuffed with loose stuffing or with a ready-made form. You have as many possible pillow combinations as your imagination will allow!

Shape, Color, and Fabric

Most pillows start from basic geometrical shapes: squares, rectangles, circles, and triangles. But there is nothing to prevent you from venturing forth into trapezoids, hearts, shamrocks, stars, or hexagons.

You can make an infinite number of different pillows, all from just two basic designs.

Many quilting stores carry coordinating fabrics in fat quarters. You can make three pillows from a half-dozen fat quarters of coordinating fabrics.

Decide on the look you want to create. If you want formal, stick to squares, rectangles, and possibly circles. Choose brocades, velvets, satins, or plain heavier-weight fabrics. Keep the trim to a minimum, such as maybe one large self-covered button in the center or tassels on the corners. Use pleats instead of gathers if you want a ruffle effect.

To lighten a room, choose bright colors and make several pillows from the same fabric, but of different shapes. For a child's room, pick funky, bright primary colors of a sturdy material.

> **Fringe Benefits**
>
> In quilting stores, catalogs, and online, you can purchase several pieces of color-coordinated fabric. Some come in packets of *fat quarters*, which, at 18 by 22 inches, are just the right size for a pillow. If the packet has 6 fat quarters, you will be able to mix and match and make 3 pillows, each with a different front and back, yet all coordinated.

Stuffing

You can stuff pillows one of two ways: with loose stuffing or with ready-made forms.

With loose stuffing, you can make the pillow any shape or size you like. Loose stuffing can be messy, though, and it's a little more difficult to recycle the stuffing if you change your mind. One solution to that problem is to make an inner lining to hold the stuffing, and then you can re-cover it with decorator fabrics whenever you want. Unless the old pillow is highly embellished with buttons, tassels, ruffles, or bows, you can just put a new cover over the old one.

There are two basic kinds of loose stuffing:

- **Feathers and/or down.** A feather- or down-stuffed pillow is soft and cozy. However, feathers are expensive and are very difficult to stuff. Feathers were designed for flying, and that's just what they do—they fly. They fly everywhere when you are trying to stuff them into your pillow cover. For some reason, feathers do not like to stay evenly distributed in the pillow and you have to keep fluffing them.

Occasionally, the ends of the feathers poke out through the material, and the pillow becomes scratchy.

✂ **Cut It Out!**

Before you make a feather pillow, check to see if any of your friends or family are allergic to feathers.

◆ **Fiber filling.** Available in most fabric stores and most large chain stores that have a sewing, notion, or home crafts department, fiber fill is practical and inexpensive. It is also nonallergenic, so your allergy-burdened friends will be happy.

Bags of fiber filling are inexpensive and available in most craft and fabric stores.

If you don't want to stuff, you can use ready-made forms, available in basic shapes and sizes in most fabric and large chain stores in the home decorating departments.

Ready-made forms are relatively easy to recycle. If you want to change the cover, just take off the old cover and put on a new one! You have little control over the size or shape, though, and you have to make your cover fit the shape. With some pointy-corner forms, it is difficult to get the stuffing in the ready-made form to fill out the corners of your new cover. Ready-made forms are nonallergenic and will keep their shape when washed.

🧵 **Fringe Benefits**

If you want to use a ready-made form but can't find the shape you want, buy a foam block and cut it to shape. This won't work if you've purchased a stuffed knife-edge pillow form, though. Those are stuffed with loose stuffing, not made from a block of foam. Look for foam blocks instead. They're not usually covered; they're just foam. Some foam even comes by the yard or by the sheet.

Now that you're stuffed with size, style, and filling know-how, let's make a pillow! There are two basic styles of pillows: the knife-edge pillow and the box-edge pillow. All other pillows are variations on these two standard styles.

Knife-Edge Pillows

Knife-edge pillows are the easiest to make and the most common for accent pillows. Knife-edge pillows start with two same-size pieces of fabric, usually squares, rectangles, or circles, one for the top or front, and one for the bottom or back. You don't even have to have two pieces of the same material. Any two pieces of fabric you have left over from other projects or that appeal to you and go with your décor will work. Let your imagination take flight.

The pillows are plump in the middle and have a knife edge along the seam. With two pieces of material and some stuffing on hand, you will be able to make a simple knife-edge pillow in less than an hour.

Here are the basic directions for making a stuffed knife-edge pillow:

1. Cut two squares of material on the grain to the size you want for your pillow.

2. With the right sides together and using a ½-inch seam allowance, sew around the edge, leaving an opening in the middle of one side large enough for your hand. Don't leave the opening on a corner.

3. Trim the corners.

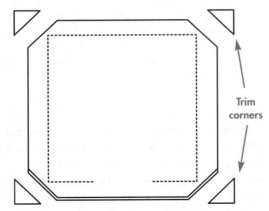

Trim corners

To eliminate corner bulk when making pillows, trim the excess fabric from the corners with a diagonal cut.

4. Turn the cover right side out. Press to make the edges and corners sharp and neat.

5. Stuff with stuffing, pushing the stuffing into corners. Use 8 to 12 ounces of stuffing for an 11-inch pillow. Adjust the plumpness to your taste.

6. Slip stitch the opening closed.

The most popular and the simplest decorator pillow to make is the knife-edge pillow.

Here are the basic directions for a ready-made-form-filled knife-edge pillow:

1. Cut two squares of fabric on the grain 1 inch wider than the form or finished pillow.

2. With the right sides together and using a ½-inch seam allowance, sew around the edge, leaving an opening in the middle of one side large enough to squeeze the pillow form through.

3. Trim the corners.

4. Turn the cover right side out. Press to make the edges and corners sharp and neat.

5. Stuff the form into the cover.

6. Slip stitch the opening closed.

Fringe Benefits

The nature of a knife-edge pillow is to be plump in the middle, which causes the corners to stick out like ears. To keep the corners from sticking out too noticeably, fold each fabric square into quarters. Make a mark ¼ inch in from the corner, make another mark at the mid-point of each side between the folded edge and the open edge, then draw a line between the points. Cut on the line, creating a slight taper at the corners.

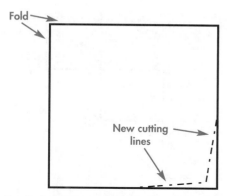

To eliminate ears on you knife edge pillow, make the stitching line near the corners as shown here.

Flange Pillows

The flange pillow is a knife-edge pillow with a wide edge, usually about 2 inches deep. Flanges can be single, double, or fringed. You can stuff them with either loose stuffing or a ready-made knife-edge form.

Single-Flange Pillows

Here are the basic directions for a single-flange pillow:

1. Cut two squares of fabric on the grain 5 inches larger than you want the pillow to be or 5 inches larger than the ready-made form.

2. With the rights sides together and using a ½-inch seam allowance, sew around the edge, leaving an opening in the middle of one side large enough for your hand or to squeeze the form through.

3. Trim the corners.
4. Turn the cover right side out. Press.
5. Topstitch around the cover 2 inches in from the edge, leaving an opening in the same place as in step 2.

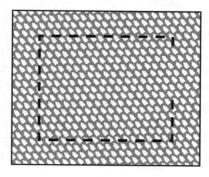

6. Stuff the form or filling into the cover.

7. Pin the opening closed on the 2-inch line, being careful not to get any stuffing or the form in the seam line. Put the pins in on the line with the heads toward you when the pillow is under the needle. This will help you pull out the pins as you go.

9. Finish topstitching across the opening at the 2-inch line using a zipper presser foot.

10. Slip stitch the opening closed at the edge.

Sewing the opening closed at the 2-inch line is difficult—even if it is well marked, pinned, and taped and you're using a zipper foot—because the bulge of the pillow gets in the way. You have to use both hands to hold the seam line under the needle, one in front of the presser foot and one behind. You can also use your left shoulder to help push on the bulge of the pillow, if you need to. It might take some practice to keep the stitches straight.

Here are a few other hints:

◆ Machine-stitch only on fabrics that do not show stitching. Try brocades, for example.

◆ Don't stuff the pillow too full.

◆ Use a fancy stitch that has a lot of fill, such as a satin stitch, on the 2-inch line. Before sewing the top to the bottom (step 2 in the basic steps for a flange pillow), put a line of fancy stitching on one side of the top and one side of the bottom. Proceed with steps 2 through 5 using the fancy stitch and leaving one side with the already-sewn stitches open. Put in the stuffing, and instead of machine-stitching across the opening, hide hand-sewn stitches in the fancy stitch already there.

◆ Put a closure on the bottom piece and use a ready-made form. (See the "Removable Pillow Covers" section later in the chapter for some closure ideas.)

Double-Flange Pillows

Here are the basic directions for a double-flange pillow:

1. Cut two squares of fabric on the grain 9 inches larger than the ready-made pillow form.

2. On each piece, press a 2½-inch hem to the wrong side on all 4 sides.

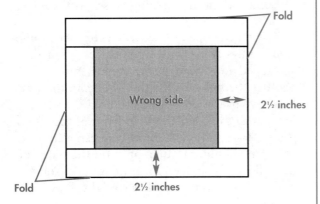

3. Open out the pressed sides.

4. Fold each corner diagonally so the fold lines match exactly, then press.

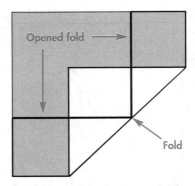

5. Open out the corners.

6. Fold the cover diagonally, with right sides together.

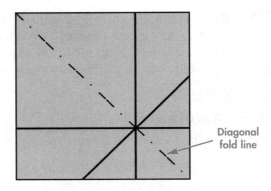

7. Pin and stitch on the fold you made in step 4.

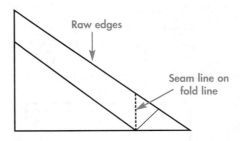

8. Trim the seam you just made to ⅜ inch. Repeat on all corners.

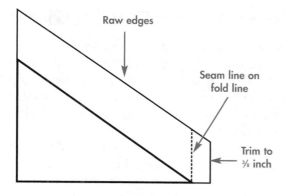

Raw edges

Seam line on fold line

Trim to ⅜ inch

9. Press open the seam.
10. Turn out the corners and press. Poke out the corners to get a crisp point.
11. On the right side of the top piece, put tape 2 inches in from each edge.
12. With the wrong sides together, place the top piece on the bottom. Stitch along the tape line on three sides and about 1 inch from each end of the fourth side.
13. Slide the pillow form into the pocket you made in step 12.
14. Pin the fourth side on the 2-inch line, being careful not to catch the pillow, with the pins straight on the line and the heads toward you when the pillow is under the needle.
15. Topstitch the fourth side at the 2-inch line using a zipper presser foot, removing the pins as you go.

As with all the flange pillows, it will be easier if you use one of the closures suggested later. However, these are basic directions, so adjust your project accordingly.

Fringed-Flange Pillows

Here are the basic directions for a fringed-flange pillow:

1. Cut two squares of fabric 4 inches wider than the desired size of the pillow. Be sure to cut on the grain, vertically and horizontally.

Fringe Benefits

Use a fabric that is loosely woven and has strong threads. Brocades, wools, or burlap will work well.

2. On the right side of the top piece, put tape 2 inches in from each edge. If fabric has a nap, do not use tape; use the 2-inch seam guide on your machine instead.
3. With the *wrong* sides together, topstitch around three sides at the 2-inch line and about 1 inch from each end of the fourth side.
4. Insert the pillow form into the pocket you made in step 3.
5. Pin the fourth side on the 2-inch line, being careful not to catch the pillow, with the pins straight on the line and the heads toward you when the pillow is under the needle. Also, be sure the raw edges are even.

6. Topstitch the fourth side at the 2-inch line using a zipper presser foot, removing the pins as you go.

7. Pull threads to make a fringe.

> ### Fringe Benefits
>
> Before pulling threads to make a fringe, clip the edge to within ½ of the stitching line about every 2 to 3 inches. This will make it easier to pull the threads, and they won't get as tangled up.

To have even fringe all around your pillow, be sure to cut the fabric on the grain.

Corded, Welted, or Piped-Edge Pillows

Another way to finish a knife-edge pillow is to put cording or piping, sometimes called welting, in the knife-edge seam. This gives the pillow a nice, neat edge that's not like every other pillow edge in the house. Cording covered with plain fabric works well with busy fabrics or if you have a needlepoint or embroidered top you want to show off. You can buy some already-covered piping, but the color selection is limited. You can easily make your own covered cording to match your fabric.

Here are the basic directions for making piping:

1. You will need enough piping to go around the perimeter of your project. Measure around the pillow or calculate how much you will need, then add at least 6 inches to that number.

   Buy the uncovered cord at a fabric or home decorating center. It usually comes by the yard. Round up if you are in doubt as to how much you need. You don't want to have to piece it at the last minute. It also comes in a variety of diameters. Select the diameter you think will work best with your fabric and pillow shape.

2. You will also need a rectangular piece of fabric from which you will make *bias strips*.

> ### Sew You Say
>
> **Bias strips** are strips of fabric cut on the bias or at 45 degrees from the selvage. Bias strips are used primarily as finishes on curved edges, but they can also be used to finish hems and other raw edges. You can purchase bias strips or make them by cutting a piece of fabric into strips on the bias. Homemade strips can be cut to any width. Bias strips are also used to cover cording for use as piping.

3. Square up the fabric. Be sure the grain lines are straight on the cut edge and the selvage. Check to see if the true bias is really at 45 degrees from the cut edge and the selvage.

4. With the fabric right side down, on the wrong side of the fabric, draw a line on the bias using one of these methods:

   Method 1: Fold the fabric on the diagonal, being sure one of the crosswise-cut edges meets the selvage smoothly and there are no wrinkles in the fold. If you're sure you have the fold on the true bias, carefully press the fold. On some fabrics, the bias fold might want to wiggle around.

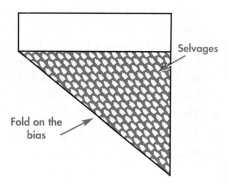

   Method 2: Use a plastic ruler that's the shape of a right triangle. Put the right angle of your triangle ruler where the selvage meets the cut edge. The hypotenuse (or the longest side) of the triangle should be on the bias of the fabric. Slowly draw a line on the fabric along the hypotenuse of the ruler. The fabric might want to bunch up and wrinkle.

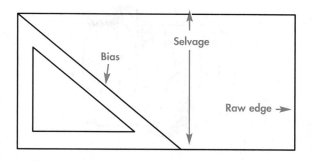

5. If your cord is ¼ inch, you will need to cut your bias strips 1½ inches wide. If the cord is wider, measure the circumference and add 1 inch. That will be the width of the bias strips you will have to make.

6. From the pressed or marked line on your fabric, draw parallel lines of the desired width. For more lines, cut the triangle from one end, stitch it to the other end, and keep drawing lines.

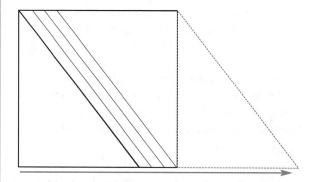

7. With the rights sides together and in the configuration shown in the following figure with all the lines matching, except offset by 1 line, sew a ¼-inch seam to form a tube.

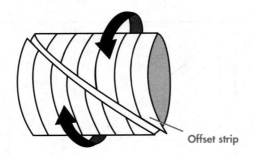

Offset strip

8. Make one continuous cut following the marked line to produce a long bias strip.

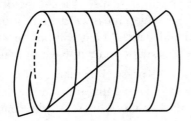

9. Fold the bias strip over the cord, wrong sides together. Using a zipper presser foot, stitch as close to the cord as possible, keeping the raw edges even and together. They might try to slip around!

In the following table, I've given you a few examples of how many yards of bias strip you can make from 1 yard of fabric, depending on the width of the fabric and the widths of the strips you want.

Here are the basic directions for using piping to finish the edge of a pillow:

1. On the right side of the top piece of the pillow, with the raw edges of the piping and the cover together, baste the piping to the edge all the way around. (The piping cording will be toward the center of the pillow top.) At the corners, make a clip in the piping seam allowance from the raw edge to the cording. Be careful not to cut the piping stitching.

2. Place the right sides of the top and bottom pieces together.

3. Using a zipper presser foot, stitch around the pillow with the presser foot as close to the piping as possible. If you have basted the piping in, stitch on the basting line. Even though you can't see it, you will be able to feel it. This should also be at the ½-inch seam allowance. Be sure to leave an opening for stuffing.

4. Trim the corners.

5. Turn the cover right side out, and stuff.

6. Slip stitch the opening closed.

Yards of Continuous Bias Strip Made from 1 Yard of Fabric

Fabric Width (Inches)	Width of Bias Strip (Inches)				
	1.25	1.75	2.25	2.75	3.75
45	35	25	19	16	12
54	42	30	23	19	14
60	47	34	26	21	16

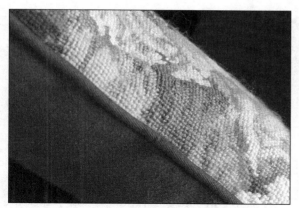

Piping gives a pillow a nice, clean edge.

Ruffled-Edge Pillows

Like piping, ruffles are inserted into the seam before you sew the top and bottom pillow cover pieces together. Ruffles can be any width, usually from 1 to 3 inches, and you have a choice of two finishes.

One way to finish the ruffle is by making a narrow, ¼-inch turned hem on the bottom of the ruffle. If the fabric has a right and wrong side, the wrong side will show when someone turns over the pillow.

The second method is to fold the fabric lengthwise so there is a fold on the bottom edge of the ruffle instead of a hem. This is the preferred method, plus it's easier and the wrong side of the fabric doesn't show.

Here are the basic directions for making a ruffled-edge pillow:

1. Measure the perimeter of your pillow, then multiply that number by 2½. This is the least amount of material you should have in your ruffle.

2. Cut strips of material on the long-wise or crosswise grain twice the width of the ruffle you want, plus 1 inch (for the ½-inch seam allowance). For example, if you want a 2-inch ruffle, cut 5-inch-wide strips.

3. Cut as many strips as you need to equal the length you calculated in step 1. For example, if you have a 15-inch pillow, you'll need to cut enough strips to equal 150 inches: $4 \times 15 = 60 \times 2.5 = 150$. Assuming your material is 44 inches wide, you will need about 4 strips: $150 \div 44 =$ approximately 4. If the material is soft, you will be able to use all 4 strips easily. If the material is stiff, you might want to go with 3 strips. In general, fuller is better.

4. Stitch the strips together with a ½-inch seam allowance, and press open.

5. Stitch both ends together.

6. Fold the strip wrong sides together, and press.

7. Stitch the gathering line along the raw edge using one of the methods suggested in Chapter 7.

8. Mark quarter and eighth points on the ruffle.

9. With the right sides together, pin the ruffle's quarter marks to the corners of the top piece and the ruffle's eighth marks midway between the corners. Adjust the gathers to evenly distribute them around the pillow top. Make a clip in the seam allowance of the ruffle at the corner.

10. Baste the ruffle to the pillow top on the ½-inch seam allowance line. With the raw edges together, the bottom fold of the ruffle will be toward the center of the top.

11. With the right sides together, place the top on the bottom, matching the raw edges. Be sure the ruffle doesn't get into the seam. This takes a little friendly encouragement. Gently pull the raw edges with one hand and the bottom of the ruffle with the other. Stitch around the edge, staying on the basting stitches you made in step 10. Be sure to leave an opening for the stuffing.

12. Trim the corners.

13. Turn the cover right side out, and stuff.

14. Slip stitch the opening closed.

Ruffles can be any size.

For a more formal look, use pleats instead of gathers. This takes a little more calculation and patience to get the pleats even, but the more formal look might be worth it to you.

> **Fringe Benefits**
>
> You can use these directions for round pillows as well. Just be sure to clip the seam allowance about every inch all the way around the curve.

Box-Edge Pillows

Box-edge pillows look like, well, boxes. They have a length, width, and depth because they are formed from a block of foam. Box-edge cushions are used primarily as seats on chairs and sofas. Select durable fabric because these pillows will experience more wear than accent pillows.

There are two basic styles of box pillows: fitted and contemporary.

Fitted Box-Edge Pillows

The edges of box-edge fitted pillows or cushions are clearly defined, usually with piping. The cover is made from three pieces: the top, the bottom, and the side, or the *boxing strip*.

Here are the basic directions for making a fitted box-edge pillow:

1. Measure the length, width, and depth of the foam.

2. Add 1 inch to the width and length measurements from step 1 for the seam allowance, and cut two squares of fabric on the grain, one for the top and one for the bottom.

3. Measure the perimeter of the cushion or calculate the perimeter with this formula: $(2 \times length) + (2 \times width) = perimeter$. Add 1 inch to both the length and width measurements for the seam allowance.

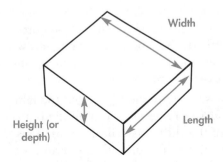

Width

Height (or depth)

Length

4. Using the measures in step 3, cut out the strips either on the lengthwise grain or on the crosswise grain.

> **Cut It Out!**
>
> If you cut on the crosswise grain, you probably will have to have more than one strip. Be sure to add in the extra seam allowances. If the fabric has stripes or is a plaid, you will have to adjust the length of your strips accordingly to match pattern.

5. Attach piping to both the top and bottom pieces as described in the earlier "Corded, Welted, or Piped-Edge Pillows" section.

6. Sew the side piece together at both ends. Mark the side piece at the width and length points: width, length, width, length (see the following figure). If part of the cushion will always be facing out, try to arrange the markings so no seam will be on the front face.

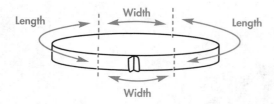

7. Stay stitch just inside the ½-inch mark on the top and bottom of the strip at each marked point. Clip the seam allowance to the stitches.

8. With the right sides together and the marked notches matching at the corners, pin the side to the top. Use a zipper foot, and stitch as close to the piping as possible. When you get to a corner, back-tack a few stitches before turning the corner, and sew to the corner. Leaving the needle in, lift the presser foot, turn the corner, lower the presser foot, take a few stitches, and back-tack again. Repeat at each corner.

9. Repeat step 8 on the bottom piece, leaving an opening for inserting the foam.

10. Turn right side out, and insert the foam.

11. Slip stitch the opening closed.

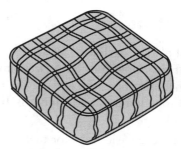

As the name suggests, box edge pillows look like boxes.

Contemporary Box-Edge Pillows

Contemporary box-edge pillows are a cross between a knife-edge pillow and a box pillow. They look like boxes but with undefined edges. There are only two pieces of fabric, the top and the bottom and are made just like a knife-edge pillow except that the corners are *mitered*.

> ### Sew You Say
> You make a **mitered** corner by sewing a seam from the diagonal to the straight edge, thereby cutting off the corner of the triangle formed when the fabric is folded on the diagonal. When you turn the cover right side out, you'll have a neat right angle.

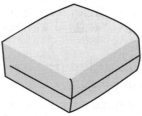

Contemporary box-edge pillows are made like knife-edge pillows with mitered corners.

Rolls or Bolsters

Rolls or bolsters are long, round tubes filled with stuffing. Some rolls have circular ends, while others just have the ends of the tubes gathered together and tied (think of Tootsie roll candy).

Here are the basic steps for making a roll or a bolster with flat ends:

1. Measure the length and circumference of the foam roll. (If you can't find a ready-made roll to suit your needs, you can make one by rolling up a sheet of polyester batting.)

2. Add 1 inch to the length and 1 inch to the circumference for the seam allowance.

3. To make the circular ends, measure the diameter of the end of the foam roll. Add 1 inch to this measurement for the seam allowance. Fold a piece of paper into quarters. Attach a piece of string to a pencil. Hold the string the length of the radius of the circle (diameter ÷ 2 = radius) at the corner where the folds in the paper come together. Draw an arc on the paper, being sure the radius remains the same all the way around. Cut out this circle, and use it as your pattern piece. (See the "Going Around in Circles" section of Chapter 12 for more on working with round cuts of fabric.)

4. Using the circle pattern piece, make two circles of fabric.

5. Fold the rectangular piece of fabric in half lengthwise, with the right sides together. Do not crease the fold. On each end and with a ½-inch seam allowance, sew a short seam from the end of the tube toward the middle, leaving space in the middle to insert the foam.

6. With the right sides together and using a ½-inch seam allowance, attach one end of the circle to the tube you made in step 5. Be sure to clip the circle in the seam allowance in several places. You might want to stay-stitch the circle first before sewing the circle to the tube.

7. Repeat on the other end of the tube.

8. Turn the cover right side out, and insert the foam.

9. Slip stitch the opening closed.

Removable Pillow Covers

If you want to be able to remove a cover from the pillow to wash it or change to a different cover, you need to put in an opening. You can put three basic openings on a pillow: envelope; snap, hook and loop, or button opening; and the zipper opening. These openings make it easy to remove the cover if you want to clean it or change it. It's also easier to make some pillow cover treatments, such as flange, as a removable cover.

On knife-edge pillows, the openings are usually placed on the back of the pillow. On box pillows, the openings are placed either on the back or in the boxing strip (most often the latter).

When you're putting the pillow cover together, put the closure opening in first and then treat the piece with the closure as if it didn't have an opening.

Envelope Openings

Here are the basic steps for making an envelope opening (assuming you're making a square pillow):

1. Measure the width of the pillow and add 1 inch for the seam allowance.

2. Using the measurement you got in step 1, cut one square of fabric for the front. For example, for a 15-inch pillow, you'll cut a 16-inch square. This will be the front of the pillow. Remember to always cut on the grain of the fabric unless the directions tell you otherwise.

3. You'll need two same-size rectangles for the back. One dimension of the rectangle will be the width of the pillow plus 1 inch. For the other dimension, divide the width-plus-1-inch measurement by 2 and then add 5 inches. For example, for our 15-inch pillow: 15 + 1 = 16. 16 ÷ 2 = 8. 8 + 5 = 13 inches. Therefore, you'll need 2 (16 × 13-inch) rectangles.

Front 16 × 16

Back 16 × 13
(cut 2)

4. Make a 1-inch double hem on one edge of each of the two back pieces.

5. With right sides together, place the back pieces on top of the front piece, overlapping the hemmed edges and matching the raw edges all around four sides. Pin and stitch with a ½-inch seam allowance.

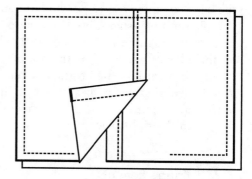

6. Turn the cover right side out, and press.
7. Insert the pillow.

Fastener Openings

Here are the basic steps for making an opening with fasteners (assuming you're making a square pillow):

1. Measure the width of the pillow and add 1 inch for the seam allowance.

2. Using the measurement you got in step 1, cut one square of fabric for the front. For example, for our 15-inch pillow, you'll cut a 16-inch square. This will be the front of the pillow.

3. You'll need two same-size rectangles for the back. One dimension of the rectangle will be the width of the pillow plus 1 inch. For the other dimension, divide the width-plus-1-inch measurement by 2, and then add up to 4 inches.

4. Make a 1-inch double hem on one edge of each of the two back pieces, then finish the edges as appropriate for the fasteners you plan to use—snaps, hook and loop, or buttons. Attach the fasteners so they're on the edge of what will be the top piece when the cover is turned right side out. You'll have to experiment a little to figure out where to put the bottom fasteners so they're in the right place

> ### Fringe Benefits
> If you want to use buttons as your fastener, skip the button holes, use snaps for the opening, and cover the snaps with decorative buttons.

5. With right sides together, place the back pieces on top of the front piece, overlapping the hemmed edges and matching the raw edges all around four sides. Pin and stitch with a ½-inch seam allowance.

Zipper Openings

If you'd rather put in a zipper instead of buttons, snaps, or hooks and loops, that's easy enough. Follow the directions in the "Fastener Openings" section earlier in this chapter, but add 1 inch for the zipper seam allowance on each of the back pieces. Follow the directions in the "Centered Zippers" section in Chapter 10, then finish as in this chapter's "Fastener Openings" section.

The Least You Need to Know

◆ You can make a wide variety of different pillows from two basic pillow styles: knife-edge and box.

◆ You can make a simple yet pretty knife-edge pillow in less than an hour.

◆ You can stuff your new pillows with two kinds of easy-to-use pillow stuffing: ready-made forms and loose fiber fill.

◆ You can close a pillow cover in three basic ways: zipper; envelope opening; or closures with snaps, buttons, or hooks and loops.

In This Chapter

- ◆ Selecting tablecloth fabric
- ◆ Measuring for a variety of tablecloth designs
- ◆ Selecting the appropriate "drop" for the occasion
- ◆ Straightening tablecloth material

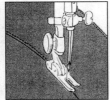

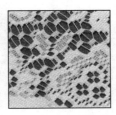
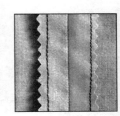

Chapter 12

Adorning Your Table

Why make a tablecloth when they are readily available in most stores? The answer to that question might be another question: "Why buy a tablecloth when they are so easy to make?" (Of course, depending on where you shop and what you want, one or the other might be more or less expensive.)

Besides appealing to your "I made it myself!" need, there are at least two other good reasons to make your own tablecloth. First, it will probably be easier to find fabric to match your decorating tastes than to find a manufactured tablecloth of the right color. Also, you can make the tablecloth any size and shape you want. If you have an old antique table, for example, it might not be one of the current typical sizes. Round and oval tablecloths come in only a few standard sizes and are not always available.

Getting Your Table's Measurements

The first step to making your own tablecloth is to measure the top of your table. Think geometry: circles, squares, rectangles, and ovals. For ovals, squares, and rectangles, you need to know the width and length. For circles, you need to know the diameter.

For all size and shape tables, you need to decide how much fabric you want hanging down from the top of the table. This is called the "drop." There are a few traditional lengths of drop:

◆ **Floor-length** tablecloths are just that—the drop reaches to the floor. This length is great for accent tables, buffet tables, and tables whose legs have been scratched by the cat; for hiding some storage containers; and for once-in-a-while elegant dining.

Fringe Benefits

Tablecloths aren't limited to the dining room table. If you have an old relic of an accent or end table that needs painting, skip the paint and cover it with a cheery tablecloth. It's much easier to make a tablecloth than paint a table. Besides, you can change the tablecloth on a whim, whereas refinishing a table is a time-consuming event.

◆ For **formal-length** tablecloths, the drop is between 16 and 24 inches from the edge of the table. When the chairs are at the table, the cloth rests on the chair.

Cut It Out!

The problem with floor-length tablecloths for regular meals is that the cloth often gets in the way and it's difficult to know where to put your legs. Do you lift up the cloth and have some of it in your lap, or do you just push in? On square and rectangular tables with floor-length tablecloths, it's difficult to push in because there isn't much extra fabric. It is easier to push in on circular floor-length cloths because of the fullness.

◆ **Seat-length** tablecloths have a drop that reaches to somewhere near the top of the seat, usually 10 to 12 inches. This helps with the problem of deciding where to put your knees!

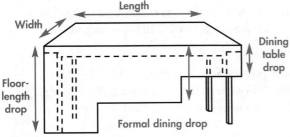

Before making a tablecloth, you need to know your table's dimensions.

Fringe Benefits

You might want to measure all the tables in your home at one time while you have your tape measure out. I give you a place to put the measurements in Appendix D. Tear it out and keep it in your purse. You never know when you're going to see the perfect fabric for your table. This way, you'll have your measurements list handy so you'll know how much to buy.

Selecting Fabric

The fabric selection for table linens today is practically endless. You can change the mood of a room easily by just changing the fabric and color of the tablecloth.

How do you want your table to look? Consider the following when you're selecting fabrics for your tablecloth:

◆ Is the table you're covering an accent table that will have little or no use other than decoration?

◆ Are the children going to be eating on it daily?

◆ Are you covering the table for a one-time elegant evening party?

◆ Do you want a bright and cheery look?

◆ Do you want a formal, subdued look?

◆ What other home décor colors and styles are you trying to match?

◆ Is the tablecloth to be the center of attention, or is what's on the tablecloth—the place mats, table runner, or napkins—to be highlighted?

◆ What other table accessories will you be using—flowers in vases, candlesticks, name place cards, or party favors?

◆ Is this tablecloth for a breakfast, brunch, lunch, tea, dinner, or dessert table?

◆ Is this a buffet table?

◆ On the average, how much and what is going to be spilled on the tablecloth?

Changing the tablecloth and napkins changes the mood of your table setting.

I'll Be Darned

In the "old days," linen was the fabric of choice for tablecloths. That's why you'll sometimes hear "table linens" in reference to tablecloths, even though the fabric might be polyester or wool.

Once you've thought about some of these questions and you've measured the table and decided on the drop, you're ready to go to the fabric store.

Make your first stop in the fabric store the home décor section. (Most general fabric stores have this section, but some quilting fabric stores might not have it.) Here you'll usually find bolts of fabric specifically for table linens, curtains, and drapes. These fabrics are wide— around 60 inches—and come on rolls.

Fringe Benefits

Also in the home décor department, you can find flannel-backed vinyl material sold by the yard. This is inexpensive, comes in a variety of colors and designs, and is great for picnics or if you have children.

If you can't find what you want in the home décor section, look around the store.

Don't despair if you find the fabric you want but it's not wide enough for your table (most fabric is 44 inches wide, so this might be the case often). You can still work with it. Also read the fabric care instructions on the end of the bolt. Fabric that stains easily and is difficult to clean does not make very good dining-table tablecloths.

When you've decided what fabric you want, it is time to figure out how much you need. If you filled out the chart from Appendix D and stuck it in your purse, you'll know at a glance how much you need to buy.

Widening the Fabric

Unless your table is very narrow, you'll most likely have to make the width of the fabric wider. If you've chosen a fabric that's narrower than the width you need (taking into account hems, drops, and the width of table), you'll have to purchase double the length measurement.

First you should check to see if the grain lines are straight. The cross-grain threads should be perpendicular to the selvage. If they aren't, try pulling on the bias in both directions.

For most soft home furnishings such as curtains, draperies, tablecloths, and napkins, it's important to have the fabric square. To do this:

1. Fold the fabric in half lengthwise, with the right sides together. Be sure the fabric is smooth and there are no bubbles.

2. Cut a nick into both selvages near the cut ends.

3. Open the fabric to a single layer. Mark a line across the fabric connecting the nicks. This line should be perpendicular to the selvage.

4. Cut on the line you marked in step 3. You should end up with a perfect rectangle, with all four corners at 90 degrees.

When you're sure your fabric is square, cut it in half crosswise so you have two equal pieces of fabric: A and B. Because you don't want the seam down the middle of your table, cut one of the halves (B) lengthwise into two pieces: now C and D. Sew C and D onto each side of piece A.

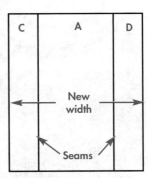

To make the fabric wider, rather than sewing two pieces together with the seam down the middle, arrange the fabric so the seams fall at or just below the top of the table.

The widths of the side pieces C and D will vary. For example, if you need to add 44 inches to create the desired tablecloth width, cut B into 2 equal parts, each 22 inches wide. If you need only 20 inches, cut 2 strips from B, each 10 inches wide. Remember to add in seam allowances where appropriate.

You might have a reason to cut both A and B. For example, you might want the seam to come exactly at the edge of the table. In this case, you might also have to cut A to the appropriate width and then cut B to the desired drop.

Going Around in Circles

For a circular tablecloth, you'll first make the fabric wider, as you did in the earlier "Cutting and Sewing" section. When you finish piecing, you'll want to have a square of fabric. Then just treat the seamed fabric as if it was a one-piece square.

Here are the basic instructions for making a circle:

1. Fold your fabric square into quarters, matching the seam lines.
2. Find a piece of string that doesn't have any give, such as dental floss.
3. Tie one end of the string to a pin and the other end to a marking pencil.
4. Make the string the length of your desired radius.
5. Pin the string to the corner where the folds come together.
6. Draw an arc, then measure the radius the arc in a few places to be sure it is the same everywhere.
7. Cut through the 4 layers of fabric and you have a circle.

You can also make a paper pattern first. You might have to piece together several pieces of newspaper to get the paper big enough. If you make a paper pattern, you have to make only a quarter of the circle, then just place the straight edges (the radius) on the folds of the folded fabric.

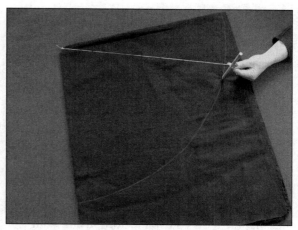

All you need to make a perfect circle is a pin, a string, and a marking pencil.

Oval Tablecloths

To make an oval tablecloth, measure and prepare your fabric as if it were a rectangle, but do not hem it yet. Place and center the fabric on the table. Put some weights or books on top so the fabric won't slip around. Measure the drop on the sides and ends, being sure the fabric is centered. These four measurements should be equal. Continue measuring the fabric all the way around the table, marking the measurement with pins. Be sure to keep your ruler perpendicular to the floor. Don't tilt it, or you won't get an accurate measure.

When you've marked the fabric with pins, remove the fabric from the table and carefully fold it into quarters. Be sure the ends and sides meet, there are no bubbles or creases in the fabric, and the layers of fabric are close together on the fold lines. Adjust the curves by moving any pins so all four corner curves look about the same. Trim, then proceed with your choice of hem.

Fringe Benefits

If it doesn't matter to you if the rounded corners are exactly the same length as the drop on the sides and end, fold the fabric in quarters carefully and round off the corners with a large dinner plate.

Hemming

You can use any of the hem finishes described in Chapter 9 on your tablecloth, using your machine or hemming by hand. For round and oval tablecloths, use a very narrow hem, which will keep the edge from twisting. For an informal look, try putting on a ruffle. This also helps keep the hem from twisting. On square and rectangular tablecloths, use a narrow hem or a 1-inch double turned hem. If you choose the double turned hem, be sure to miter the corners (see Chapter 11 for mitering tips).

You can also choose from a wide variety of trims, fringes, and laces to add to the hem of your tablecloth. Or you can embellish the hem with hand-embroidered stitches or with a fancy stitch you find on your machine. Go wild. Try something new.

Fringe Benefits

For an extra special look, make two tablecloths of coordinating fabrics but with different amounts of drop. They'll look great layered on your table.

Napkins

The fun of making napkins comes in choosing the fabric. You can select fabric that coordinates with your other table decorations, or you might want to match the napkins to the tablecloth or table runner or place mats. You might want to have a plain tablecloth and have your napkins match your flower centerpiece.

Napkins are just hemmed squares. The sizes vary somewhat, from 10-inch cocktail napkins to 18- to 20-inch dinner napkins. Don't be tempted to make dinner napkins that are too small. You can easily get 4 napkins from 1 yard of 44-inch fabric.

The purpose of napkins, remember, is to keep spills off your lap, to wipe your hands, and to occasionally dab at your face. Select fabric that is stain resistant and not too scratchy. It also helps if the fabric is easy to iron after it's washed. It's often a good idea to preshrink the fabric before cutting it. If the fabric wrinkles badly and is difficult to iron after preshrinking, you might want to find a different fabric.

Fringe Benefits

Before you cut the fabric, be sure the grain is straight both horizontally and vertically. Cut the napkins on the grain lines. This is particularly important if you are going to pull threads and fringe the edge.

Napkins often have very narrow hems (see Chapter 8 for instructions for narrow hems), but choose the hem finish that most appeals to you.

Napkins aren't often embellished with ribbons, lace, buttons, or ruffles. Keep it simple. Let the decorating statement be in the fabric.

Preshrinking

Some fabrics shrink in the wash, and some fabrics claim to be preshrunk. Use your judgment about these. If the fabric needs to be dry cleaned, you might want to take the fabric to the dry cleaners for preshrinking before you start.

For curtains, tablecloths, or napkins that will be washed regularly, it's a good idea to first preshrink the fabric. You can do this in many ways, but it's probably safest to wash the fabric the way you'll wash the tablecloth or napkins when you throw them in the laundry.

Cut It Out!

Sometimes long pieces of material such as tablecloths get wrapped up and tangled in the dryer. If you have mesh washing and drying bags, these might help.

The Least You Need to Know

- Tablecloths are functional and decorative—and are easy to make yourself.
- Tablecloths have three measurements: width, length, and drop.
- Even round and oval tablecloths start out as rectangles.
- Napkins are basically just hemmed squares.
- To be on the safe side, preshrink your fabric in the same manner you will clean the finished product.

In This Chapter

◆ Designing table runners

◆ Creating place mats

◆ Making a quilted project (without quilting anything!)

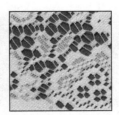

Chapter **13**

Table Runners and Place Mats

One of the easiest ways to set a pretty table is to use place mats or a table runner. You can vary your decorations seasonally by having a stash of different runners and mats readily available in your linen closet. You can make a bunch of seasonal runners all at once with a little cutting, a little glue, and possibly a little hemming.

You make table runners and place mats the same way. The only difference is size and shape. Table runners tend to be long and narrow and go down the middle of a table, and place mats are usually rectangles sized to hold a place setting of china and silverware.

Table Runners

The size of your table runners depends on the size of your table (or bureau or side table). If the runner is to remain on the table during the meal, it should be narrow and short enough not to bump into anyone's place settings or place mats. If you want your runner to overhang the edge of the table where guests will be sitting, be sure it's wide enough to accommodate a place setting of china and silverware. A highly ruffled runner might not be appropriate for this occasion.

Runners can be any shape. They are traditionally rectangular and about 12 inches wide and vary in length. But they don't have to be rectangle. If your table is round, why not make a round table runner? The corners don't have to be square, either. Ovals, rounded-cornered rectangles, and triangular pointed ends all work.

Table runners can be made from any fabric and can be single-sided, quilted, or lined. Of course, the simplest table runner is just a hemmed rectangle of your favorite fabric. In Chapter 5, I gave you directions for a simple no-sew table runner. The hems and trim on that runner were put together with glue, but you can also hand- or machine-sew your runner. The butterflies on that runner were attached with double-sided fusible webbing, but you could instead hand- or machine-*appliqué* them if you like.

> ### Sew You Say
>
> **Appliqué** is the process of sewing one piece of fabric on top of another. The edges of the applied piece are turned under and attached with invisible or decorative stitches, zigzagged, or glued.

Here are the basic directions for a simple table runner (assuming you're making a rectangle table runner):

1. Cut a rectangle of fabric the size you want.

2. Measure 2 pieces of decorative trim the length of the runner, plus enough extra on the ends to equal the width of the trim. Measure 2 pieces of trim for the width of the runner in the same manner.

> ### Fringe Benefits
>
> If you are going to bind the edge of your runner or place mat with a bias edging, rounded corners are easier to finish than square corners. Find a plate and round off all the corners before you finish the edge. If you're making a fringed edge, you do need to have straight sides and square corners.

3. With right sides together and using a ½-inch seam allowance, sew the trim to the runner on two opposite sides, leaving enough extra on both ends to equal the width of the trim.

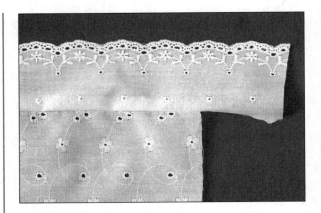

4. Sew the trim to the other two sides of the runner, leaving enough extra on both ends, as in step 3.

5. Miter all four corners of the trim.

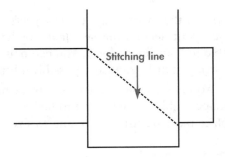

Stitching line

6. Trim the mitered corners, then press flat.

> ### Fringe Benefits
>
> For a simple and simply elegant runner or bureau scarf, use a piece of nice white, ecru, or off-white linen. Trim the edge with a soft antique lace that lays relatively flat, with not too much ruffle. Try two different shades of white for the laces, one slightly narrower than the other, placed on top of each other, and sewn to the linen.

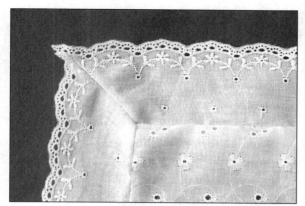

Mitering the corners gives a nice finish and enables the runner to lay flat.

Place Mats

Place mats can make a table—or make a table look completely different, depending on what you want. You can find place mats made from almost any material—plastic, bamboo, rush, cork, or fabric.

Place mats are usually 12 by 18 inches. If you have a round table, consider making trapezoid place mats instead of rectangle ones, as trapezoids will fit on the table better. For place mats that will go on a round table, you might want to make them with a rounded bottom or top edge.

> **Cut It Out!**
>
> Remember, place mats will be placed under food that might be spilled. When buying fabric, consider how easy or difficult the fabric will be to wash and press and also how stain resistant it is.

Follow the table runner directions for making place mats, except make them shorter, and make several alike or that complement each other in some way.

Seasonal Runners and Place Mats

You can make a seasonal set of runners very quickly and easily by using plain, stiff material for the background (such as Trigger fabric), any fabric for the appliquéd designs, fusible webbing, and cookie cutters. Here's how:

1. Trace cookie cutters onto the appliqué fabric. Don't cut them out yet, but cut around them, leaving about ½ all around. You don't have to be neat on this step!

2. Following the manufacturer's directions for the fusible webbing, press the webbing to the wrong side of the appliqué shapes.

> **Fringe Benefits**
>
> After you have made the table runner, you can make cookies to match! If you can't find the cookie cutters you want, make your own design templates from stiff cardboard.

3. Cut out designs and press the cut-out shapes onto the plain background fabric.

4. Make a narrow hem on the wrong side of background fabric. If you're finishing the edge with trim, fold ¼ to ½ inch to right side, and sew or glue the trim over the raw edge.

The following table lists some suggestions for seasonal runners.

For other occasions, such as someone's birthday, choose a design meaningful to that person. If you celebrate religious holidays and it's appropriate to your faith, use your religious symbols on the runner.

Season or Holiday	Background Color	Shapes	Shape Color
Winter	Blue	Snowflakes	White
	Blue	Snowpeople	White
Spring	Pale yellow	Eggs	Multicolor
	Pink	Daisies	White
	Light green	Bunnies	White or pink
Summer	Primary colors	Sunflowers	Yellow-gold
		Boats	Multicolor
		Butterflies	Multicolor
Fall	Ecru	Leaves	Orange
	Tan		Gold
	Brown		Yellow
Valentine's Day	White	Hearts	Pink and red
St. Patrick's Day	White	Shamrocks	Green
July 4th	Red, white, blue	Stars	Red, white, blue
Thanksgiving	Gold	Turkeys	Brown

Cut It Out!

If you'll be putting dining accoutrements on the runner, it helps if the surface of the runner is smooth, without a lot of ruffles and bumps. Even some quilted surfaces are not smooth enough to keep the salt and pepper shakers from falling over, and tall bud vases don't stay vertical very long if the runner is too soft and lumpy.

Quilted Table Runners and Place Mats

Even if you've never quilted, here are two very easy ways to make quilted runners or place mats. (The first way is really cheating, but no one will know.)

Faux Quilted Runners and Place Mats

You can probably find prequilted material sold by the yard in your local fabric shop. It has top and bottom pieces with batting in between and has been machine-quilted to hold the layers together. Some of the quilted material is the same on the top and the bottom, and some has different but coordinating fabrics on the top and on the bottom.

You'll need enough prequilted material for your place mats or runner (you can get 6 (12×18-inch) place mats from 1 yard of material) and enough packages of double-fold bias tape to go around each mat without having to piece the bias tape.

Cut It Out!

You might also find prequilted fabric that has an obvious right side and a wrong side. This is not what you want for this project. You want to be able to use either side as the top.

Here are the basic directions:

1. Cut out the shape you want, and bind the place mat or runner with matching or contrasting double-fold bias tape. Round off the corners if you want to (a large dinner plate makes a nice template).

2. Top-stitch or zigzag the bias tape to the edge of the place mat. When you get to the end, overlap the bias tape. Before you sew the 2 ends together, fold the end under ¼ inch.

If you have trouble finishing the end on your machine, finish it by hand. Sometimes the bump at the end causes the stitching to get messy. It's also difficult to be sure the folded under bias tape on the underside stays in place.

Another way to finish the intersection of the bias is to butt up the two ends against each other. Start with the raw edge folded under ¼ inch. After you have sewn all around, cut off the excess binding, leaving just enough to fold under the last raw edge ¼ inch and have the two folded ends of the binding meet. Hand-sew the folded edges together with tiny invisible stitches.

I'll Be Darned

Double-fold bias tape comes in several widths, so choose the one that suits your taste. For place mats, the ½-inch extra-wide tape works well. When you look at the bias tape, you'll notice that one edge is slightly narrower than the other. When you're applying the bias tape to the edge of the place mat, be sure the narrower edge is up. This way, you'll be sure to catch the other side of the tape when you sew it in place because it's sticking out a little more.

Easy Mock Quilted Runners and Place Mats

This method of making runners or place mats or a variety of other items such as vests, jackets, or pot holders or hot pads really isn't quilting, but it ends up looking like quilting. (It's not exactly cheating, but …)

You'll need …

- Enough fabric of your choice for the backing pieces.
- A packet of fat quarters or a variety of large enough scraps to make the strips needed.
- Lightweight *batting* material with a low loft.
- Double-fold bias tape or enough fabric to make your own.

Sew You Say

Batting looks like thin pillow stuffing and is used between two layers of fabric, such as in a quilt. It comes in various weights and sizes, or you can buy it by the yard. It comes in various thicknesses called loft. High-loft batting is good for a winter quilt; low-loft batting is better for table runners and place mats.

Here are the basic directions:

1. Cut a piece of backing fabric wider and longer than the finished project by about 2 inches in each direction.

2. Cut a piece of batting the same size as the backing fabric.

3. Cut several strips from a variety of fabrics long enough to reach across the width of the backing fabric on a slant. The angle of slant is up to you. The strips can be a variety of widths from 1¼ inches to 3 inches, or they can be all the same width. Be sure to cut all the strips on the straight of grain. If you have a cutting mat and rotary cutter, this is the perfect time to use them.

4. Lay the batting to the wrong side of the backing fabric. It might help to hand-baste the backing to the batting with long stitches, to keep it in place and keep the batting square with the backing fabric.

5. Take two different fabric strips and, with right sides together and one raw edge of each strip matching, lay the strips at a slant on top of the batting. Pin the strips in place. Using a ¼-inch seam allowance, stitch the strips to the backing. If you have a walking presser foot, this would be a good time to use it.

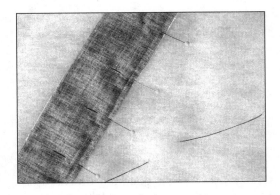

6. Open and finger press the seam.

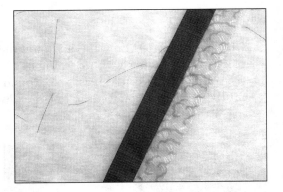

7. Place another strip on one of the two sewn-on strips, right sides together. Pin in place, and sew to the backing.

8. Open and finger press the seam.

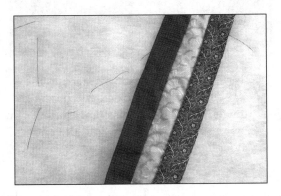

9. Continue like this until you've sewn on enough strips to cover the backing and batting.

10. Trim the place mat or runner to the size and shape you want.

11. Bind the edges.

You can also bind the edges using the bias tape you made. If you plan to have rounded corners, cut the strips for the binding on the bias (see Chapter 11). If you plan to have square corners, you can cut the strips for the binding on the grain.

Here are the basic instructions:

1. For a ¼-inch finished binding, cut strips 1¼ inches wide. For a ½-inch finished binding, cut strips 3¼ inches wide.

2. Sew the strips together to make one long strip.

3. Press in half length-wise with wrong sides together.

4. With the right sides together, sew the strip's raw edge to the right-side raw edge of the place mat or table runner with a ¼-inch seam allowance.

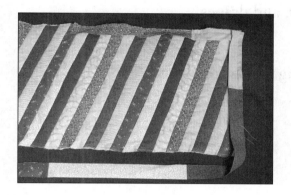

5. Fold the strip over the raw edge, and slip stitch it to the back. (See Chapter 4 if you have forgotten how to make a slip stitch.)

Other Finishing Methods

If you want to have a lined place mat, treat it as you would a knife-edge pillow (but obviously don't stuff it). If you include a little padding, try basting the batting to the wrong side of the top, and proceed as with the knife-edge pillow directions (see Chapter 11).

You can insert a small ruffle or piping or other trim into the seam as with the pillows, too. You can also fringe the edges. Put a line of stitches, either straight or a narrow zigzag, in from the edges to prevent the whole thing from unraveling. Where you place the stitching depends on how mow much fringe you want.

Hot Mats

You can make hot mats or pot holders the same way as runners or place mats, using any shape that appeals to you. Choose a heavier batting or one with more loft, or use two layers of lighter-weight batting for a little heat-proofing.

Fringe Benefits

For extra heat-proofing in your hot mat, put a piece of silicone-protected, heat-resistant fabric (find this in fabric stores sold by the yard) between the batting and the backing, with the silver side toward the batting.

The Least You Need to Know

◆ You can make place mats and table runners quickly and easily.

◆ Table runners and place mats use basically the same "pattern," adjusted to the size you want.

◆ Place mats and table runners don't have to be square or rectangle! Why not try triangles or ovals?

◆ With prequilted fabric from your fabric store, you can make quilted projects without really quilting.

In This Chapter

◆ Making curtains, valances, and drapes

◆ Lining drapes

◆ Choosing window-hanging hardware

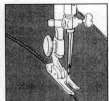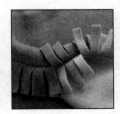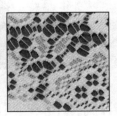

Think Rectangles: From Valances to Drapes

Ninety percent of all curtains, drapes, and valances is just hemmed rectangles (some valances have ventured forth into triangles and trapezoids). If you can measure, cut a rectangle, and make a hem, you can make your own window treatments.

You can hem your curtains by hand, using your sewing machine, or using glue or fusible webbing. The rectangular shape of basic curtains and drapes, and their lack of wear and tear, make them good choices for gluing.

All the instructions in this chapter assume you're using a sewing machine, but choose the method that works best for you.

Drapes, Valances, or Curtains?

Ask 20 people what the difference is between drapes and curtains, and you'll probably get 20 different answers. When I asked some window covering authorities, they said: "Drapes move, and curtains don't"; "Curtains hang on a rod and are rarely ever pushed or pulled on the rod. How you arrange them is how they will stay. Drapes are hung on rods that go back and forth"; "Drapes hang by the side of the window during the day to let in the light and are pulled together at night to keep out the cold"; and "Curtains hang in the middle."

Others say that drapes tend to be made of heavier-weight fabric, are often lined, and look more formal. Curtains tend to be made of lightweight fabric and are more frilly.

Many reference books use *drapes* and *curtains* interchangeably, as I'll do in this chapter. There's less confusion with valances. They're short curtains that hang across the top of the window.

Regardless of what you call them, they are mostly all just hemmed rectangles.

Defining Your Curtain Style

Most curtains are purely decorative, but others are both functional and decorative. Curtains can also create an illusion in the room, depending on where they are placed in relationship to the window. You can make windows appear longer or shorter, narrower or wider, just by changing the curtains. For example, if you have a tall, skinny window and you want to create the illusion that it's a wide window, hang the curtains so that most of the curtain hangs outside the window frame and not over the window.

You can change how large or small your window looks just by changing how and where you hang your curtains.

When designing your window treatment, you'll first have to decide whether the curtains are to be decorative, functional, or both. This decision will help you select the right type of fabric and hardware and will determine whether or not you'll line the curtains. Before you pick

out the fabric, think about the answers to some of the following questions:

◆ What look are you trying to create— formal, informal, somber, light, or cheery?

◆ Are these curtains decorative only, functional only, or both?

◆ Are you trying to keep out light or let in light?

◆ Will these curtains be opened and closed daily?

◆ Do you have small children in your home?

◆ Will these curtains be in a bathroom, where there is a great deal of moisture?

◆ Are you trying to keep the cold out and the heat in?

◆ Are these curtains the primary décor statement, complementary, or just in the background?

With the answers to these questions in hand, now you're ready for a trip to the fabric store.

Deciding on the Hardware

What hardware will you use to hang your curtains? You have an endless number of choices in terms of design, but only a few in terms of function.

There are two basic kinds of hardware: those that allow the curtains to be opened and closed (traverse rods), and those on which the curtains remain stationary (curtain rods).

Traverse Rods

If you plan to open and close the curtains daily, you will need a traverse rod. In general, the curtains are attached with hooks to sliders on the rods. You open and close the curtains either by pulling on a cord or by pulling the curtain by hand.

Another style of traverse rod consists of a rod and rings. In this case, the curtains are attached to the rings. The rings slide easily across the rods and you can pull the curtains open and closed by hand without any cords. If the rod is designed for long curtains, there might be a rod you use to pull the curtains open and closed.

Cut It Out!

The traverse rods that have cords can be difficult to install, and many come with long cords that hang loosely on the edge of the curtain window frame. These cords present a strangulation danger to small children. On some brands of traverse rods, the cords are encased in a bracket that's mounted to the wall. These are better if you have small children.

Curtain Rods

Curtain rods hold curtains that will not be slid back and forth. Some are purely functional and are never seen, and others are part of the overall decorative effect of the window treatment. Most are very easy to attach.

Some rods are spring loaded. These don't need to be attached to the wall because the rod fits snugly inside the window frame. These are great for apartments and for lightweight fabrics.

Some of the traditional curtain rods come with two rods, one slightly deeper than the other, that almost nest and are fixed to the wall on the same bracket. Use these if you have panels that cross over each other, called Priscilla curtains, or if you want a valance to hang over the top of the panels.

Measuring the Windows

Windows come in all kinds and shapes, and you'll need to make several measurements for each window. You'll need the inside dimensions as well as the outside dimensions. You'll need

to decide how far outside the window frame you want the curtains to hang, depending on whether you are trying to make the window look wider or narrower.

Cut It Out!

If you're mounting rod fixtures to the wall instead of the window frame, be sure to fasten the rod to a stud. If you don't, and if the curtains have any weight at all or you open and close them regularly, the curtains will fall off the wall. Find the studs before you determine the width of the curtains. If your walls are concrete, you'll need the right kind of screws to fasten the fixtures to the wall. Consult your local hardware store for help.

Next, decide how long you want the curtains to be. The traditional lengths are as follows:

- To the top of the sill
- To the bottom of the sill
- To the top of the *splashboard*
- To the floor
- To a *puddle*

Sew You Say

Some homes have **splashboards** running around the room at floor level. These boards are attached to the wall, vary in height, and are usually painted or naturally finished.

To make curtains **puddle,** they need to be very long—so long that the bottom of the curtain not only reaches the floor, but also lies on it in a puddle or pile. This is currently chic, but it seems like a vacuuming nightmare to me!

Calculating Cutting Lengths

One of the good things about making curtains is that you have so many options. But for each option, you have many decisions to make. There are some generic customs in the curtain manufacturing industry, and you can decide to go with convention or not. For example, the typical curtain hem is a 4-inch double folded hem. Does it really matter if yours is 3½ inches or 4¼ inches? Not in the least! Don't be discouraged by all the measuring and calculating. The dimensions are only suggestions. If you miss by an inch or two, nobody is going to notice, and certainly nobody is going to care. Just remember, curtains are only hemmed rectangles.

One thing that might astonish you is how much fabric you need to make curtains. If money is a consideration, think short, simple, and unlined.

I give you a picture of a generic window and a fill-in measurement chart in Appendix E. Use this as a guide, or draw a picture of your windows. Then, fill in the chart for each different type of window you want to cover.

Hems

As I mentioned earlier, most curtains have a double folded hem, unless it has a ruffle. The double folded hem adds weight to the bottom of the curtain and helps it hang better. For full-length curtains, a 4-inch double folded hem is standard, which means you will have to add 8 inches for the hem when calculating length. For shorter, to-the-sill café curtains, a 2-inch double folded hem is standard.

Casings

On some curtains, the rod goes through a pocket sewn into the top of the curtain. This is the casing. The size of the rod determines the size of the casing. If the rod is round, measure its circumference, divide by 2, and add at least ½ inch for ease. This would be the minimum width of the casing. If the rod is flat, measure the width and add at least ½ inch for ease.

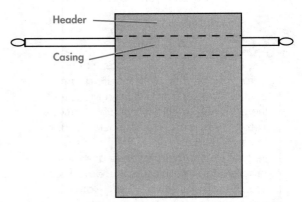

Some curtains have casings, and some have headers and casings. The rod goes through the casing, while the header is purely decorative.

Headers

Some curtains have headers or headings. The header sticks up above the rod to the top of the curtain. It's purely decorative and optional. If you want a valance, you don't need a header; if you want a header, you don't need a valance over it. Headers are usually between 1 and 5 inches, but you can make yours any size you want. When you're calculating the amount of fabric needed, multiply the desired width of the header by 3.

Fringe Benefits

On heading-less curtains, the fold at the top of the casing sometimes rests directly on the rod. To avoid this, sew a line of topstitching in the casing about ½ inch down from the fold at the top of the curtain. This creates a tiny heading. Be sure to allow for this inch when calculating how much fabric you need for the casing.

Ruffles

Ruffles are found on lightweight curtain fabrics such as sheers and cottons. The ruffle generally goes on the inside and bottom edges. On some curtain styles, like Cape Cod curtains, the ruffle goes all the way around. Sometimes there's also a ruffle across the top that looks and acts like a valance but is attached to the curtain, hangs down from the top of the curtain, and not on a separate rod. Very often, when curtains have ruffles, the tiebacks are also ruffles.

To determine how much fabric you'll need for the ruffle, measure all the edges that are going to have a ruffle, including the tiebacks. Multiply that number by at least 2½; multiply by 3 if the material is really filmy. If you're cutting across on the crosswise grain, divide that number by 44 or 60, depending on the width of the fabric. That is how many widths you will need.

Then decide how wide you want the ruffle, plus enough for top and bottom narrow hems. Multiply this number by how many widths you need, and divide by 36. This will be how many yards of material you will need just for the ruffle.

For example, this is the amount of material you'll need for a ruffle for 1 pair of Pricilla curtains 60 inches wide and 72 inches long:

Bottom edge	60
Middle edge	72
Top edge	60
Tieback	24 (Tiebacks can be any length you want; this is a typical length.)
Total	216 inches × 3 (for sheer) = 648 inches

If you want a 6-inch ruffle, add 1 inch for the 2 top and bottom ½-inch hems, for a total of 7 inches.

Then, if your material is 60 inches wide:

648 (inches) ÷ 60 = 11 widths (always round up)

11 widths × 7 inches wide = 77 inches

Rounding up, 77 inches is 2½ yards for 1 panel. So just for the ruffle for one pair of curtains, you will need 5 yards of material.

> **Fringe Benefits**
>
> To determine how much ruffle you need, measure the perimeter of the curtain where the ruffle will be, as well as the tieback. Using the preceding example, 216 ÷ 36 = 6 yards of ready-made ruffle per panel, or 12 yards per pair of curtains.

Tiebacks

Tiebacks come in all shapes, colors, designs, and fabrics. You can make tiebacks to match the curtains exactly, or you can use decorative cords with tassels or ribbons and bows. The quickest and easiest tiebacks are braided cords that attach to the window frame or wall with a cup hook.

Top Edges

Before you calculate the cutting length, you have to figure out how the curtains are to be attached to the rod and how easily you want them to slide. The simplest top edge is one that is straight across, has no heading, has a casing for the rod, and does not slide.

You can attach the curtains to the rods in many ways. Look in the home decorating section of your favorite store or at pictures in advertising flyers to get some ideas of what you like and don't like. Once you've decided what you want for the top of the curtain, adjust the calculations accordingly.

For example, if you have chosen hooks that are meant to be seen, put a hook on the rod and measure the length you'll need from where the hook attaches to the curtain rather than to the rod. If you want to attach the curtains with ribbons and bows, test where the top of the curtain is going to be by using a scrap of material, then measure accordingly. Depending on the type of top you want, you might have to do a little fiddling until you get the correct measurements.

Some curtains hang from tab loops.

You can also use any of a variety of tapes that will help with pleats or use *shirring* at the top. The tape is sewn or glued onto the inside top of the curtain. Hooks are slid into the pockets on the tape to create pleats.

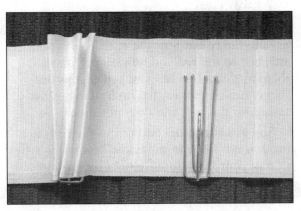

You can easily make a pleated top edge using pleater tape and hooks.

> **Sew You Say**
>
> **Shirring** is a method of decorative machine gathering used to take in fullness stitched in many rows across fabric.

Side Edges

For unlined curtains, you'll have to hem both side edges of each panel. These hems are double folded hems between 1 and 1½ inches. If you're putting a ruffle on the inside edge, you don't need the hem.

Fullness

To determine the approximate width of the fabric you'll need, measure the width of the area you are going to cover with one panel. Multiply by 2 if the fabric is heavy. If the fabric is very light, multiply by at least 3. Curtains generally look better if there's some fullness, so don't skimp!

If the curtains are going to close on a traverse rod and you'll be using pleater tape, measure the window and divide by 2 if you want 2 panels. The style of pleater tape you choose determines the width of each panel. The tape will come with suggestions about how much fullness and how much pleater tape you'll need.

> **Fringe Benefits**
>
> The width of the panel depends on how much window you want to cover, how much wall you want to cover, how full you want the curtains to be, whether you're going to pleat or gather the top, whether the curtains are going to open and close, and how many panels you're going to use. If you have a bay window, for example, you might want one panel to hang on each side of the bay window, or you might want a panel to hang at each corner.
>
> Make a diagram of what you want to do. Measure a lot. Then measure again.

Straightening and Matching

Curtains need to be cut on the grain. Before cutting, be sure you straighten the fabric (see Chapter 12). When you're calculating the amount of fabric to buy, plan on some extra to allow for straightening.

Also, if the fabric has a pattern like a plaid, you'll want the pattern on each panel to match at the center opening. This will require some extra fabric.

It is always a good idea to buy extra fabric anyway. You can always put the leftovers in your stash and make a scrap quilt or an accent pillow when you have some spare time!

Linings

Linings help keep your curtain fabric from fading. If the primary fabric is very expensive and you want to preserve it from the sun, consider lining the curtains. White or off-white cotton sateen is a typical curtain lining material. You might also find special linings that block out heat and/or light.

Making lined curtains is easier than hemming the edges on unlined curtains. You hem the linings with the same hem allowance as the curtains, but you make them 2½ inches shorter in overall length so they don't show behind the curtains. To account for this, cut the lining 6 inches narrower than the curtain width.

Wide Curtains

If your curtains will be wider than 44 or 60 inches, you'll have to piece the fabric. If possible, line up the seams with any vertical frames in your window. Use your judgment on where to put the seam. In some cases, even with a lining, when the sun shines on the curtain, you will be able to see the seam. If the fabric is sheer or frays easily, make French seams (see Chapter 7).

Plain Curtains

Plain straight curtains are the easiest to make, but you have to decide on the rod arrangement first. You can make a casing for the rod to fit in, or you can hem the top and use clips that slide on the rod.

1. Preshrink (optional, depending on the fabric) and straighten the fabric.
2. Cut the panels to the desired length remembering to adjust if you use clips.
3. Make a double fold hem on the bottom.
4. Make a double fold hem on the sides.
5. If you're using curtain rods, stitch the header line (optional).
6. Stitch the casing line. Repeat on both panels, press, and hang.
7. If you're using a clip and rings, make a double fold hem on the top instead of a casing. Repeat for both panels, press, and hang.

Lined Curtains with Pleater Tape

To determine the width of each panel when you're using pleater tape, insert hooks into uncut tape the way you want them spaced in the finished curtain. Then attach the hooks to the rod, adjusting the amount of tape needed to cover the window. Then, mark the tape, and remove the tape from the rod and the hooks from tape. Measure the length of the tape. This will be the width of the fabric you need for each panel plus 6 inches.

1. Preshrink and straighten the fabric.
2. If necessary, piece fabric to make it wider. Cut the fabric and lining on the straight of grain, matching any patterns.
3. Make a double fold hem on the bottom of both the curtain and the lining. Blind stitch on the curtain; topstitch on the lining.

4. Pin the lining to the curtain, right sides together, matching raw edges. The fold at the bottom of the lining hem should fall just below the fold at the top of the curtain hem.

5. Sew a ½-inch seam on both sides. Notice that the curtain is wider than the lining.

6. Lay the curtain, lining side up, on a large flat surface. Adjust the lining so it's centered in the middle of the curtain, right sides still together. If necessary, trim the top edge of the lining to match the top edge of the curtain. Pin the top edge, raw edges even. Sew a ½-inch seam across the top, then trim the corners.

7. Turn the curtain and liner right side out, then press the edges flat. Be sure the folded-in edge of the curtain is the same size all the way down the side of the curtain. If the fabric was cut on the grain and your seams are straight, the lining should lay square on the curtain.

8. Adjust the pleater tape so there's a pocket near the edges of the curtain. Follow the manufacturer's directions, and sew the pleater tape to the lining near the top of the curtain.

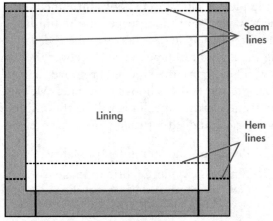

If you don't want the curtain lining to show, make the lining with narrower than the curtain fabric width.

9. Finish the bottom corners. If you want to, sew a curtain weight into each corner before you finish it off.

Cut It Out!

Some pleater tape comes with iron-on adhesive. Even if you use the iron-on tape, topstitch across the top and bottom of the tape on lined drapes. (You don't need to do this step on unlined drapes.)

If the lining of the curtain is part of the decorative value of the curtain and, for example, will show, cut the lining the same width as the curtain. After you make the hems, and with right sides together, sew the lining to the curtain around the sides and top. Then, turn right sides out and press the edges to make it look sharp.

Unlined Tiered Ruffled Curtains

A basic set of curtains consists of four panels and a valance, although some have the ruffle valance sewn to the top panels. The panels and valance go on traditional curtain rods. There are usually tiebacks for the top panels. How you arrange the four panels and valance is up to you. You might want all four panels to be the same length. You might want long tops and short bottoms, or vice versa. You might not want any tops, just bottoms and a valance. You might want a separate valance (which will require the nested rods, if you're using a top layer), or you might want the valance attached to the top panels. The combinations are nearly infinite. Look in magazines, flyers, and catalogs for ideas on the look you want.

For detached ruffle valances, add the heading and casing dimensions to the width of the ruffle. You won't have to ruffle this valance, so treat it as just another hemmed rectangle with a heading and casing.

Choose lightweight or sheer fabric. If you're new to sewing, try cotton or broadcloth.

Once you've determined how many panels you want and how long you want them, the rest is easy:

1. For the typical window and 44-inch fabric, use one width of fabric for each panel.

2. Round off the inside bottom corners with a plate.

3. Make the ruffle, or purchase ready-made ruffle trim. You'll have to piece together the ruffle in many places. Use ½-inch seams and finish them neatly. When you're sewing the hems, be sure the seams are to the wrong side.

4. Finish each end of the ruffle with a narrow, ¼-inch hem.

5. You can attach the ruffle to the panel in one of two ways:

   Method 1: Hem the bottom of the ruffle with a narrow hem. Put a gathering stitch about ½ inch from the top edge. Attach the right side of the ruffle to the right side of the panel. Sew the ruffle to the panel. Finish the edges together with a zigzag stitch.

   Method 2: Make a narrow hem on the top and bottom of the ruffle. Put a gathering stitch 1 inch from the top edge. Hem the panel with a ½-inch double fold hem. Lay the wrong side of the ruffle to the right side of the panel. Put the gathering thread on the top of the hem stitching of the panel, then stitch on the gathering stitch. This method requires many pins. You might want to baste by hand. This method is also a little more time-consuming, but it gives a nice finish to the ruffle.

6. Treat the valance as a very wide rectangle. Make a casing on the valance. When you put the valance on the rod, it will look like a ruffle.

Cape Cod curtains are tiered and have ruffles all around.

The Least You Need to Know

◆ Most curtains and drapes are hemmed rectangles.

◆ Measure, measure, and measure again.

◆ Lining draperies is easy.

◆ Curtain hardware comes in a variety of functional and decorator styles.

In This Part

Creating Your New Wardrobe

It's time to take a look in your closet. With very little effort, you can start to redefine who you are by creating clothes that truly reflect you. If you can sew a seam and read a pattern (you'll learn the latter in Part 4), you can start creating your new wardrobe.

Many patterns include skirts, tops, jackets, and pants in the same envelope. Buy one pattern, enjoy hours of fun and creativity, and end up with a whole new look! This part will show you how.

In This Chapter

- ◆ Taking your measurements
- ◆ Finding your size and shape
- ◆ Changing your fashion as your body changes

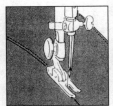

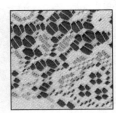
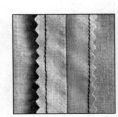

Chapter 15

Measuring Up

Throughout the history of fashion, clothing sizes and styles have varied widely. In some cases, it was difficult to tell whether style dictated size or size dictated the style. If you've seen *Gone with the Wind*, you might remember the scene when Scarlett O'Hara's maid was diligently pulling in Scarlett's corset to make her waist as small as possible. Pictures of Queen Elizabeth I reveal her fashion that was so extreme that she appeared to have no bust at all— only hips. Even in the last half of the twentieth century, pattern manufacturers have changed their sizing suggestions.

Just as everyone has unique fingerprints, everyone has a unique body shape. Not all size 12 bodies look alike. When you're making clothes for yourself or others, remember that all patterns are just starting points. Almost every pattern has to be adjusted here and there. Because of the looseness and lack of fitted quality prevalent in today's fashion, one person might fit into many sizes, and many different-shape people can wear the same size.

What to Measure

Before you start any clothing project, you must know your measurements and what shape you are. You can take a couple approaches to measuring. If you're making a casual-wear garment, you can take a minimalist approach to measuring; if you're making more technical and formal wear, you'll need much more accurate measuring.

The latter, more technical approach calls for more than 50 measurements, which might be a bit overwhelming for our purposes here. In this chapter, we'll use the minimalist approach of measuring, plus add a few embellishments. You can probably get by with knowing four measurements.

For Women	For Men
Bust	Chest (just under the armpits)
High bust	Waist
Waist	Hips
Hips	Length of outside leg

If you're shaped like I am, you might want to take a measurement around the belly, too. With these measurements, you can find a pattern close to your size that you can alter to fit your body. And don't be surprised if you're a different size on the top than you are on the bottom.

> **Fringe Benefits**
>
> To learn more about making clothes really fit every body shape and size, check out Pati Palmer and Marta Alto's book *Fit for Real People*.

Top Measurements

You'll need to take two bust measurements. The first is the *high bust*. When measuring your high bust, the tape measure should be directly under your arms and across the top of your breasts.

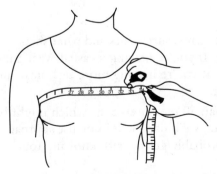

Measure your high bust with the tape directly under your arms and across the top of your breasts.

The second measurement is around the *full bust*. The tape should go around the tips of your breasts.

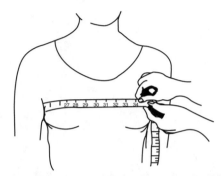

When measuring your bust, the tape should go around the tips of your breasts.

Bottom Measurements

The third measurement you need is your *natural waist*.

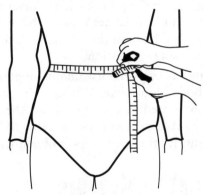

Use your natural waist for this measurement.

The fourth measurement, usually labeled *hips*, can vary according to your shape. Try several different measurements between your waist and your thighs. In what used to be called the typical shape, the hip measurement was about 7 to 9 inches below the waist. On some bodies, it might be as high as 3 inches below the waist; on other bodies, the widest part might actually be somewhere around the thighs. This is important to know, because if you buy a straight skirt pattern according to your waist size, it might not be big enough in the thigh area if you have larger thighs.

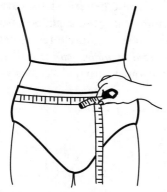

Take your hip measurement at your widest point. Also note the distance from this point and your waist.

Fill in the following measurements table so you'll have them all in one place. You'll notice that some additional measurements are listed there. These might be helpful to you, depending on what you plan to make.

What to Measure	My Measurement
Height	_____
Weight	_____
High bust	_____
Full bust	_____
Waist	_____
Hips: 7 to 9 inches below waist	_____
Tummy: 3 inches below waist	_____
Fullest part of your hips	_____
Length from waist to crotch	_____

What to Measure	My Measurement
Length from base of neck to line from underarm to underarm on back	_____
Length from underarm line to waist	_____
Length from crotch to floor	_____
Outside leg (from waist to desired length)	_____
Inside leg (from crotch to desired length)	_____
My body shape	_____

You can determine your body shape by studying the following figure and seeing how you shape up.

Measuring Tips for Women

If you want the clothes you create to fit properly, you need to start with good measurements. The following are a few tips to help you get accurate measurements:

◆ You don't have to show anyone your measurements, so be honest with yourself. Don't pull the tape measure too tight. Comfortably snug is what you want.

◆ When you measure yourself, try to use the undergarments you'll most likely wear when you wear the outfit. Because bras tend to change the fullness of your bust and even the lines and location of your bust, measure your bust line with the appropriate bra.

◆ Don't let your fingers get between your body and the tape measure.

◆ If you wear control-top pantyhose or undergarments, try taking your hips and belly measurements with them on and also with them off to see if there's a difference.

Many different methods and techniques are available for how to measure and what to measure. Don't let this worry you. Try different methods until you find the one that works best for you and really reflects your measurements, and then stick with it.

Misses' Petites, Half-Size, Women's, etc.

For the most part, the labels for women's clothing sizes are all variations on a theme. When you're buying manufactured clothes, some of these designations help you find the best fit. When you're making your own clothes, though, you almost always can use a Misses' size pattern and make it fit your body. Choosing from one of the other groups might save you some alterations, but you probably won't have as many choices.

In the following table are some of the pattern companies' suggestions for each of the clothing categories. All numbers are approximate and should be considered guidelines only. Because the guidelines keep changing, depending on styles and assumptions about the human body, these might change at any time.

Label	Height	Waist	Bust	Other
Misses' Petite	5'2"	larger than Misses	average	short-waisted
Half-Size	5'2"	larger than Misses	low C cup+	short-waisted
Women's	5'6"	larger than Misses	average	rounder in back

Note: Misses' Petite and Half-Size are not available from all pattern companies.

What Shape Are You?

When you have your primary measurements, you can determine what your generic shape is. The names of these generic shapes aren't the most flattering—*hourglass, apple, pear*—so I'll use the somewhat less-pejorative terms *hourglass, triangle, inverted triangle, round,* and *rectangle.* Find one that most nearly describes you:

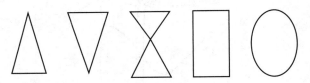

What shape are you? From left to right: triangle, inverted triangle, hourglass, rectangle, and round.

- **Triangle.** Shoulders are narrower than hips.
- **Inverted triangle.** Upper body is wider than hips.
- **Hourglass.** Shoulders and hips are the same width; waist is about 10 inches smaller.
- **Rectangle.** Waist has little or no indentation.
- **Round.** Wider in the middle.

Remember, not everyone fits neatly into one category. These are only generalities and guidelines.

When Your Body Changes

Some people reach a size when they're in their teens and never change size again. That probably isn't true for most of us, though. We go on diets; we gain weight; we go on diets. In spite of our tendency to try to find the Fountain of Youth, our bodies do change with age. For the most part, we get a little shorter, our waists get a little thicker, and our bust seems to get a little lower.

As our bodies age and change, it might become increasingly difficult to find just what you want to wear in manufactured garments. The manufactured clothing industry caters to the average size that sells the most. The choices become less interesting the more we stray from Misses'. Don't despair. When you make your own clothes, you have endless variety, and you always have something that fits perfectly.

The Least You Need to Know

◆ There are nearly as many different shapes and sizes of the human body as there are humans.

◆ You can make your own clothes that fit you perfectly.

◆ Knowing your measurements will help you select the perfect pattern for your size and shape.

In This Chapter

◆ Perusing pattern books

◆ Picking a pattern

◆ Getting familiar with the pattern

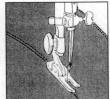

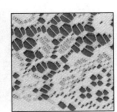
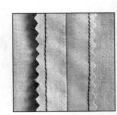

Chapter**16**

Picking a Pattern

You've learned the sewing basics, from sewing a seam to hemming, to putting in a zipper. You have all your measurements handy, and you're ready to find a pattern you like and start filling your closet with custom-made-for-you clothes.

Picking out a pattern to sew can be fun. There are so many options available, from traditional patterns like Simplicity, Vogue, Butterick, and McCall's, to newer manufacturers like Burda and New Look. With the advent of the World Wide Web, you can even download patterns as well as pattern-generating software.

With all the options available to you, the hardest part might be making up your mind!

Finding the Perfect Pattern

Even if you have no intention of buying a pattern, it's fun to go to your local fabric store and look through the pattern books to see what the current styles are. In addition to the pattern books primarily focused on women's fashion, you'll find pattern books for home furnishings, children's clothes, men's fashions, and costumes during the Halloween season.

You can also subscribe to pattern magazines, if getting to a fabric store is difficult—or you just want the patterns to come to you!

Most fabric stores have a large number of different pattern books available for you to browse through.

If you tend to be overwhelmed when confronted with too many choices, start with the smallest pattern book you can find or just look in a specific section of the book that displays a certain type of garment, like blouses. (Pattern books are divided into color-coded sections to help you narrow your search.)

Fringe Benefits

When you go to the fabric store to buy a pattern, take a pad of tiny Post-its with you. When you find a pattern that interests you, put a Post-it on that page. I used to put my fingers in each page, but I soon ran out of fingers! If you don't have Post-its, you can always write down the page numbers. Leave the Post-its in the book until you get the pattern because sometimes the pattern isn't in stock in your size, and you might have to go with your second choice.

Most patterns are arranged numerically in large drawers, so when you've decided on a pattern, go to the right drawer and get the pattern you want. Some patterns aren't listed in books and don't live in drawers. These are found on racks instead.

Reading Pattern Books

The first things you'll notice when you look at pattern book pages are pictures of models wearing all the garments made from the one pattern advertised on the page. Variations on the pattern will be shown, too. For example, you might have a choice of necklines, types of sleeves, or skirt length.

Cut It Out!

It helps to imagine the design in a fabric or color you like. If the model's wearing green plaid and you don't care for green plaid, image the garment in your favorite color. We have a tendency to be attracted to our favorite colors and ignore our least favorite colors. Don't ignore a great style just because the model is wearing a color that's not your favorite.

If you have a good first impression of the garment, check to see if you really like the neckline, waistline, sleeves, and hemline. Somewhere on the page should be a section showing a line drawing of the garment. This will help you get an idea of what the basic shape is and also what the back will look like.

On many pattern pages, you might find the same symbols for body shape you identified in Chapter 15. Remember, these are guides. If the only shape suggested for this particular pattern is an hourglass and you are clearly round, this probably won't be the best pattern for you.

Many pattern books will indicate whether making the pattern is simple, medium, or advanced. Other helpful information includes whether or not the pattern is suitable for knits or wovens, or whether it will work on fabric with a nap or one-way design. It might also state whether the garment will look good with obvious diagonals or plaids. Take these suggestions into consideration when selecting both the pattern and the fabric.

For the More Adventurous

When you've looked through enough pattern books, you might start to think everything looks the same, especially if you look at the black-and-white drawings of the garment outline. This might be because there really are only a few basic concepts, with an infinite number of variations on each concept.

If you're not crazy about any ready-made pattern you've seen and you're daring and want to set off on your own creative path, here are two possibilities:

◆ Buy the most basic pattern you can find that's been adjusted to your particular body shape. Some pattern companies call these "Basic" patterns, for example, Vogue's 1004 or 1005. From this pattern, you can make any other pattern you like. You can change the neckline, the hemline, or the waistline. You can move the darts around. You can add collars or cuffs, ruffles or pleats. Find one of the many books available on simple pattern drafting if you want a little guidance, then go for it.

◆ Or buy several patterns, each highlighting a feature you want, then put the pieces together in different ways.

Some patterns are very expensive, and this might not be the best option if you're on a limited budget. However, patterns are often on sale. If you're making your wedding dress, for example, it might be worth the extra expense to get exactly what you want and use the neckline from one pattern, the skirt from another, and the train from yet another.

What Size Do You Need?

Once you've decided on your pattern, it's time to decide what size you need. Don't assume that just because you've always bought a size 10 in manufactured clothes, you should buy a size 10 pattern. Also, don't assume that just because you used a size 10 pattern last time, you should buy a size 10 this time. Trust your body measurements from Chapter 15. No manufactured pattern will fit you perfectly; all patterns are just approximations. You'll have to adjust the pattern to your body somewhere.

Find the small chart of numbers on the pattern book page or on the back of the pattern envelope. Using your measurements and the manufacturer's size chart, follow these general guidelines for selecting the best size pattern for you for this project:

◆ If your bust is 2 inches larger than your high bust measurement, use the high bust measurement when selecting your pattern size.

◆ To be on the safe side, if you're buying a pattern with a wide skirt, find the size nearest your waist size. If the pattern is for a straight skirt, select a pattern nearest your hip size.

◆ When selecting a dress pattern, always select a pattern nearest your bust or high bust size.

Don't be surprised if you have to buy two patterns—one for your top and one for your bottom. You can almost always adjust one or the other as needed, though.

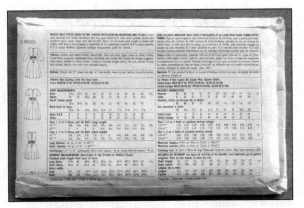

The back of the envelope gives you information on the approximate size you should consider making.

Fringe Benefits

If you're picking individual pieces from several patterns, it's best to stay with the same pattern company so the pattern markings and symbols will line up with each other.

Reading the Pattern Envelope

For such a small space, it is amazing how much information the pattern manufacturers fit on the back of the pattern envelope.

Near the top of the envelope, you'll see a section called "Suggested Fabrics." This doesn't mean you're limited to just these kinds of fabrics. The makers of this list have usually taken into account the lines of the garment and the drape of the material and have suggested what will work best. If you've chosen a long, flowing skirt pattern, you probably won't find cotton duck as one of the choices suggested by the manufacturer. If you've chosen to make a winter coat, the list probably won't include chiffon or Georgette. The "Suggested Fabrics" list will also suggest other fabrics you will need for linings, interfacings, trims, etc. For the most part, the suggestions are helpful.

Fringe Benefits

Fabric store owners group their fabrics in many ways, and one way is by kind of fabric. The "Suggested Fabrics" list can help you narrow where to start looking. For example, if a suggestion is for challis, start with that part of the store. You also can ask a sales clerk if challis is in any other sections of the store or where any fabric that drapes like challis is.

When you've decided on the fabric and the size, use the chart to determine how many yards of fabric you need. Buy the amount suggested by reading down the size column. Don't forget to look at naps, one-way designs, border design, plaids, or any other feature of either the pattern or the fabric that might require more fabric.

I'll Be Darned

It might be my imagination, but it seems that "in the old days," the amount of fabric suggested was always more than I ever needed. Today it seems the amount of fabric suggested is exactly what I need, with barely enough left over to save for my stash.

Don't Forget the Notions!

Somewhere on the back of the envelope you'll also find a list of suggestions for the notions you'll need to finish your project, such as zippers, snaps, buttons, and elastic. Get everything you need all at once—and don't forget the thread.

Fringe Benefits

Get in the habit of putting all of each project, including pattern and thread and all the notions, in either a 2-gallon plastic bag or some other clear container. This will make working on the project easier, and you'll be able find everything you need when you come back to it.

The Least You Need to Know

◆ Pattern books can help you select a pattern.
◆ Read the back of the pattern envelope. It can help with everything from the selection of fabric to how much you need.
◆ Refer to the envelope for a list of notions you need, and be sure to pick up everything you need for your project at once—including thread.

In This Chapter

◆ Familiarizing yourself with the pattern

◆ Learning what all the pattern marks mean

◆ Understanding pattern directions

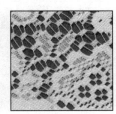

Chapter 17

Reading and Working With a Pattern

In the last 100 years or so, patterns and pattern directions have been greatly improved. Today's patterns are much easier to use, and the directions are much simpler to follow. If you're new to sewing or using patterns, that might not be apparent at first. As you look at this big piece of tissue paper covered with solid lines, dotted lines, triangles, diamonds, circles, arrows, and more, it can be overwhelming! You might even be afraid you'll rip it if you handle it!

In this chapter, we look at a pattern and directions so it's not so confusing and overwhelming. I discuss what all those symbols and lines mean, and I even tell you how to place the pattern on your fabric.

By the end of this chapter, a pattern won't be so scary.

Looking at the Pattern

Many patterns are printed on very large, almost unmanageable sheets of tissue paper. Many patterns also include more than one size on each sheet.

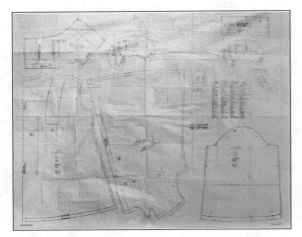

Many pattern pieces are printed on large sheets of tissue paper.

Before you take out the tissue pattern sheets, take out the directions. These are usually printed on regular paper.

Somewhere near the left column of page 1 will be a diagram showing all the pieces you need for each variation of the garment. If, for example, you have a pattern of a dress that also has a jacket and you only want the dress, you can identify which pieces you will need. The pieces are numbered. Circle the ones you want.

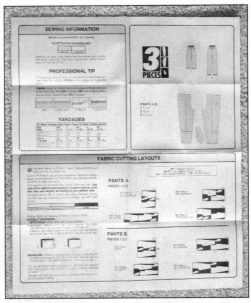

The directions are printed on newsprint.

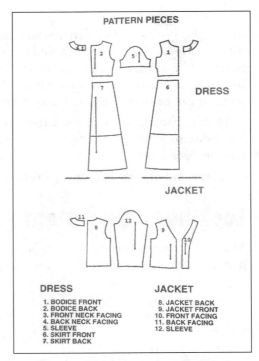

On the first page of the directions, you'll find a small diagram showing all the numbered pieces.

Also, when a pattern offers more than one size, sometimes the different sizes are printed on one pattern piece and the sizes are indicated by different lines. Sometimes, though, each size has a separate piece. This is particularly true of facings.

Dots, Triangles, Squares: Reading the Pattern Marks

Depending on the complexity of the pattern, there will be a variety of marks on the pattern pieces. Most patterns have big and little dots. Sometimes you match notches; sometimes you match dots, depending on where they are. Notches (the triangles along the edge) are almost always matched on seams.

Here's what the symbols mean:

◆ Dots sometimes mark the beginning and end of gathering stitches or ease, particularly on sleeves.

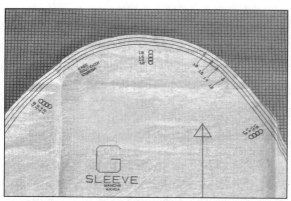

Dots sometimes mark the beginning and end of gathering stitches or ease, particularly on sleeves.

◆ A large dot marks the top of the sleeve where it meets the shoulder seam.

◆ Dots also mark the end of stitching in a seam if part of the seam is to be left open, like for a zipper.

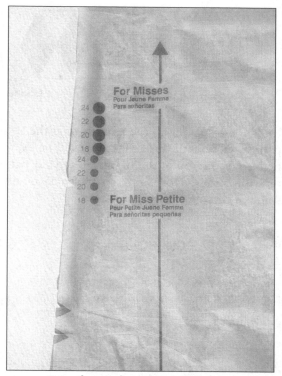

Dots also mark openings in seams.

◆ Along with dashed lines, dots mark darts.

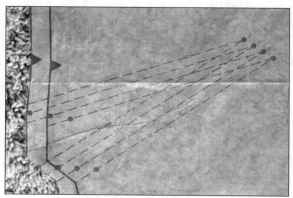

Darts are marked by dashed lines and dots.

◆ Big and little squares often mark where pleats are called for.

◆ Triangles mark the notches you match when sewing seams together (see the next section).

Triangles mark the notches you match when sewing seams together.

Don't despair at all the markings on the pattern pieces. All these markings will be explained at the top of the first page of your pattern directions. Most simple patterns have only some of these markings.

> **Cut It Out!**
>
> You might be tempted to ignore all these little triangles, dots, and squares, but don't do it. Transfer every mark to the wrong side of the fabric, even if it seems like a waste of time and energy. You will thank yourself later.

What Are These Triangles For?

All around the edge of your pattern, you'll notice little black triangles. Sometimes they're single triangles, sometimes they come in pairs, and occasionally they come in threes. These triangles help when you're sewing seams together. The directions will always say to sew the seams together, "matching notches." These little triangles are the notches.

These notches are also helpful because single notches are placed on what will be the front, and double notches are placed on what will be the back. This comes in very handy on the top edge of sleeves because it's very easy to switch the sleeves accidentally. The double notches always go to the back.

When you look at the pattern directions, you'll probably notice that the pattern artist indicated these notches by having them stick out past the cut line. You can cut around the triangles so they stick out, and many sources do

suggest this. It's not easy to cut the notches exactly right, though.

I suggest that you cut off all the notches when you cut out the pattern pieces. Cut smoothly along the cutting edge of the pattern after it's pinned to the fabric, passing by all the notches. When you've cut out all the pieces, go back and put a snip into each triangle in the seam allowance. If the garment has sleeves, always put a snip into the seam allowance at the top of the sleeve. There will be a dot on the pattern to mark the spot.

> **Cut It Out!**
>
> When you're working with fabric that is very slippery and frays a great deal, snipping at the notches might not work well. Instead, put a piece of tape in the seam allowance and then cut the notch snips. Don't forget to remove the tape after you've sewn the seam!

Other Pattern Markings

Other pattern markings provide useful information to help make your sewing experience a pleasure. The information depends on the pattern. For example, if there are no darts, you won't see any dart markings. Pattern manufacturers and designers are always trying to make the patterns easier to read. If you pick up an old pattern at a garage tag sale, some of the symbols might be different, but they're usually described on the directions page of the pattern.

Reading the Pattern Directions

On the front side of the first page of the pattern directions, you'll see several diagrams for laying out the fabric. Notice they're arranged both by size and by width of fabric. Find the one that matches the size and width of your fabric. There might also be a diagram for one-way designs and naps.

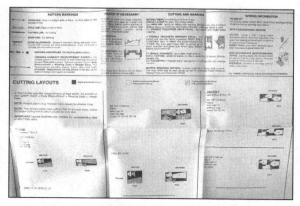

On the front side of the first page of the pattern directions, you'll find several diagrams for laying out the fabric.

It helps to circle the layout diagram you're using so you can easily find it as you lay out the pieces. If you've made any of your pieces wider or longer (see Chapter 18), you will have to adjust accordingly.

Sometimes a pattern piece is cut singly, sometimes it's cut on the fold, and sometimes you cut it out more than once. The number of pieces you'll need to cut is clearly marked on the pattern and on the layout sample.

The directions will tell you where to fold. If a pattern piece is used more than once, it will be shown in a different color on the directions.

Cutting the Pattern Pieces You Need

Open the pattern and find the pieces you need. Keeping in mind how you chose to cut (or not) the notches, cut out each pattern piece you need on the cutting line and set it aside. Put the unused pieces in a bag for future use.

Fringe Benefits

Folding a pattern is worse than trying to fold a road map! It's nearly impossible to get it back to the original shape and into the envelope, particularly after you've cut some pieces. My advice: Don't even try. Get some clear, gallon-size resealable plastic bags and put all the unused pieces in the bag. Cut the envelope along the edge and put the front, with the picture facing out, in the bag on one side of the pattern pieces and the back side of the envelop facing out on the other side of the pieces. As you remove the pattern pieces from the fabric later, just slip them into the plastic bag. Plus, this helps you keep your patterns in one place. The plastic bags are slippery, though. Commercial bags available from sewing notion companies work better if you want to spend a little more.

The Least You Need to Know

◆ Reading and following a pattern is easy once you get to know it a little.

◆ The dots, triangles, squares, and other pattern marks are all there to help you sew your project.

◆ Follow the pattern directions for a successful sewing experience.

In This Chapter

- ◆ Adjusting patterns to fit
- ◆ Using darts and seams to your advantage
- ◆ Lengthening and shortening pattern pieces

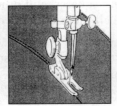

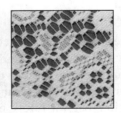
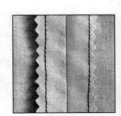

Chapter **18**

Custom-Fitting a Pattern

You're armed with your pattern and now the knowledge of how to read it—including what all those markings mean—but before you start cutting your material, you need to consider if you'll have to make any fitting adjustments to your pattern.

How a pattern fits depends somewhat on your taste. Some people like their clothes nice and tight, while some like the loose, baggy look. In spite of all the differences in taste, fashion, and body shape, there are still a few simple rules you should follow when you're changing a pattern to fit a particular body.

Adjusting to the Body's Lumps and Bumps

The human body is not a tall, two-dimensional, flat paper doll or fashion magazine advertisement. The human body has lumps and bumps, more or less but not exactly in the same places.

The female body's lumps and bumps—the back shoulder blades, the bust, the waist, the hips, the tummy, and the derriere—have to be considered when designing a pattern. Trying to accommodate those lumps and bumps is what the fashion industry and pattern industry are all about. Sometimes fashion designers try to emphasize these areas; sometimes they try to hide them entirely.

People with entirely different shapes may still all start with the same size pattern.

I'll Be Darned

If you look in a history of fashion book, you'll notice that certain parts of the body were prominent at certain times. For example, in the 1500s, wide hips were the fashion. During the late nineteenth century, bustles emphasized the derriere. During the 1920s, fashion de-emphasized all bumps and lumps.

Going from the flat of the fabric to the contours of the body is accomplished mostly through darts, gathers, and seams. For a pattern to fit correctly, even loose-fitting garments, you need to consider the location of the seams and darts.

Locating Seams

On most apparel, the basic seams are the shoulder seams and the side seams. Some garments have a front seam, and many have a back seam.

If the garment has a fitted sleeve, there will be a seam where the sleeve meets the shoulder. Dresses might have a seam that attaches the top to the skirt. Most other seams are decorative. Some seam lines are for contouring.

For basic, nondecorative seams, keep the following general placement rules in mind:

◆ The side, back center, and front center seams should be perpendicular to the floor.

Cut It Out!

In some cases, as with the A-line skirt, "perpendicular to the floor" does not mean straight up and down from the floor, but that the seam doesn't slant to the front or the back.

◆ The shoulder seam should be on the middle top of the shoulder and should not point toward the front or the back.

◆ If a waist seam attaches a top to a skirt of a dress, for example, this line should be parallel to the floor.

Although all rules in fashion have been broken and will continue to be broken, these are the general guidelines.

Placing Darts

Remember darts from Chapter 7? You can use them to get around all the lumps and bumps. Or you can use gathers or pleats instead of darts in many locations (also in Chapter 7).

Here are some dart-placement tips:

◆ The darts for the wide part of bust can start almost anywhere in the shoulder seam, the side seam, the waist, or some combination of all three. The bust dart points to the tip of the bust. It doesn't go to the tip, it just points to it. For B cups, the end of the dart should be about 1 inch from the tip of the bust; for A cups, a little less; and for C and D cups, a little more. It is very important that the darts point to the tip of the bust, not to the floor or the sky.

◆ Use small darts in either the shoulder seam or the waist line in the back to shape the shoulder blade.

◆ Start tummy and derriere darts at the waist and make them perpendicular to the floor.

Cut It Out!

If you're making a dress that has a waist line seam, and the bust darts and the shoulder blade darts start from the waist, the bust and the tummy darts must match up at the waist seam line in the front. Likewise, the darts for the derriere and the shoulder blade must line up in the back.

◆ On fitted skirts, adjust for the hip bump in the side seams.

I'll Be Darned

On men's shirts, use a yoke instead of darts to accommodate the shoulder blade bump. Most of the other shaping on men's apparel happens in the seams. Some men's pants do have pleats at the waist to help shape the pants around the tummy or derriere.

The Princess Seam Line

Garments with a princess seam line don't use darts. All the shaping is in the seam line. There are two princess lines. One starts in the shoulder seam and runs directly over the fullest part of the bust, then continues to the waist, hip, or hemline. The second princess line starts in the armhole curve, goes near the fullest part of the bust but not over it, and continues to the waist, hip, or hemline.

Fitting the Pattern to Your Body

The easiest way to fit the pattern to your body is to find a friend to help you. After you have trimmed the pattern pieces to the cutting line and to the size you think most nearly represents your body, try some of the following to see how it really fits. It helps if you wear a leotard. If you have a form that has been shaped to your size, use her.

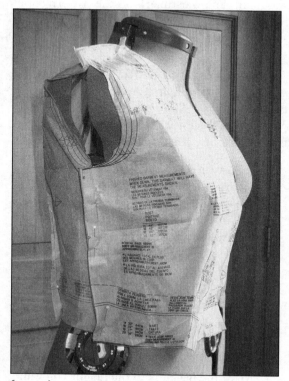

If you plan on sewing many garments, a dress form is very helpful.

1. Pin all the darts together.

2. Clip all the curved edges into the seam allowance.

3. Pin the bodice's center front lines to your center front line.

4. Pin the bodice's center back lines to your center back line.

5. Pin the side seams of the pattern together.

6. Pin the shoulder seams together on your shoulder.

7. Pin a piece of elastic around your waist.

8. Tuck the skirt pieces up under the elastic so the elastic falls on the seam line.

To have a perfect fit, the front, back, and side seams should be perpendicular to the floor. The darts should point to the tip of the bust. The shoulder seam line should be at the center of your shoulder. The waist mark on the pattern should be at your waist. The width of the shoulder should be appropriate for the design of the garment.

If you don't have a perfect fit, the following suggestions might help (for more complicated fitting, read *Fit for Real People* by Pati Palmer and Marta Alto). Follow them in order, and stop when the pattern fits; you don't have to try them all.

1. Adjust the back first so the back center seam is perpendicular to the floor. Adjust the darts. If, after adjusting the darts, it still doesn't fit, slit the pattern vertically. Separate if the pattern is too small, or make a vertical tuck the length of the pattern if it's too large. Rearrange the darts. Be sure the shoulder blade dart points to the shoulder blade.

2. Adjust the front, taking in or letting out seam lines and darts so the center front line is perpendicular to the floor.

3. Mark the neckline to the height you want it.

4. Adjust the length of the pieces on the lines provided on pattern.

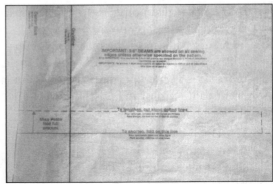

Adjust the length of the pieces on the lines provided on the pattern.

> ## Fringe Benefits
> When lengthening or shortening a garment piece, do so on the places marked on the pattern. You lose some of the shaping if you lengthen or shorten from the bottom.

5. Adjust the shoulder seams.

6. Rearrange the dart lines, adjusting the point and the size of the dart as necessary.

7. Adjust the sleeves.

8. Adjust the skirt by pulling it up under the elastic until the front and back seams are perpendicular to the floor and the hem line is parallel to the floor. The side seam should also fall perpendicular to the floor.

When you've finished marking the pieces, you might want to make another pattern out of another piece of paper. Don't forget to move all the other marks on the pattern as well.

> ## Fringe Benefits
> If you've made major adjustments on every seam and dart, maybe you started with a wrong-size pattern. Try again with a different size pattern.

Fabric drapes differently than paper, and if you really want to know if this pattern fits you well, use the pattern to make a sample of the finished garment from gingham or muslin. Use long stitches of a very different color to make the seams and darts. This makes it easier to take them out if you want to move them. Try on the practice garment, and fine-tune the pattern. When you have what you feel is a good fit, you're ready to continue with your project.

Fringe Benefits

You can find software to custom-fit your patterns to you. You just input all your dimensions, select the style you want, and, before you can blink an eye, all the adjustments are made to your specifications. Then you can print the pattern pieces and get to work. Visit www.livingsoft.com for a sample of these products.

The Least You Need to Know

◆ To get the perfect fit for you, you might need to adjust a pattern.

◆ Side, back, and front seams should fall perpendicular to the floor.

◆ Bust darts should point to the tip of the bust.

◆ Gathers and pleats can replace darts for a different, less fitted look.

◆ In the princess style, all shaping is done in the seams without darts.

In This Chapter

- ◆ Getting your fabric ready
- ◆ Fitting the pattern pieces to your fabric
- ◆ Marking the fabric

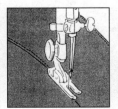

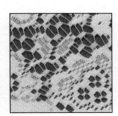
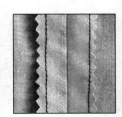

Chapter 19

Working With the Fabric

You have your pattern, and, perhaps more important, you can read and understand what all the dots and squares and various lines mean. You understand the pattern directions and how to adjust the pattern to fit you best. Now you just have to be sure your fabric is as ready as you are, including preshrinking it or straightening it, if necessary. You can start cutting and transferring the pattern markings to your fabric.

Preparing the Fabric

There are several schools of thought on how to prepare your fabric. You first have to think about whether you're going to preshrink your fabric. Preshrinking is a good idea if the garment is going to be washed often. Of course, some fabrics you would never wash, so preshrinking by washing is not an option. You could dry-clean those fabrics for shrinkage first.

The fabric is almost always folded in half lengthwise. This helps keep the rights and lefts correct. Whether you fold right sides together or wrong sides together depends on which authority you like best. It depends somewhat, too, on how you plan to mark the pattern. Wrong sides together work best if you are marking darts with a tracing wheel. It is easier to slip the carbon paper between the layers. (See the "Transferring the Markings" section later in this chapter.)

Cut It Out!

When you preshrink some fabric, you might notice that the selvage shrinks differently than the rest of the fabric and the fabric no longer lays perfectly flat. If this happens, clip the selvage in several places or neatly cut off the selvage.

For this chapter, I'll assume the selvage is straight and the crosswise grain is perfectly perpendicular to the selvage. I'll also assume that the fabric's horizontal line of the design is printed right on the crosswise grain. Now, place the selvages together, shifting one or the other so that when the fabric is placed on the table, it is flat without any bumps on the folded edge. Slide the selvages together until everything is perfectly smooth. If you're using slippery fabric, pin the selvages together in many places.

Fringe Benefits

If your material has an obvious right and wrong side, you won't have any trouble telling which is the left side and which is the right side after you've cut out the pieces. If you can't tell which is the right side and which is the wrong side, as on some plain cottons or broadcloths, it's very easy to make two lefts or two rights without even realizing it. Before you take out the pins, make a mark in the seam allowance to indicate the wrong side.

When putting selvages together, be sure you smooth out all the wrinkles.

Cut It Out!

Unfortunately, we don't live in an ideal world. If the crosswise grain is really a long way from being perpendicular to the selvage, consider a different fabric. Also, if the printed pattern is more than ½ inch off the crosswise grain, you might want to use a different fabric.

If you're having trouble getting the fabric to lay flat, try pulling on the bias in both directions and in many places up and down the fabric. You can also try clipping the selvage in several places or cutting off the selvage entirely and then pulling on the bias. If after all this it still doesn't lay flat, you might need to get different fabric.

Laying Out the Pattern

If you like puzzles, you'll love the challenge of arranging the pattern pieces on the fabric. The challenge comes in trying to minimize the amount of fabric needed, while making sure all the pieces are arranged in exactly the right way. No pieces are just plunked on the fabric and cut out.

Fringe Benefits

Before you pin and cut, loosely lay out all the pieces on the fabric to be sure you have enough fabric.

Place pattern pieces on the fabric either on the fold, on the grain, or on the bias. Place the biggest pieces that need to be on the fold first. Place the fold line of the pattern piece on the fold line of the fabric, smooth out the pattern piece, and pin here and there around the edge. Pin in the seam allowance, parallel to the edge of the pattern. If you pin across the cutting edge, it makes it difficult to cut the fabric without moving the pins.

Cut It Out!

On most fabrics, it won't matter if the pins stray out of the seam allowance into the garment because the pin holes won't show. However, you don't want to put pin holes in specialty fabrics like silk or satin.

Getting It Straight

You'll need a ruler to place pieces on the grain. Find the grain line marked on the pattern piece. It is usually marked by a long arrow with arrow heads at both ends. Place the pattern piece on the fabric, and measure the distance from the grain line to the selvage at one end of the line. Carefully move the ruler to the other end of the grain line and measure again. Move the pattern piece around until both ends of the line are exactly the same distance from the selvage. Pin the ends of the grain line, smooth out the pattern piece, and pin around the edge.

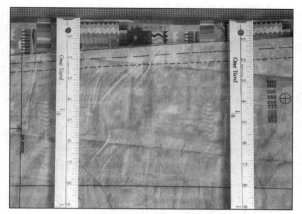

When laying the pattern piece on the fabric, be sure the grain line is equidistant from the selvage.

Watch the Naps

If the fabric has a nap or one-way design, decide which end is the top and which end is the bottom. Keep track of the direction of the fabric as you place the pieces. Any pieces that will be seen by the world will have to go in the same direction.

On fabrics with a nap, like velvet and corduroy, run your hand up and down the fabric to determine which way is up. Usually, it feels smoother as you run your hand to the bottom and rougher when you run your hand toward the top.

Be careful of crosswise folds. In fact, you can't use a crosswise fold with fabrics with a nap or one-way design. You'll have to cut the fabric crosswise and then put the two tops together as well as right sides facing each other. Be careful not to place a piece upside down.

You should continue to keep the pieces right side up when using napped or one-way design fabric, but if you're desperate for space, you can put pieces that will never show, such as facings, upside down.

Plaids and Stripes

Plaids and stripes take more fabric as well as more patience when placing the fabric. You want the plaid or stripe lines to meet at appropriate places in the seam lines and in the front, if there's an opening. You'll have to slide the pieces around a bit so they match up. While you're sliding them around, you also have to keep the grain straight. Be sure to check all seams that meet. If you have to choose between a front seam matching or a side seam, always pick the front!

Border Fabric

On border prints, you'll have to place the pattern grain line on the crosswise grain on pieces where it's necessary to have the bottom be the bottom. All other pieces that won't show the border design should be cut on the lengthwise grain.

Cutting the Fabric

After you've pinned all the pieces to the fabric, cut out the pieces, keeping in mind how you chose to cut out (or not) the notches. Leave the pattern pinned to the fabric piece until it's time to sew. Lay them flat, or clothespin them to a hanger.

> **Fringe Benefits**
>
> Some people prefer not to pin the pattern to the fabric, but to use weights instead. This method is quicker, but it's also easier for the pieces to slide around, and you run the risk of losing the grain line.

Transferring the Markings

You've cut out all the pattern pieces, but before you take the pattern off the fabric, you need to transfer the markings (those dots, squares, and triangles; see Chapter 17) from the pattern to the fabric. These markings make it easier to put the pieces together.

You can mark the pattern in a variety of ways: tailor chalk, wheel and tracing paper, marking pencils, or tailor tacks. What you use is up to you, as long as the marks are transferred from the pattern tissue to the fabric. How you transfer the markings (those dots, squares, and triangles; see Chapter 18) is a combination of what you like and the fabric you are using. If you think you're going to be using a wide variety of fabrics, be familiar with all the possibilities:

> **Fringe Benefits**
>
> All markings go on the wrong side of the fabric. In the case of a pocket placement, however, mark the *wrong* side of the fabric then hand-baste through the markings, thus making the markings visible on the right side.

- You can use pins, in some cases. They don't work on slippery fabrics or silks, satins, or leathers that will show the pin holes. Pins have a habit of falling out, though, so don't use them if you're going to wait until another day to put the garment together. Plus, pins might rust, even if you think they are rustproof.

- Tailor chalk and dressmaker's pencils are usually a good choice. They do rub off if left for a long time, so keep that in mind. Some colors are difficult to see on certain fabrics. Do not use very dark-colored pencils on very light-colored and lightweight fabric; the markings will show through.

◆ Liquid markers wash or fade out in time. Be sure to test your marker on a scrap of fabric before you mark your garment.

Cut It Out!

Not all marking tools are good for all kinds of fabric. If in doubt, test on a piece of scrap material. If the directions say that the marking pen washes out, be sure that that is true for your fabric.

◆ Snips work well on any markings in the seam allowance.

◆ A tracing wheel and tracing paper are great for marking darts. The tracing wheel might damage some fabrics, so test this method on a scrap first. The tracing wheel isn't very helpful for marking dots and notches.

◆ Tailor tacks are sewn by hand with a double thread. Insert needle into dot on the tissue pattern and through both layers of fabric. Take a small stitch, and bring the needle back up through the dot. Leave a very long tail. Repeat the process through the same dot so that a small cross is made on the under fabric. Leave a large loop on the top, and cut the thread, leaving a long tail. When you remove the tissue from the fabric, pull the thread gently through the tissue. Gently pull the fabric pieces apart, being sure there are tails showing on both pieces of fabric, then cut the tailor tack in half. If the tails are not long enough or the fabric is flimsy, however, sometimes the threads fall out. The threads of the tailor tacks get sewn into the stitching and are sometimes difficult to remove.

Tailor tacks are made with thread as one way of transferring markings from the pattern to the fabric.

I'll Be Darned

On some old patterns, the dots on the patterns were actually holes. When you made a tailor tack, you didn't go through the tissue paper, but just through the hole. Today you have to go through the tissue paper. After you've made the tailor tack and pulled the crossed piece of the tailor tack through the hole, sometimes it doesn't go easily and the tissue rips in different directions. If you don't remove the little piece of tissue paper before you sew the dart lines, sometimes the paper gets sewn into the dart. This paper can be very annoying to try to get out!

The Least You Need to Know

◆ To preshrink or not to preshrink? Be sure your fabric is ready to go before you start cutting out pattern pieces.

◆ Match the pattern grain line to the fabric grain line when laying out the pattern pieces.

◆ Always transfer markings to the wrong side of the fabric.

◆ Test marking pens on scrap material before you use them on the real thing.

In This Chapter

◆ Putting together a garment

◆ Following directions

◆ Working with facings and sleeves

◆ Straying from the directions—when it's okay to

 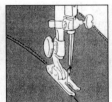   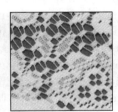 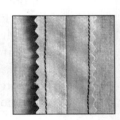

Chapter **20**

Putting It All Together

You've read your pattern and directions and understand what all the marks mean. You've cut out your pattern pieces and transferred the markings to your fabric. The time has come to put your garment together.

There's nothing tricky about this part. Basically, all you have are seams and hems, maybe a gather here or there, and possibly a zipper. Remember, almost everything is your choice. How you finish the seams and hem is up to you. The pattern directions will offer suggestions, but it's ultimately your choice.

The pattern will also suggest how to put in the zipper and what kind of zipper to use, but you have a choice here, too. I like invisible zippers, so whenever a pattern calls for a zipper, I almost always use an invisible one. Sometimes a pattern calls for buttons and buttonholes. If you're nervous about making buttonholes, or if your machine makes it difficult to put in a nice, neat buttonhole, use your imagination. Put in snaps and use the buttons for decorative purposes only.

If in doubt, follow the directions. In most cases, there's a reason for doing things in the order suggested by the pattern. It's almost always true.

First Things First

Before you start to sew, read through all the directions. Identify the pieces that go together. Lay them out more or less in order. In your mind, work through the parts you don't understand, and get help before you start.

In addition to sewing pieces together, pressing is important. When the directions tell you to press, press! Don't skip this step. It might mean that you have to run back and forth to your iron, but do it anyway.

Likewise, if the pattern tells you to clip, clip! This will help when you turn the garment to the right side.

Follow the seam allowances suggested. The patterns have been sized for the given seam allowances.

After each section is put together—for example, when the skirt is together—try it on. Its easier to make final adjustments to darts and seams as you go rather than after the garment is finished.

Following Instructions

If this is the first time you'll be making a garment from pattern instructions, follow them *exactly*. Later, when you have some experience working with patterns, you can fiddle around with the directions.

You learned about seams, hems, and zippers earlier in the book. When you're following the pattern instructions, you might come across a few other terms and techniques you'll need to know.

Neck Facings

There are myriad kinds of facings. Dresses and tops usually have neck facings, whether or not the garment has a collar. If the garment is sleeveless, there might be an armhole facing. Jackets and blouses that open in the front will probably have front facings. (There are also a variety of ways of finishing neck and arm holes that do not include facings.)

If a garment does not have a collar, it almost always has a facing. The facing is cut from the same fabric as the garment, in such a way that it fits the neck opening exactly. When the facing is sewn to the garment, there should be no puckers or gathers.

Facings are usually *interfaced*. Select the weight of the interfacing suggested on the pattern or for the look you want to accomplish and one that is suitable for your fabric. If you choose fusible interfacing material, follow the manufacturer's instructions.

When you're putting in the facing, always *grade* it. After you've sewn the facing to the garment, you'll notice that you have several layers of fabric in the seam allowance. To help the facing lay flat, and so the neck hole doesn't have a big bump of fabric, trim each layer to a different width.

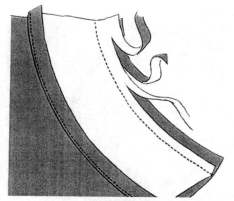

Grade the seam to eliminate bulk and help the garment lay flat.

Trim the curve by clipping each layer in a different place. This will help keep the clips from showing through. Be careful not to clip the stitching, though.

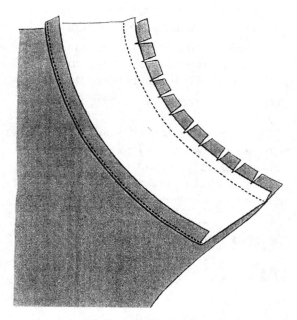

Whenever you sew a curve, be sure to clip the curve in several places before you turn the piece right side out.

After you've graded the seam, and to prevent rolling, press all the seam allowances toward the facing. *Understitch* by stitching through the facing and seam allowances close to the seam.

> ### Sew You Say
>
> To **understitch**, press and stitch all the seam allowances to the facing very close to the seam line. Understitching is used primarily on all faced edges, to prevent the facing from rolling and showing on the right side of the garment.

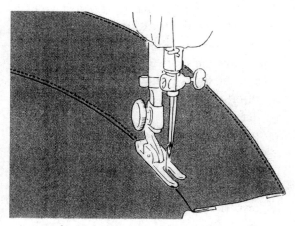

Understitch to prevent facings from rolling.

Press the facing to the inside. You might want to tack the facing in place. To avoid having the stitches show on the right side, stitch the facing to any available seam allowance, such as the shoulder seams for neck and armhole facings.

Armhole Facings or Sleeves

A garment will have either an armhole facing or a sleeve. When you're putting in the armhole facing, follow the same directions for the neck facing.

Then, to put in the sleeve, sew the shoulder and side seams of the garment, sew the underarm seam of the sleeve, and then set the sleeve into the garment.

Some things to take into consideration include the following:

1. Be sure you've marked the sleeve before you start.

2. Put a gathering thread on the stitching line between the two dots on the sleeve before you sew the underarm seam.

3. Unless otherwise directed by the pattern, be sure to press open the seams of both the sleeve and the garment before you start to pin them together.

4. When pinning the sleeve to the garment, be sure the single notches match in front and the double notches match in back.

5. Pin the top of the sleeve dot to the shoulder seam.

6. Pin the underarm seam together.

7. Pin from the underarm seam to both the front and back dots where the gathering stitches begin. There should be no tucks or gathers in this section.

8. If this is a set-in sleeve, you shouldn't have any gathers showing where the sleeve meets the shoulder. The best way to eliminate gathers is to use as many pins as possible to ease the top of the sleeve to the garment. Some fabrics ease in easier than others, and pins really help here. You cannot use too many pins; the more pins, the better. After all the pins are in, gently pull the sleeve gatherings to the left and the seam allowance to the right. Check to be sure you haven't accidentally put in a tuck on the garment side. This step takes patience and practice. The key is in the number of pins you use. When all the pins are in and there are no puckers, carefully and slowly stitch on top of the gathering thread.

9. If the sleeve is to have a gathered top, gather evenly around the top, and pin. Here again, using lots of pins helps.

10. Reinforce the underarm by making another row of stitches between the notches. Then trim between the notches.

11. Press, following the pattern instructions.

Don't get discouraged if your first attempt at putting in sleeves seems impossible. Start with light- to medium-weight fabric, but not sheer or something slippery. For tips that make putting in the sleeve a little easier, keep reading.

When to *Not* Follow Instructions

Sometimes pattern directions go with the tried-and-true methods of doing things, and creative sewers have come up with easier and sometimes streamlined methods. Almost all patterns use conventional zippers, for example. Almost all patterns put in sleeves as described earlier, although some are changing their methods on sleeves. Here are two alternative methods you might want to try, one for zippers, and one for sleeves.

Zippers

Conventional patterns usually call for conventional zipper placement, either centered or lapped (see Chapter 10 for instructions on how to put in these kinds of zippers). But if you're making a dress that has a top and a bottom, the top and bottom have to be sewn together, the back seam sewn to the bottom of the zipper opening, and the zipper opening basted before the zipper can be inserted.

If you want to use an invisible zipper, don't sew the back seam first. Put in the zipper first. If you use an invisible zipper, you'll have to re-arrange the order of steps for the entire garment.

Sleeves

Most patterns suggest sewing together the shoulder and side seams on the garment and then sewing together the underarm seam and the sleeve before attaching the sleeve to the garment. Sewing the armhole seam is difficult with all the material and pins. Trying to keep the gathers from puckering and the garment from getting tucks takes practice. When you're putting sleeves in children's clothes, it's even more difficult because everything is so small.

An alternate way to put in sleeves is to put the sleeves in before you sew the underarm seam on the sleeve and the side seam on the garment. Just sew the shoulder seam. Putting in the sleeve is easier because everything lays flatter, and it's easier to maneuver the sleeve and the garment under the needle. Once the sleeve is attached to the garment, sew the side and underarm seam as one seam. If you use this method, you'll have to reorder how the pieces go together.

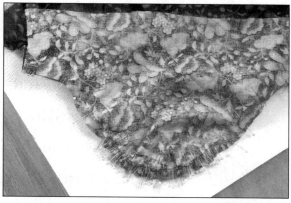

It's sometimes easier to put in a sleeve before sewing the underarm and side seams together.

Cut It Out!

If you're making a garment with sleeves and are using an invisible zipper, you have to decide what to do first. I suggest making the back if it has a top and a bottom. Put in the zipper, and then sew the back seam. Put the front together if it has a top and a bottom, put in sleeves, then sew the side seams.

Read the pattern directions first. Then figure out what you need to change, rearrange the directions, then start sewing.

The Least You Need to Know

- ◆ Grading a seam eliminates bulk in facing seams.
- ◆ Understitching keeps the facing from showing on the outside of the garment.
- ◆ Following directions exactly is helpful in almost every case.
- ◆ If it's easier, you can rework the instructions a bit when you're putting in invisible zippers and some sleeves.

In This Part

No Pattern? No Problem!

Here, at the start of the twenty-first century, let's keep two things in mind: Our ancient ancestors never had a pattern picked out of a pattern book, and the current fashion is easy and free-flowing. The designs of the ancients and the fashions of today vary only in types of fabrics available. Most garments were made with two to four seams. Most of the garments described in the following chapters are made with two to four seams. The difference between our ancestors and us is that they had to sew the seams together with bone needles. We have steel needles. If you choose to use a sewing machine, you can make most of the garments in Part 5 in less than 3 hours, assuming you have the materials on hand.

In This Chapter

- ◆ Making a simple top
- ◆ Varying neck and armhole facings
- ◆ Adding pockets

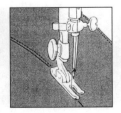

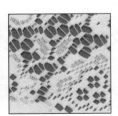
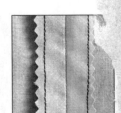

Chapter 21

Sewing a Simple Top

Most simple tops start with a rectangle. You can make a top from one or two rectangles for casual as well as fancy evening dress by just changing the fabric. For example, if you want an everyday casual top, scrubs, or a maternity top, choose cotton or some other lightweight synthetic or a knit. If you want loungewear, try velour, terrycloth, or fleece. If you need a night out on the town, try challis or a synthetic silk. For a really formal affair such as a wedding, try velvet or a shimmery fabric. The occasion dictates the fabric, and the fabric dictates the look.

All these tops can be made from one or two rectangles, two to four straight seams, three simple edge finishes, and a hem.

Choosing a Neckline

Before you begin your top, you have to decide what style neckline you want. Most are simple and easy to make on garments with or without a front or back center seam.

All necklines need to be faced in some way to prevent fraying on the curve and to add a nice finish to the garment. Choose a finish that's appropriate to the fabric and to the look you want. For example, if you want something fancy, you might want to choose velvet or a shimmery fabric for the top and face the neck and armholes with a satin-covered piping.

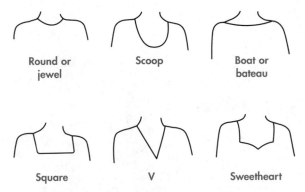

Round or jewel

Scoop

Boat or bateau

Square

V

Sweetheart

Choose a neckline from one of these, or design your own.

Deciding on Armholes

There are no set-in sleeves for these easy-to-make tops. However, you can create the illusion of a cap sleeve by adjusting a few lines.

This easy scrub top has the illusion of sleeves.

Like necklines, armholes have to be faced or hemmed. If the line is straight, a simple folded hem will work. If you want a curve to the armhole, I'll give you finishing options in the later "Shoulders and Armholes" section.

Long or Short?

The length of the top is entirely up to you. The bottom edge can hang just below your bust, to allow some of your midriff to show, or it can go to your waist or hips—even your thighs, knees, or ankles. This basic pattern is for a bottom edge just above the hips. For all other lengths, see the tips in the later "Variation" section.

A Simple Top Without a Nap or One-Way Design

This top is easy to make because it is very loose and virtually shapeless. However, with a little ingenuity and some trim here and there, you will be able to wear it anywhere.

1. Measure from the top of your shoulders to where you want the bottom to be. Multiply that number by 2.

> **Fringe Benefits**
>
> If you're using bias tape to face the edges, add a few inches to the measurement determined in step 1. This is the amount of material you need to purchase. If you're making your own bias binding, add at least ½ yard of material to make the bias strips.

2. Measure around your bust. Divide that number by 2, and then add 6 inches.

   If you plan to have the top go below your hips, and your hip measurement is larger than your bust measurement, use the hip measurement.

3. Cut a single rectangle the length and width determined in steps 1 and 2.

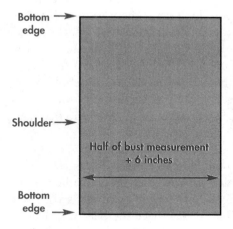

4. Fold the rectangle crosswise and then lengthwise. Mark the point of the folds.

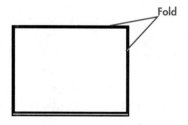

5. With the fabric still folded, cut the curve for the neck opening around the point of the folds in the shape you want. When you're cutting a round or jewel neck, be sure the opening is large enough that you can get your head through. You also might want the front lower than the back so you won't choke.

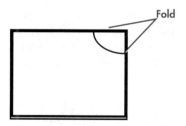

6. Face the opening. See the later "Neck Openings" section for some facing possibilities.

7. With the right sides together, sew the side seams, leaving a 7- to 8-inch armhole opening.

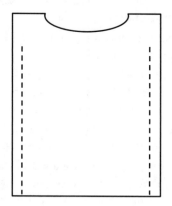

8. Face the armhole openings. See the later "Shoulders and Armholes" section for some possibilities.

9. Hem the bottom.

> **Fringe Benefits**
>
> If the fabric doesn't have much stretch and the bottom of the garment falls below your hip line, consider leaving the side seams open a few inches at the bottom. Hem the side seam openings with a narrow double folded hem in the seam allowance. This will give you some ease when you're putting on the top and also add a decorative touch.

A Simple Top with a Nap or One-Way Design

If your fabric has a nap or one-way design, you'll have to cut the fabric crosswise and add shoulder seams:

1. Measure from the top of your shoulders to where you want the bottom to be.

2. Measure around your bust. Divide that number by 2, then add 6 inches.

   If you plan to have the top go below your hips, and your hip measurement is larger than your bust measurement, use the hip measurement.

3. Cut 2 rectangles the length and width determined in steps 1 and 2.

4. Pin the rectangles with right sides together and the tops matching. Remember which side is the top!

5. Sew across the top, forming a shoulder seam, but leaving the neck open.

6. Cut the neck opening around the point of the folds. When you're cutting a round or jewel neck, be sure the opening is large enough that you can get your head through. You also might want the front lower than the back so you won't choke.

7. Face the opening. See the later "Neck Openings" section for some facing possibilities.

8. With right sides together, sew the side seams, leaving a 7- to 8-inch armhole opening.

9. Face the armhole openings. See the later "Shoulders and Armholes" section for some possibilities.

10. Hem the bottom.

Variations on a Theme

You can vary these simple tops many ways just by changing the necklines or the sleeves, trimming the bottom, or adding pockets. Here are a few ideas for adding a little variety to the basic pattern.

Changing the Neck

The front and back necklines don't have to match. If you don't want them to match, in the earlier step 4, just fold the fabric lengthwise. In step 5, cut the neck back one way and the front neck another. You might want to cut the front a bit lower than the back, to prevent choking. If the front is already low, this isn't a problem.

If you want to change up your neckline, here are some facing options:

◆ Use matching or contrasting purchased double fold bias tape. (See Chapter 12 for more on how to sew on purchased double fold bias tape.) Place the bias tape over the edge, and sew. This facing will show. See Chapter 13 for finishing tips.

◆ Make double fold bias tape from same fabric and sew down over the edge. This facing will show. See Chapter 13 for finishing tips.

◆ Sew the right side of single fold bias tape to the right side of the neckline, then clip the neckline. Fold the bias tape over so it doesn't show on the front side, understitch, fold to the wrong side, then slip stitch in place with tiny stitches. This facing should not show.

◆ Make piping as for knife-edge pillows from the same fabric or a contrasting one. Baste piping to the neck edge. Sew the right side of single fold bias tape to the right side of the neckline, and snug it up to the piping using a zipper foot. Clip the neckline, then fold the bias tape to the wrong side, and slip stitch in place with tiny stitches.

◆ Stay stitch around the neck opening. Clip to the stitches, then fold on the stay stitches to the right side. Glue or baste, then cover the raw edge with trim.

◆ Make a front or back slit. Here's how:

  1. After cutting the neck hole, mark the front or back slit on the lengthwise fold line from the crosswise fold line.

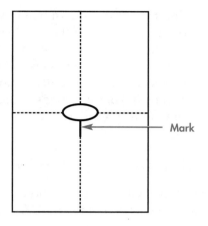

2. Draw a V about ½ inch wide at the neckline and 5 inches long.

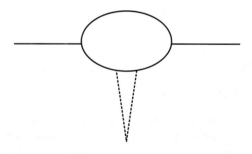

3. Stay stitch just inside the marked lines.

4. For the facing, cut a rectangle 3 inches by 6 inches. Finish one short side and both long sides. (See Chapter 7 for a variety of ways to finish an edge.)

5. Place the center of the facing over the center of the V, with the right sides together.

6. Stitch along the marked lines, reinforcing the point by shortening the stitch length.

7. Cut through to the point of the V.

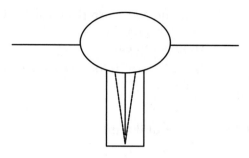

8. Turn the facing to the inside, and press.

9. Finish the rest of the neckline, using one of the methods suggested earlier.

◆ Make facings like you usually find on manufactured tops. This will require extra fabric. Be sure the front and back lines are on the grain.

1. After you've cut the opening on the garment and it's the way you want it, place the garment on a piece of paper and trace the opening onto the paper.

2. Mark the center front, center back, and center shoulders.

3. Remove the garment from the paper. By hand, draw another line on the paper about 2½ inches outside the first line.

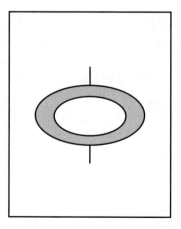

4. Mark the center front and back points. Cut out the paper pattern.

5. Lay the pattern on the fabric, making sure the center front and back lines are on the grain.

6. Cut out, and finish the outside edge. (See Chapter 7 for a variety of ways to finish an edge.)

7. See Chapter 20 for how to sew in a facing.

✂ Cut It Out!

If the part of the facing that goes across the shoulder of the garment is wider than the shoulder, you'll have to adjust something. Either make the facing narrower or use one of the other facing methods suggested.

Working With Shoulders and Armholes

We are not square boxes, and some of us have a few more bumps than others. If you would like to add a little shape to any of the tops in this chapter, you can slant the shoulder seam by making a dart where the traditional seam would be with the wide end toward the arm and the point toward the neck. Trim the dart and press open. You could also use one of the following suggestions:

◆ If you'd like a small, capped sleeve, move the side seams in and make a gentle curve to the edge at the armhole. Trim the seams, then finish as in the earlier directions.

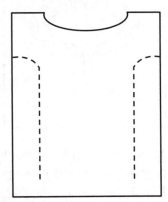

For a small capped sleeve, move the side seams in and make a gentle curve to the edge.

◆ Sew the middle of a ribbon to the middle of the underside of the shoulder on the fold line. Bring the ribbon to the front, and tie it with a bow. This will gather the shoulder line and add decoration. You can also tie in your bra straps at the same time so they won't show.

Playing With the Bottom Line

One of the easiest places to show your creativity is at the bottom of the top! Try adding:

◆ lace or a ruffle,

◆ one or two strips of different-color fabric, or

◆ fringe or other decorative edging.

Adding Pockets

Patch pockets are easy!

1. Make a square or rectangle the size you want, plus ½ inch added on 3 sides for the turn-under hem and 1¼ inches on the top edge for the top-of-pocket finishing.

2. Stay-stitch ½ inch on the 2 sides and the bottom.

3. Hem the top with a single ¼-inch fold-over hem.

4. Fold the top over, right sides together, 1 inch. To keep the hem from flopping open, slip stitch the hem to the pocket or tack it down with a decorative top stitch.

5. Seam both sides of the top of the pocket with ½-inch seams. Turn right side out, and press.

6. Fold the sides and the bottom to the wrong side on the stay stitching, and press.

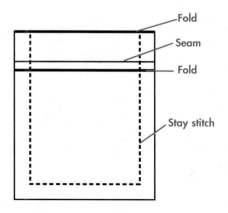

7. Pin the pocket on the top where you want it.

8. Topstitch the pocket in place. With a few back-tacks, reinforce the top where the pocket meets the garment.

The Least You Need to Know

◆ With one simple top pattern, you can create many fun tops just by varying a few details.

◆ From scrubs to a maternity top to a glitzy night-on-the-town top, the fabric you choose for your top can change the look of your top.

◆ You can finish a neck or armhole in so many ways.

In This Chapter

- ◆ Raising (or lowering) hemlines
- ◆ Making a waistband casing
- ◆ Sewing a simple skirt

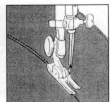

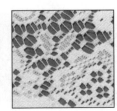
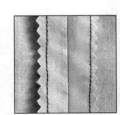

Chapter 22

Sewing a Fun Skirt

One of the simplest garments to make is a skirt. With just two or three seams, a fold-over waistband, and a hem, you can make a skirt in a snap. For example, depending on your body shape, you might be able to make a mini-skirt with less than 1 yard of material in about an hour.

There are no rules about how high off the floor to place the hem, save what you have in mind. Practice with the simplest skirt (I'll give you some directions later in this chapter), then let your imagination take over.

Skirt Shapes

There might seem to be myriad skirt designs, but there really are only a few basic skirts, each with a host of variations. The lingo is always changing, so some of the following definitions will vary in the industry.

Straight

For a straight skirt, think rectangles! The straight skirt consists of two or three rectangles and a waistband, which is also a rectangle. Usually there's one rectangle for the front and one or two rectangles for the back, depending on whether you put a zipper in the back seam.

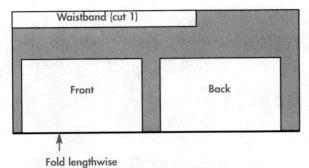

Fold lengthwise

You can make a straight skirt from three rectangles.

Circle

Think circles! The circle skirt consists of two semi-circles or one semi-circle and two quarter-circles, depending on whether you put a zipper in the back seam. A circle skirt might also have one rectangle for the waistband.

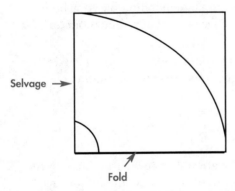

You can make a circular skirt from two semi-circles.

Flared

The flared skirt is similar to the circle skirt, but instead of a whole circle, it's more like wedges. In the circle skirt, the waistline has no gathers or darts and is shaped to match the waist. On the flared skirt, the waistline is cut wider than the actual waist measurement, to allow for either gathers or darts.

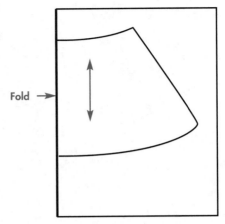

You can make a flared skirt from two or more wedge-shape pieces.

A-Line

The A-line skirt is halfway between the straight skirt, which is made from rectangles, and the flared skirt, which is made from wedges. The seam lines are straight, and the degree of A-ness varies according to the angle you choose.

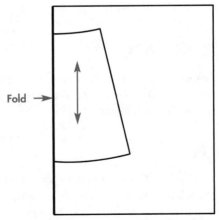

The A-line skirt is halfway between a straight skirt and a flared skirt.

Gathered

Gathered skirts are, again, rectangles—very wide rectangles. All the fullness is gathered in at the waist. With two seams, a hem, and a fold-over waistband, or an attached waistband and two rectangles, you can make a gathered skirt in less than two hours.

The rectangles can be square rectangles, or they can have a slight curve at the waist and the hem. As a guide, the center front, center back, and side seams should be the same length; body shape can change that, however. To hem a gathered skirt, try on the skirt, then place the hem the same distance from the floor all around. The fullness is entirely up to you.

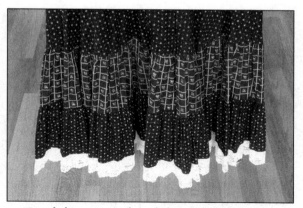

Tiered skirts are gathered skirts made from any number of rectangles that increase in width from the waist to the hem.

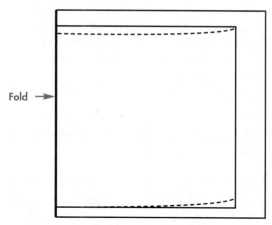

Make a gathered skirt from wide rectangles gathered at the waist.

Tiered

Tiered skirts are gathered skirts made from any number of rectangles that increase in width from the waist to the hem. Typically, different fabric is used for each rectangle. Because a tiered skirt has the smaller-width rectangle at the waist, there's less fabric to distribute in gathers around the waist and, therefore, it tends to be more flattering than a simple gathered skirt.

The Long and Short of It

Skirts can be any length—just look around you or in any fashion magazine. Whatever length you want is just right for you. Traditionally, though, some names are associated with the different lengths.

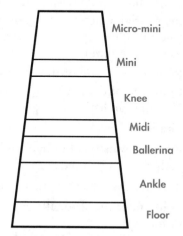

Micro-mini

Mini

Knee

Midi

Ballerina

Ankle

Floor

The length of your skirt is up to you.

At the Waistband

Skirts have a variety of finishes at the waist. Some skirts have no waistbands, some have fold-over bands, and some have attached waistbands. Some are tight-fitting, some have a drawstring in a casing, some have elastic in a casing, and some are just elastic.

Nonelastic Attached Waistbands

A waistband is just another rectangle. The length is your waist measurement plus ½ inch for ease, 1¼ inch for the seam allowance, and at least 1 inch for overlap if there is an opening, such as a zipper. Skip the 1 inch for overlap if the skirt has no opening. The width is twice whatever width you want, plus seam allowances. Here's how it works:

1. Cut the rectangle lengthwise on the grain. One of the long edges could be on the selvage.

2. Cut a piece of fusible waistband interfacing the same size as the waistband minus all the seam allowances.

3. Fuse the interfacing to the waistband following the manufacturer's directions.

4. Mark the seam allowance on one end and the overlap amount on the other end. The amount of overlap is up to you; 1 inch is usually minimum.

5. Pin the right side of the waistband to the right side of the garment between the markings and stitch.

6. Grade the seam.

7. Fold the waistband in half, right sides together, and stitch the ends. Trim the corners.

8. Turn the waistband right side out.

9. Fold under the seam allowance on the inside.

10. Slip stitch the inside edge of the waistband to the garment.

Cased, Elastic Waistbands

A waistband with casing and elastic is a pretty simple waistband to make:

1. When you're cutting the fabric for the casing, extend the length of the garment above the waistline by twice the width of the elastic you plan to use, plus ¼ inch for a hem.

2. After the garment has been put together, press the top fold at the designated width of the elastic.

3. With a ¼-inch hem, sew the casing to the garment, leaving an opening in the back to insert the elastic.

4. Cut a piece of elastic the measurement of your waist, with some overlap. The amount of overlap is up to you; 1 inch is usually minimum.

5. Thread the elastic through the casing using a safety pin or bodkin, being careful not to twist it. Use a safety pin to pin the ends together. Try on the garment, and adjust the elastic tightness accordingly. When you have the tightness you like, sew the elastic ends together.

6. Slip stitch the casing closed.

7. To help keep the elastic from curling, vertically stitch through the elastic and the casing in a few places.

If you'd rather, you can eliminate the elastic and use a cord. You'll have to make a buttonhole slit for the cord if you want it to show on the right side. (Follow your sewing machine use manual to make a buttonhole.) After you've threaded the cord through the casing, find the middle of the cord and tack it to the middle of the back of the casing. This will prevent it from slipping all the way out.

A Simple Straight Skirt

If you want to try your hand at a skirt, try the simple straight skirt first. Decide on how much hem you want. This might depend on the material you select. For example, if you select denim, you might not want any hem at all; just finish with a natural fringe.

1. Cut two rectangles on the grain. The length of the rectangles should be your desired skirt length plus hem allowance plus twice the width of the elastic and ¼ inch turn-under for the waistband. The width of the rectangles should be your hip measurement at the widest part divided by 2, plus 2 inches for ease and seam allowances.

2. If the fabric is 44 inches, you might need 2 lengths, depending on how wide your hips are. If the fabric is 60 inches, you should need only 1 length.

   For 44-inch fabric and 2 lengths: Fold the fabric lengthwise. Cut 2 rectangles on the fold.

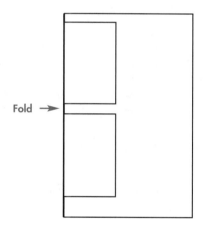

   For 44- or 60-inch fabric and 1 length: Fold the selvages to the middle of the fabric. Cut a rectangle on each fold.

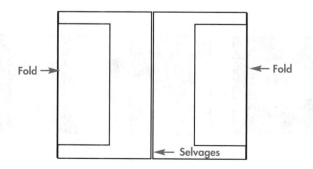

3. With the rights sides together, sew the side seams. If you want, leave a slit on one or both sides in the seam at the hemline. Make a narrow, double-fold hem in the seam allowance.

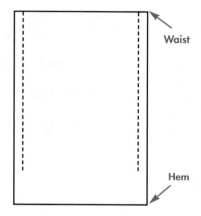

4. To finish the waistband, follow the instructions in the earlier "Cased, Elastic Waistbands" section.

5. Hem.

That was pretty easy, wasn't it? With this skirt and Chapter 21's simple top, you're ready for a night out!

The Least You Need to Know

- Making a pull-on skirt is quick and easy.
- You can change your look just by varying your hemline or skirt fullness.
- You have options when you put in a waistband, and most are pretty easy to do.
- Straight skirts start with rectangles.

In This Chapter

- ◆ Making easy pull-on long pants
- ◆ Looking at the long and short of pant styles
- ◆ Changing the fabric to change the look

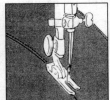

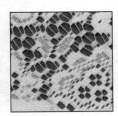
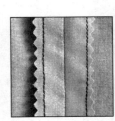

Sewing Easy Pull-On Pants

If you want to be really comfortable, try loosely fitted pull-on pants. These pants are easy to make and need only three seams, a fold-over waistband, and two small hems. Then you're good to go.

The design is casual, but by changing the fabric to something shimmery or shiny, these pants can be worn to the most formal of occasions. For lounging around home or for sleep attire, choose a nice, soft, snuggly fabric.

And whereas most of everything else in this book starts with a simple rectangle, pants have an added feature to work with—the crotch. Once you've established the crotch line, everything else is simple.

Basic Pants Styles

There seems to be a wide variety of styles of pants, but they all more or less have the same shape. The length of the leg determines the name, but the names vary somewhat depending on the width of the leg. In some cases, it's difficult to tell just by looking what the style is. For example, the difference between pedal pushers and toreadors is only inches and might look different on tall or short people. Don't worry about the names, and make your pants any length you want!

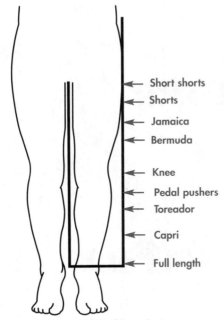

Pants come in a variety of lengths.

To get a general idea of a crotch line for you, fold a pair of your favorite pants so the side seams are together, and lay them flat on a piece of paper. Trace the crotch line on the paper. For these casual pull-on pants, an approximation is enough. When you've found a crotch curve you're comfortable in and with, save it to use on other patterns.

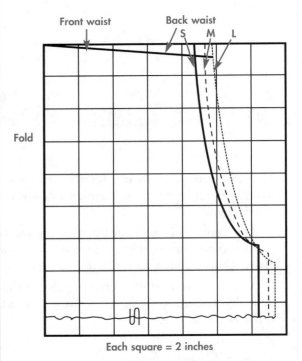

Each square = 2 inches

Use your favorite pants as a pattern for your crotch curve.

Pants vary in fullness both around the hip line and in the leg. Pants can be tapered from fullness at the top of the leg to narrow at the bottom hem; they can be straight from thigh to ankle; or they can flare, narrow at the thigh and wide at the hem.

The ankle finish can vary, too. Some baggy pants have either elastic or a tight cuff at the ankle.

The Crotch Line

On tailored pants, the crotch line should fit snuggly and not be too baggy in the seat. On pull-on casual pants, the crotch line should fit comfortably, and if it's high or low by a little bit, it doesn't matter. On more formal pants, the front and back crotch lines differ slightly, with the extension slightly longer in the back. For casual pants, this doesn't matter so much.

Baggy Pull-On Pants

The following directions are for basic long, baggy pull-on pants. Feel free to add your own creativity and styling to the basic pattern (I offer some variation suggestions in the next section).

You'll need 1 or 2 lengths of 45-inch fabric, or 1 length of 60-inch fabric. I suggest you use a lightweight cotton. Challis also makes great pull-on pants. You'll also need some elastic for the waistband. Two-inch–wide pajama elastic works well.

1. The waist dimension should be your hip measurement plus a few inches for fullness and seam allowance. Again, as with most of these easy-fit clothes, the amount of fullness is up to you. The same is true of seam allowances. The company standard is ⅝ inch, but there is nothing wrong with ½ inch. If the top of the pants is smaller than your hips, you won't be able to get them on!

2. Measure from your waist to your ankle. Add to this length twice the width of the elastic for the waist, plus the top and bottom hem allowances.

3. Fold the fabric lengthwise, as described in Chapter 22, depending on the fabric width. Transfer the measurements to the fabric, putting in the crotch line you made earlier in this chapter, or loosely trace the crotch line of your favorite pants. Remember, these are loose-fitting, baggy pants, so you just need an approximation.

4. Cut 2 pieces alike.

Fringe Benefits

There are no side seams on these pants. The fold will be where the side seams would normally be.

5. With right sides together, stitch the center front and center back seams from the waist to the crotch.

6. Place the inner leg seams together, and stitch to form the legs. Remember where the front and back seams are. You don't want to sew the wrong legs together!

7. Make the casing, and insert elastic as suggested in Chapter 22.

8. Hem.

Pant Variations

Once you've found the perfect crotch line, you can use it to make a variety of pants. Here are some suggestions for changing the look of your pants:

◆ Change the length. (See the first figure in this chapter for some ideas.)

◆ Put a narrow elastic casing at the ankle.

◆ Gather the bottom and put on a cuff. Cuffs are the same as waistbands, only smaller (follow the directions in Chapter 22).

◆ Put on patch pockets (see Chapter 21).

◆ Change the fullness by adding more than 2 inches to your hip measurement.

◆ Leave and finish an opening in the front of the waistband. Use a cord in the waistband instead of using elastic.

The long version of these pants are incredibly comfortable. Try making them from challis. You'll soon discover that you will want several pairs of different colors.

The Least You Need to Know

◆ Pull-on pants are quick and easy to make.

◆ Use a favorite pair of pants to get a crotch line approximation, then save it and make yourself a new favorite pair.

◆ You need only one basic pattern to make a wide variety of pull-on pants.

◆ You can easily change your look by changing the length of your pants.

In This Chapter

◆ Making a simple dress

◆ Changing the look of the dress

 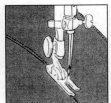   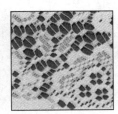 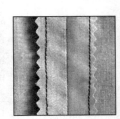

Chapter 24

Sewing a Three-Hour Dress

In less than 3 hours, and with minimal effort, you can easily make a simple, loose-fitting, hang-around, fun dress. (These dresses make great maternity dresses, too.) How fancy or how simple is up to you and the fabric you choose.

Because the top piece is placed horizontally, this dress does not work well with a nap or one-way design. Keep this in mind when you're picking your fabric.

A Simple Dress

To make this simple dress, you'll need 3 rectangles of 45-inch-wide fabric. The 2 rectangles that make the skirt are the same length. The length of the dress is up to you, so the size of the rectangles is up to you. Measure from somewhere under your bust to whatever length you want. The width is determined by how full you want the skirt.

The length of the third rectangle will be the distance between your shoulders. The width is two times the length from your neck to somewhere below your bust.

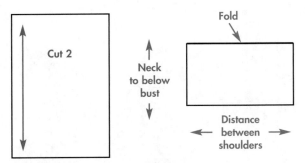

You'll need these rectangles for this dress.

1. Cut out the 3 rectangles.
2. Sew gathering lines across the top raw edge of the front and back skirt rectangles.

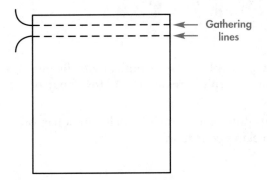

3. Fold the third rectangle into quarters.
4. Follow the directions in Chapter 21 for cutting the neck opening. Remember, this piece is going crosswise.

Cut It Out!

To cut the neck, start with a small slit or circle. Then, test to see if your head will fit through, gradually making the opening the size and shape you want. It's easier to keep making the opening bigger than to make it smaller!

5. Face the neck, as described in Chapter 21.
6. Sew top to bottom front and back, gathering as needed.
7. Sew the side seams, leaving the arm hole openings about 7 to 8 inches wide.
8. Face the arm hole openings the same way you faced the neck opening. If the line is straight, you can sew a narrow double folded hem.
9. Hem.

In 3 hours and with 3 rectangles, you have a comfy dress.

Dress Variations

You can vary the look of this dress many ways:

◆ Try velour for a cozy, hang-around-the-house-on-a-cold-evening dress.

◆ Try two bath towels for a nice cover-all beach robe. You need one large towel to cut in half crosswise and one medium towel for the horizontal piece. Leave the bottom side seams open. You don't have to hem the bottom or the sleeves. Towels with fringe are particularly nice.

With two towels, you have a beach robe.

◆ Make the neckline deeper for a jumper effect.

◆ Make the top piece wider from elbow to elbow for a different sleeve effect.

◆ Use two different fabrics, one for the top piece and one for the bottom pieces.

◆ Make the "dress" really short, to wear as a top with pants or a skirt.

◆ Cut a slit from top to bottom on the front, then shape the neck to a V for a vest if it's short or for a duster if it's long.

◆ Add two patch pockets.

If comfort is what you want, and if your sewing time is limited, this is the dress to start with. Don't forget to add your own creative touches to make this dress uniquely you.

The Least You Need to Know

◆ With three rectangles, you can make an easy dress in a couple hours.

◆ If you want to make a beach robe, use two towels.

◆ You can easily adapt the dress pattern in this chapter to make just about any style and length dress you'd like.

In This Part

Part 6

The Joy of Giving

You've mastered all the basic sewing skills and even created a few nice things for your home and your wardrobe. Now consider giving away some of your creations. Just think of how pleased your friends and family will be when they receive a gift made especially for them by you. How much more personal the gift will be when you add your own creative touch and personalize the gift.

In the following chapter are very simple gifts you can make with the skills you've learned in this book. Remember, the following are only the basics. Don't be afraid to embellish to create something special!

In This Chapter

◆ Making simple gifts to give to friends and family

◆ Creating lavender sachets

◆ Creating blankets for sleepovers or chilly sports games

◆ Stitching a tote bag or wine bottle bag you can fill with goodies

◆ Making a hooded toddler bath towel

◆ Recycling pieces of denim into a pillow

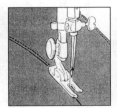

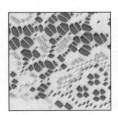
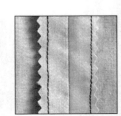

25

Gifts to Give to Friends and Family

Experience the special joy that comes when you give your friends and family personalized gifts you have made. Enjoy the fun of surprising them when it isn't a special holiday or their birthday. Do the unexpected, and those times will create the memories.

You have all the skills necessary to make the gifts suggested in this and the next chapter. The directions are only here to get you started. Then embellish, embellish, embellish.

Take-It-with-You Blanket

This blanket can serve many purposes: for a child to take to a sleepover, to be stowed in the car for emergencies, or to carry to an outdoor sports event or picnic. Choose the fabric design to match the receiver's personality or the purpose of the blanket. I chose trains for my grandson.

What you'll need:

> A length of fleece. The length is somewhat determined by the purpose of the blanket and the intended recipient, but 2 yards is good for most occasions.
>
> 1 yard of (1-inch-thick) webbing to match the fleece
>
> 2 buckles that fit the width of the webbing
>
> Matching thread
>
> Contrasting embroidery floss or yarn (if you want to make it fancy)

1. Square off both ends of the fleece.
2. Finish both ends. Remember, you can easily slip stitch the end, use your machine to make a small hem, or use iron-on tape if you're in a hurry. If you want to be fancy, try the blanket stitch around the edge.

3. Fold the fleece in half, then in quarters lengthwise, and roll.

4. Mark the fleece about 1 inch in from the folded edges. Measure the distance between the marks.

5. Cut a piece of webbing to this length plus 1 inch.

6. Divide the remaining webbing in half.

7. Unroll the fleece.

8. Place the webbing in an H pattern on the marks on the fleece.

This blanket is easy to make and perfect for taking with you.

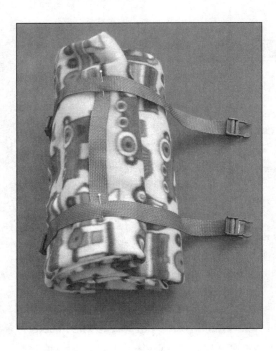

9. Stitch the webbing firmly in place.

10. Attach the buckles to the ends of the webbing.

11. Fold and roll the blanket with the webbing to the outside. Snap the buckles together. Off you go!

Autographed Wine Bag

Wine bags are in! Make this wine bag from a material you can easily write on with a fabric pen. Sign your name and write the date. When you give the bag and a bottle of wine to your friend, also give them the pen. Tell them to sign their name and write the date on the bag when they pass the bag along to someone else.

What you'll need:

>A rectangle of fabric about 28 to 30 inches long by about 16 inches wide
>
>2 circles of fabric approximately 5 inches in diameter
>
>A cord with tassels
>
>A fabric pen
>
>A bottle of wine

1. Stitch the rectangle along the long edge, leaving a small opening for turning.

2. Stay-stitch within ½ inch on both circles.

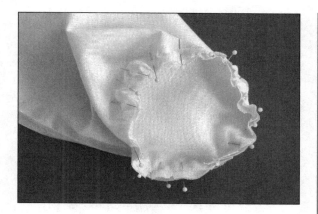

3. Sew one circle to each end of the tube you made in step 1.

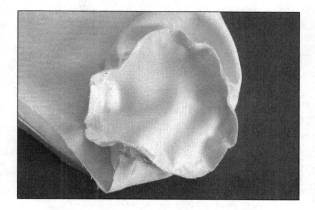

4. Clip the curve.
5. Turn to the right side. Slip stitch the opening. Push one end of the tube into the other end to make a lined bag. The folded edge is now the top of the bag.
5. Stitch the cord about 2 inches below the top.
6. Autograph the bag. Put the wine bottle in the bag, and attach the pen. Then, give it to a friend.

Your friends and family will love receiving this personalized wine bag.

Pocketed Tote Bag

This easy tote bag has the added feature of a personalized pocket.

What you'll need:

> ½ yard heavy-weight fun fabric without nap or one-way design
>
> A piece of plain, heavy-weight fabric
>
> Enough webbing for 2 handles
>
> Fabric paint
>
> Various trims (optional)
>
> Thread

1. Decide on the approximate size finished bag you want.
2. Cut a rectangle that's the width of the bag by twice the length plus 2 inches for the top hem and 2 to 3 inches for the bottom.
3. Cut a rectangle of the plain fabric for the pocket.

4. Finish the pocket as described in Chapter 22.

5. Personalize the pocket with fabric paint or other decorations.

6. Fold the bag rectangle in half with wrong sides together.

7. Center the pocket on the bag, and pin it in place. Be sure to pin through one layer of the bag only. Unfold the bag, and stitch the pocket to the bag. Reinforce the top of the pocket where it meets the bag.

8. Fold the bag rectangle in half with right sides together.

9. Stitch the seams, then finish the seam edges.

10. To make the bottom flat, sew across the corners, about 2 to 4 inches deep.

11. Tack the corners to the seam.

12. Press a 1-inch fold to the wrong side of the top.

13. Pin the webbing to the top edge of the bag in four places. Be careful to not twist the webbing. The end of the webbing should be about ¼ inch above the raw edge of the folded top. Tack in place.

14. Fold the top edge, including the webbing, over another inch.

15. Topstitch at the hem fold at the top of the bag. Put reinforcing stitches on the webbing in a decorative pattern, such as a boxed X or zigzags.

16. Fill the bag with goodies, or give it away empty.

As easy as this fun tote is to make, you can personalize one for everyone on your gift-giving list (or for yourself!).

Coordinated Napkin Set

This set of colorful coordinated napkins makes a nice hostess gift.

What you'll need:

> A packet of fat quarters that are soft to the touch, somewhat stain resistant, and do not have a right and wrong side
>
> Thread to match

1. Make a square from each fat quarter. The napkins will be approximately 18 inches square.
2. Fringe all the edges, or finish with a narrow hem.

Fringe Benefits

If the fabric fringes easily, make a narrow zigzag line about ½ inch from each edge. Snip the edges to the stitching in several places to make it easier to fringe. Fringing is a good sitting-in-front-of-the-TV-with-a-good-movie activity.

3. Fold and press the napkins. Stack, and tie with a ribbon.

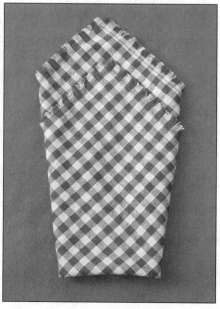

With a few simple steps, you can have several of these great napkins handy for giving.

Christmas Tree Skirt with Matching Doily

There are an infinite number of possibilities for making a tree skirt. Seasonal fabrics abound! You can go plain or simple. The following directions are basic. Please embellish at will.

What you'll need:

> 1½ yards of fabric (I used burgundy velveteen.)
>
> 1½ yards matching lining fabric
>
> 3½ yards of fringe (I used gold.)
>
> ½ yard narrow trim (optional)
>
> 5 decorative buttons
>
> 5 large snaps
>
> Other decorations, sequins, beads, appliqués (optional)

1. Cut a 42- to 48-inch square from the 2 fabrics, depending on the width of the fabrics.

2. Fold each square into quarters, and make a circle using the pin-and-string method described in Chapter 12. Draw the largest circle you can that will fit the square.

3. Make another circle with a 2-inch piece of string for the center hole.

4. Cut out the circles. Cut the small circle carefully so you can make a fancy doily from it later.

5. If you're going to add any other decoration or appliqué to the tree skirt, do it now.

6. Cut a straight line from the outer circle edge to the inner circle edge on both fabrics.

7. With right sides together, stitch the fabrics together using a ½-inch seam allowance and leaving an opening for turning on one of the straight edges.

8. Clip the seams, curves, and corners.

9. Turn the skirt right side out, and stitch the opening closed.

10. Sew fringe around the edge.

12. Sew on buttons and snaps.

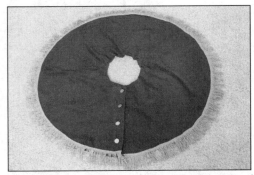

You can easily make a tree skirt from a circle of seasonal fabric.

Bonus doily:

1. Finish the circle cut from the center of the tree skirt.

2. Sew on some trim.

From the circle cut from the tree skirt, make a bonus doily.

Lavender Sachets

Sachets of lavender are always a welcome gift. A sachet is only a small knife-edge pillow filled with lavender or some other nice-smelling herb. Use all the same fabric or 3 coordinating fabrics..

What you'll need:

> 2 (5-inch) squares of fabric for each sachet
>
> A very small amount of stuffing (Cotton balls will work.)
>
> Matching thread
>
> 2 tablespoons herbs per sachet

Fringe Benefits

You can purchase stacks of 5-inch squares as well as 10-inch squares all perfectly precut from quilting stores and catalogs. If you plan to make sachets for everyone you know, buying a stack of precut 5-inch squares might be the way to do it.

1. Follow the directions for a simple knife-edge pillow (see Chapter 11), using the 5-inch squares and ½-inch seam allowance.
2. Trim the corners, then turn the sachet right side out.
3. Stuff with a small amount of stuffing and the herbs.
4. Slip stitch the opening closed.
5. Stack three sachets together, and tie with a ribbon.

For some pretty, easy sachets, make 5-inch knife edge pillows and fill them with lavender.

Hooded Toddler Bath Towel

Most hooded baby towels are designed for babies and are very small. As the baby grows, the hooded towel no longer goes around their little bodies. Try this slightly larger size for any toddlers you know.

What you'll need:

> 1½ yards terrycloth or toweling
>
> ½ yard contrasting cotton (I used a fat quarter.)
>
> Matching thread

1. Make a square in the terrycloth approximately 42 inches on each side. Straighten.
2. From the leftover fabric, cut a right triangle, about 12 inches on two sides.
3. Make bias binding from the cotton, about 5 yards.
4. Sew the binding on the hypotenuse (long side) of the triangle, using a zigzag stitch.
5. Lay the triangle on one of the corners of the square, and pin.
6. Round off all corners with a plate. Readjust the pins on the corner with the hood.
7. Stitch the binding around the whole square using the zigzag stitch.

   You can also sew the binding on by hand if you don't have a sewing machine.

Your favorite toddler will love this hooded towel.

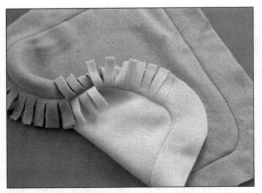

With two pieces of fleece, you can easily create a tag blanket for a special infant.

Teenager Pillow

You can never have enough accent pillows. Here is one that'll appeal to all the teenagers you know.

What you'll need:

> Old jeans or enough scraps from old jeans to make the size pillow you want
> Stuffing or a ready-made pillow form
> Thread

1. For a 16-inch pillow, cut 32 (5-inch) squares.
2. Make 2 stacks of 16 squares, one stack right side up, the other stack upside down.
3. Take one square from each stack. With wrong sides together, and using a ½-inch seam, stitch down one edge of the squares.
4. Do not cut the thread. Just keep sewing squares together until you have a chain of 16 pairs of squares.
5. Snip the threads between the pairs.
6. Make 2 stacks with 8 pairs of squares in each stack.
7. Sew the squares together as before, wrong sides together. Now you should have 8 rows of 4 squares each.
8. Snip the threads between the rows.

Tag Blanket

Babies love to feel soft blankets. This variation on a tag blanket could just become the child's transitional object. Tag blankets are incredibly simple to make yet will bring hours of joy to the baby.

What you'll need:

> ½ yard fleece (2½ yards if you want one side one color and the other side a different design)
> Matching or contrasting thread

1. Make 2 squares approximately 18 inches square. The exact dimensions don't matter.
2. Round off the corners with a plate.
3. Put fleece squares together. Topstitch all the way around, 2 inches in from the edge.
4. Cut in from the edge to the topstitch line every ¾ inch all the way around to make the "tags."

9. Pin the rows together, wrong sides together and matching seam lines.

10. Make 2 large squares of 16 smaller squares.

11. With wrong sides together, pin and stitch the cover ½ inch from the edge, leaving an opening for the stuffing.

12. Stuff the pillow.

13. Finish stitching the opening closed.

> **Fringe Benefits**
>
> My daughter is very short, so I have to cut at least 6 inches off the legs of all her jeans. The pillow pictured here was made from all the cut-off jean legs I accumulated over the years.

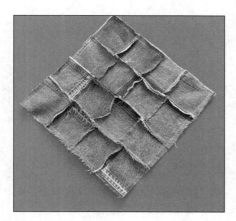

With saved scraps from your old jeans, making a pillow for a teenager is simple.

> **Fringe Benefits**
>
> The rag edge look is presently "in." This look is created by sewing wrong sides together and letting the raw edges fray at will. If you don't like this look, follow these directions, but put right sides together.

This pillow is a breeze to make and is as easy to customize. Here are some variations you might try:

◆ Use a plain piece of denim for one side of the pillow cover. You'll then need only 16 smaller squares.

◆ Use a bandana for one side of the pillow cover. You'll then need only 16 smaller squares.

◆ Cut shapes other than squares. Sew together odd shapes crazy-quilt–style until you have the size you need for the pillow.

◆ Make 9 (5-inch) squares. Cut a red bandana into 2-inch strips. Alternate squares and strips, using a ½-inch seam allowance.

This last chapter is only the beginning of your creative sewing future. Go and sew!

The Least You Need to Know

◆ On a rainy afternoon when you have nothing else to do, make several gifts at once so you have them ready when an unexpected occasion arises.

◆ Prepare stacks of napkins ready for fringing so you can fringe them while watching TV.

◆ When making a tote bag, think ahead about what you might put in it, and coordinate the fabric to the contents.

◆ Use up scraps from old jeans or recycle an old pair of jeans into a pillow.

◆ Fleece tag blankets are easy to make and will bring hours of comfort to a little one.

Appendix A

Glossary

acetate   A manufactured fiber used in taffeta, satin, and brocades. It drapes well and is inexpensive, but it fades and wrinkles easily.

acrylic   A synthetic fiber made to be like wool, pile, or fake fur. It is soft and warm, and it resists moths and wrinkles, but it pills and attracts static.

action stretch   Any fabrics that have stretch and recovery in two directions.

alpaca   A soft, silky fabric made from alpaca fur. It is used for coats, suits, and sportswear.

antique satin   A heavier satin material used mostly for draperies and upholstery.

appliqué   Usually used for decorative purposes, appliqué is the sewing (or gluing) of one piece of fabric on top of another. The top piece is a cut-out design, which is then placed right side up on the right side of the main fabric. It is sewn on with invisible stitches.

back-tack   To take several small stitches at the beginning and end of a seam to keep the seam from coming undone.

backed cloth   A layer of fabric added for extra weight and warmth.

backstitch   An extra-strong hand stitch used mostly for hand stitching seams in place of machine stitching.

bandle   A coarse linen made on hand looms in Ireland.

barathea   A pebbly, closely woven fabric used for dresses and lightweight suits.

bar-tack   Similar to a back-tack, several small stitches on top of each other used to strengthen the bottom of a zipper, the edge of a pocket, or anyplace there is extra strain on the stitching.

basting   Long running stitches made by hand or machine to hold fabric temporarily in place.

batiste   Named after Jean Baptiste, a French linen weaver, batiste is a name given to a variety of fabrics that tend to be lightweight; it is used for lightweight blouses and dresses, infants' dresses, and handkerchiefs.

batting   A layer of material usually placed between the upper and lower layers of a quilt. It adds warmth and height.

bias   The true bias is the diagonal line formed at a 45-degree angle when the lengthwise grain is folded to the crosswise grain.

binding   Narrow strips of fabric used to cover the raw edges of a garment or other project made of fabric. When used on curves, the binding is made from fabric cut on the bias.

blanket stitch   A stitch usually sewn by hand along the raw or finished edge of fabric to prevent fraying or for decoration.

blind stitch (or blind hemstitch)   A tiny stitch sewn by hand to join two pieces of fabric. The stitches are made to not show.

bobbin   A round metal or plastic holder on which thread is wound. It's usually housed beneath the needle plate of a sewing machine and holds the thread for the bottom part of the stitch.

boucle   A plain- or twill-weave fabric with looped yarns that create a nubbly surface.

broadcloth   A tightly woven cotton cloth with a slight luster. It can also be a blend of cotton and polyester or other manufactured fibers; it is used in shirts, dresses, and blouses.

brocade   A rich fabric with interwoven designs of raised pictures. It is used for dresses, drapes, and upholstery.

buckram   A very stiff fabric used as interlining, especially in hats.

bunting   A soft, plain, woven cloth used for making flags.

burlap   A coarse, canvaslike fabric used for fabric sacks (like potato sacks) and furniture construction.

button shank   On some buttons, the metal loop found on the underside of the button, used to attach the button to the fabric. Shanks can also be made of thread, to allow room for the buttonhole side of the item to fit under the button.

calico   A plain, closely woven, medium-weight, inexpensive cloth. It often has small pictures printed on one side and is used for aprons, dresses, and quilts.

cambric   A soft, white, closely woven cotton fabric with a slight gloss on the right side. It is used for undergarments, aprons, shirts, and handkerchiefs.

canton flannel   A heavy, warm cotton fabric that's strong and absorbent. It is used for interlinings and sleeping garments.

canvas   Made from cotton or linen fabric with an even weave; it is very heavy and firm. Some canvas has a stiff, open weave that makes it suitable for use in needlework. Canvas with a close weave is also used for beach chairs.

casing   A channel made by folding over the top of a project, used to hold curtain rods, elastic, or drawstrings.

challis   One of the softest fabrics, it's very lightweight, usually patterned, and is used for scarves, dresses, and blouses.

chambray   A plain woven fabric with colored warp and white filling. It's used for shirts.

cheesecloth   A plain, woven, soft cotton also known as gauze. It's used for dust cloths, costumes, and flagging.

chenille   A ribbed, velvety fabric, softer than velvet or corduroy, used for scarves and blankets. It's named after the French word for caterpillar because the yarn is furry like caterpillars.

chiffon   A thin, lightweight, see-through, flimsy fabric made from silk or rayon. It is used mostly for fancy dresses and underwear. It's also very difficult to sew.

chino   An all-cotton twill, usually used for military clothes and work pants.

chintz   A glazed cotton fabric usually printed with bright colors. It's used for draperies, slipcovers, summer dresses, and skirts.

clip   To cut into the fabric at right angles to the raw edge, to prevent distortion of curved seams, or to cut diagonally across corners to reduce bulk when an item is turned the right side out.

corduroy   A heavyweight fabric with narrow to wide ribs or wales that have a nap. It's mostly used for pants, jackets, and some dresses and skirts.

cotton   A natural fiber that's spun into many other fabrics. There are many varieties of cotton, depending on where the cotton plant was grown. Cotton is absorbent and cool, but it wrinkles and shrinks unless it's been chemically treated. It is used for almost everything.

crepe   A lightweight fabric with a crinkly surface, used in fancy dresses.

cretonne   A drapery and slipcover fabric similar to unglazed chintz, but with larger designs.

crinoline   A heavily sized, stiff fabric originally made for hoop skirts. It's used when a very stiff interfacing is needed.

crosswise grain   The direction of the widthwise threads on a fabric, running from selvage to selvage.

curtain weight   A weight inserted into a curtain hemline to improve the hang of the fabric.

cutting line   A solid, printed line on a pattern piece, used as a guide for cutting.

damask   A firm, glossy fabric (usually silk or linen) similar to brocade but flatter and reversible. It is used for tablecloths, napkins, draperies, and fine upholstery.

dart   A tapered, stitched fold of fabric used on a garment to shape the fabric around the contours of the body.

denim   A rugged, heavy cotton, usually blue with white or gray mottled effect. It is used primarily for work clothes.

dimity   A thin, sheer cotton used for aprons, needlework, bedspreads, dresses, and children's clothes.

domette   A soft synthetic fabric used for padding in curtains or under tablecloths.

Donegal   A thick Irish wool used for suits or coats.

dotted Swiss   A sheer cotton with small dot motifs that originated in St. Gallen, Switzerland, in 1750. It's used for dresses, curtains, evening wear, baby clothes, and wedding apparel.

drape   The property of fabric that causes it to fall into graceful folds.

dressmaker's carbon paper   Paper with colored coating on one side, used to trace or transfer pattern markings to fabric.

drop   The length of the tablecloth from the edge of the table to the bottom of the cloth.

duck   A cotton or linen heavy, tight-weave fabric that's very strong and the most durable fabric made. It was formally used for sails and is now used in some outerwear.

ease   The distribution of fullness without creating gathers or tucks when one section of a seam is joined to another, slightly shorter section.

edge stitch   An alternative to the zigzag stitch, used on finer fabrics to finish hems and facings to prevent fraying.

facing   A piece of fabric used to back the main fabric of a project around an opening or raw edge to give a neat finish and prevent fraying.

faille   A silk fabric with a crossways ribbed weave. It is used for coats, dresses, and handbags.

fat quarters   A variety of fabrics, often sold together, that have been cut from 1 yard of fabric. They are approximately 22×18 inches.

flat seam   A simple seam used to join two pieces of fabric with a single line of stitching.

flat-fell seam   A self-enclosed seam that is flat, strong, and hard-wearing, generally used on sportswear.

French seam A double seam in which the raw edges are completely enclosed.

gabardine A twill-weave fabric with an obvious diagonal weave. It is heavyweight and is used in household furnishings and some pants.

gathering stitch Traditionally, two parallel rows of running stitch or loose machine stitch used to make gathers such as ruffles.

gingham A lightweight woven fabric, usually white and another color woven in a square pattern. It is used for children's dresses, curtains, and other home decorations.

grading To trim the seam allowances within a seam to different lengths, eliminating bulk. Also called layering.

grain of fabric The direction in which the warp threads of the fabric run, parallel to the selvages.

heading Fabric above the casing, or at the top edge of a curtain.

hem The finished lower edge of an item such as sleeves, skirts, pants, curtains, and tablecloths.

interfacing A layer of fabric, often synthetic, nonwoven, or iron-on, used to stiffen lightweight fabrics and make them easier to handle or to lay flat.

interlining Soft fabric used to line curtains or tablecloths, for added weight and luxury.

jacquard A fabric similar to brocade or damask, with colored designs woven into the pattern with different weight yarns.

lace An openly woven design, usually geometric or of flowers. Fine lace is used in wedding dresses and for fancy dresses. Lace is also used for curtains and tablecloths.

lapped seam A seam made by overlapping the edges of the panels of fabric to be joined.

lawn A fine-weave cotton fabric used for heirloom babies and children's dresses.

layering To trim the seam allowances within a seam to different lengths, eliminating bulk. Also called grading.

lengthwise grain The direction of the lengthwise threads on a woven fabric, which run parallel to the selvages.

linen The natural fiber made from the flax plant. It is the basis for many other fabrics. Many linens have a nubby texture. Linen is absorbent and cool, but it wrinkles easily if not treated.

lining A layer of fabric added for improved wear.

Lycra One of the brand names for stretch fibers.

mercerized cotton thread Sewing thread treated to improve wear and look more lustrous.

mitered corner A diagonal seam formed when fabric is joined at or shaped around a corner.

monk's cloth A heavy, loosely woven basket-weave cloth used for draperies and upholstery.

muslin A fine, loosely woven cloth, usually in white or natural.

nap Soft pile fabric surface made by short fibers that brush in one direction, such as velvet.

net A machine-made mesh.

notch To cut a V-shape wedge in the seam allowance so pieces of fabric can be matched when they are being stitched together. They also are made to reduce bulk in curved seams when an item is turned right side out.

notion Any article, other than fabric, used in the construction of any garment or project.

nylon A manufactured fiber used in many fabrics. It's strong, warm, and lightweight but is subject to static cling. It also holds body heat.

one-way design Pattern, stripe, or check that repeats in one direction along the length of a fabric so there is an obvious top and bottom to the fabric.

organdy   A fine, stiff, open-weave cotton.

organza   Finely woven stiff silk.

overcast stitch   A stitch sewn by hand over the raw edge to prevent fraying and to make the edge look neat. Also called the overhand stitch.

paisley   An intricate pattern with elongated and curved oval patterns. It originated in India but is named after a town in Scotland famous for its textile industry.

percale   A medium-weight, plain cotton or blend fabric usually used for sheets and curtains.

piping   Trim made from bias-cut strips of fabric, used either flat or with an inserted cord to give a neat finish to an item. Sometimes called welting.

pique   A light- or medium-weight cotton fabric woven in a single color with an embossed effect.

polyester   A manufactured fiber used alone or in blends with natural fibers. It's strong and warm but is subject to static cling and stains easily.

poplin   A broadcloth with an obvious horizontal rib.

pucker   Unsightly gathering along a seam line cause by a blunt needle or a bulky seam.

rayon   The first synthetic fiber developed; it resembles silk. It's soft and drapes well, but it wrinkles and will rot if exposed to the sun.

right side   The side of a fabric designed to appear as the visible part of a finished garment or home furnishing.

ruching   Gathering fabric to create a panel of luxurious folds. Several lines of stitching worked to form a gathered area.

running stitch   A hand stitch used to make seams or gathers.

sateen   A cotton fabric with a glossy surface.

satin   A type of weave with the warp threads running over the surface of the fabric, to give a glossy finish. It's used mostly for fancy dresses and wedding dresses.

scrim   A stiff, loosely woven lightweight linen fabric used for upholstery or drapery lining.

seam allowance   The allowance around the edge of a piece of fabric for making the seam. The amount of fabric between the seam line and the edge of the fabric.

seam line   The line around the edge of a piece of fabric marking the line where stitching is to be made.

seam tape   Firmly woven narrow cotton tape used to prevent seams from distorting. The seam tape is positioned along the seam line on the wrong side of the fabric and is stitched into the seam as the layers of fabric are joined.

seersucker   A striped or checked woven fabric in which the threads are drawn tighter, creating rows down or across the fabric.

selvage   The woven, nonfraying edges of a length of fabric.

shantung   A plain-weave fabric with irregular nubs scattered throughout. It can be made from silk, cotton, or other fibers.

sheeting   A plain-weave, usually cotton fabric. It is identified by the number of threads per inch. It comes in widths wide enough for sheets.

shirring   A method of decorative machine gathering used to take in fullness stitched in many rows across fabric.

silk   A natural fiber spun by silk worms. It's soft and warm and drapes well, but it's damaged easily by sunlight and perspiration. There are a variety of kinds of silks, depending on the diet and habitat of the worms. Each kind of silk has a special name.

slip stitch   A hand stitch primarily used for hemming.

stay stitch   Machine stitching worked just inside a seam allowance to strengthen it and prevent the fabric from stretching or tearing.

straight stitch   Plain stitch used for seaming, stay stitching, understitching, and topstitching.

taffeta A plain fabric, usually silk, with a stiff, glossy finish. It's used in fancy dresses and costumes.

tarlatan A highly starched, open-weave fabric, similar in weight to muslin.

terrycloth Cotton fabric with uncut loops on the surface. Higher-quality terrycloth has loops on both sides. Terrycloth is primarily used for towels and bathrobes and is sometimes called toweling.

ticking A tightly woven fabric with a distinctive stripe, usually of blue and white, traditionally used for bed pillows.

topstitching A line of stitches used to deliberately emphasize seams or finish hems.

toweling *See* terrycloth.

trigger A blend of 65 percent polyester and 35 percent cotton; it is usually 60 inches wide. It's used primarily in home decorating, although some lighter weights are used for pants.

trim To cut away excess fabric.

tweed A plain-weave woolen fabric made from irregularly textured colored yarns. The heavier weights are used for upholstery; lighter weights are used for suits and jackets.

understitch The process of sewing a facing and all the seam allowances together close to the seam line, to prevent the facing from rolling to the right side.

velvet A woven fabric with a pile that creates a soft surface.

velveteen Fabric that resembles velvet, but it has a shorter pile and is usually washable.

voile A plain-weave, semisheer fabric, often used for children's clothes, blouses, and curtains.

warp The threads that run up and down a woven piece of cloth.

weft The threads that run across a woven piece of cloth.

welting Trim made from bias-cut strips of fabric, used either flat or with an inserted cord to give a neat finish to an item. Sometimes called piping.

whip stitch Strong, overedge hand stitch used for joining two flat edges.

wool The natural fiber made from sheep's fur. It is absorbent, warm, and resists wrinkles; however, moths love it. Some wools shrink.

zigzag stitch Machine stitch where the needle goes from side to side creating a zigzag pattern.

Practice Makes Perfect

The following pages contain three different sewing practice pages. Make several copies of these pages. Then, with your machine unthreaded—both the top thread and the bobbin— try stitching on the lines. For a further challenge, try stitching halfway between the lines.

On the straight lines, when you come to a corner, leave the needle in the paper, lift the presser foot lever, turn the paper, put the lever down, and keep going.

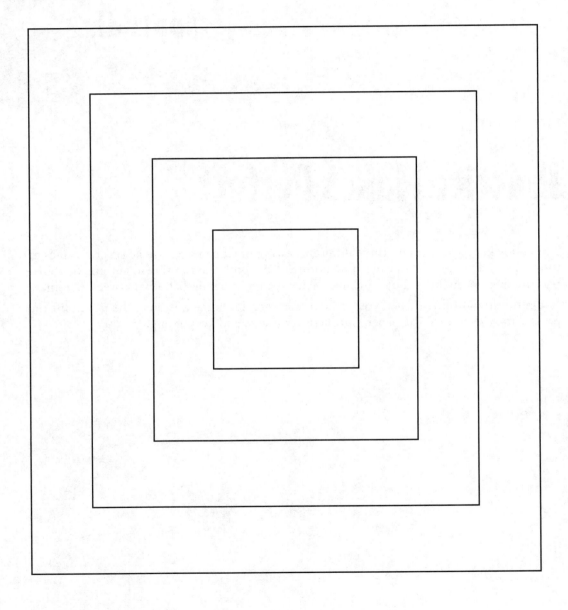

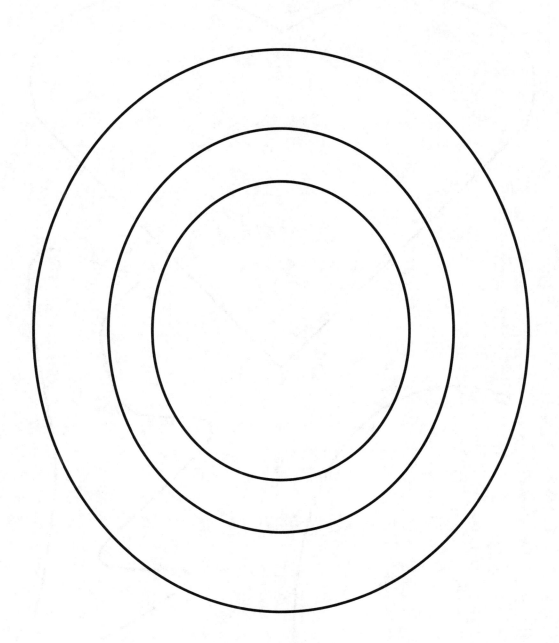

Tear-Out Sewing Machine Troubleshooting Chart

In the instruction book that came with your sewing machine, you will find a chart that will help you when something goes wrong. Keep this chart handy. If you don't want to tear your book apart and tack the page to the wall near your machine, tear out and use this one instead.

If This Happens ...	Check ...
The machine doesn't go.	Is it plugged into the socket?
	Did the plug fall out of the back of the machine?
	Is it turned on?
	Did you forget to re-engage the handwheel after you filled the bobbin?
The upper thread keeps breaking.	Is the machine threaded correctly?
	Check your instruction manual:
	Do you have the right size needle for your thread and fabric?
	Is the thread tension too tight?
	Is the thread freely unwinding from the bobbin?
	Is the bobbin case properly inserted?
	When was the last time you cleaned out the lint?
The lower thread keeps breaking.	Is the bobbin winding too tightly?
	Is the bobbin threaded correctly in the bobbin case?
The cloth doesn't feed.	Is the presser foot down?
	Is the pressure appropriate for the weight and texture of the material?
	Is the stitch length selector on 0?
	Is the presser foot attached properly?
The needle keeps breaking.	Is the needle straight?
	Does the needle have a blunt point?
	Do you have the right size needle for the fabric?
	Is the needle inserted into the clamp correctly?
The stitches are different sizes.	Is the machine threaded properly?
	Is the needle the appropriate size for the material?
	Is the needle straight?
	Is the needle sharp?
	Is the pressure appropriate for the material?

Tear-Out Table Measurements Charts

List all the tables in your home by location or other identifying characteristics.

Square, Rectangle, and Oval Tables

Table	Location	Width (W)	Length (L)	Drop (D)	Hem (H)
1					
2					
3					
4					
5					
6					

Round Tables

Table	Location	Width (W)	Length (L)	Drop (D)	Hem (H)
1					
2					
3					
4					
5					

Tear-Out Window Measurements Chart

It is very frustrating to be in the fabric store, see the most beautiful fabric that would be perfect for the windows in a certain room—and on sale!—but you can't remember the size of your windows. You might even be out of town in a store you might never frequent again.

To ease this frustration, here is a handy tear-out sheet of window measurements. Fill it out and carry it with you in your purse. Then, when the mood strikes you to buy some fabric, you will be prepared.

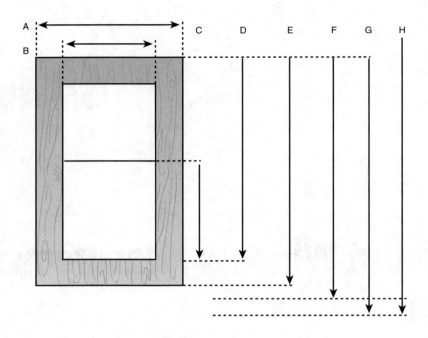

Measurements

A	Width of the outside frame	_____
B	Width of the inside frame	_____
C	Length from middle to bottom sill	_____
D	Length from top of frame to sill	_____
E	Length from top of frame to bottom of sill	_____
F	Length from top of frame to top of splashboard	_____
G	Length from top of frame to floor	_____
H	Length from ceiling to floor	_____

Further Readings

Books

Babylon, Donna. *How to Dress a Naked Window: A Step-by-Step Guide to Creating Over 30 Great Looks.* Iola, WI: Krause Publications, 1997.

Bednar, Nancy, and JoAnn Pugh-Gannon. *Encyclopedia of Sewing Machine Techniques.* New York: Sterling Publishing Co., Inc., 1999.

Betzina, Sandra. *Fabric Savvy: The Essential Guide for Every Sewer.* Newtown, CT: The Taunton Press, 2002.

Coetzee, Karen, and Rene Bergh. *Sew-It-Yourself Home Décor.* Iola, WI: Krause Publications, 2000.

Creative Publishing International, Inc. *The Complete Photo Guide to Sewing.* Chanhassen, MN: Creative Publishing International, Inc., 1999.

Cy DeCosse Incorporated. *Sewing for Special Occasions: Bridal, Prom and Evening Dresses.* Minnetonka, MN: Cy DeCosse Incorporated, 1994.

Dodson, Jackie, and Jan Saunders. *Pillows! Pillows! Pillows!* Radnor, PA: Chilton Book Company, 1996.

Dorling Kindersley. *The Complete Book of Sewing.* London: Dorling Kindersley, 1996.

Gynther, Elsebeth. *Easy Style: Sewing the New Classics.* Asheville, NC: Lark Books, 1993.

Meyrich, Elissa. *Sew Fast Sew Easy: All You Need to Know When You Start to Sew.* New York: St. Martin's Griffin, 2002.

Palmer, Pati, and Marta Alto. *Fit for Real People*. Portland: Palmer/Pletsch Publishing, 1998.

Reader's Digest. *New Complete Guide to Sewing: Step-by-Step Techniques for Making Clothes and Home Accessories*. Pleasantville, NY: Reader's Digest, 2002.

Simplicity Pattern Co., Inc. *Simplicity's Simply the Best Home Decorating Book*. New York: Simplicity Pattern Co. Inc., 1993.

Soto, Anne Marie, ed. *Simplicity's Simply the Best Sewing Book*. New York: Simplicity Pattern Co. Inc., 2001.

Zieman, Nancy. *Essential Sewing Guide*. Birmingham, AL: Oxmoor House, 1998.

———. *Sewing with Nancy's Favorite Hints*. Iola, WI: Frause Publications, 2002.

Periodicals

Clotilde's Sewing Savvy
23 Old Pecan Road
Big Sandy, TX 75755
www.ClotildesSewingSavvy.com

Creative Needle
1 Apollo Road
Lookout Mountain, GA 30750
www.creativeneedlemag.com

Fiberarts
PO Box 469125
Excondido, CA 92046-9125
www.fiberartsmagazine.com

SewNews
Golden, CO
741 Corporate Circle, Suite A
Golden, CO 80401
sewnews.com/
sewnews@sewnews.com

Threads
63 S. Main Street
PO Box 5507
Newtown, CT 06470-9874
www.threadsmagazine.com

Websites

The number of websites sewers would find helpful and fun is almost endless. These are just a sample of the possibilities that exist:

www.carolharrisco.com
Go here if you plan to sew for children, want to make fine linens, or just want to look at beautiful vintage lace and fabrics.

www.clotilde.com/cl/
Try this site if you want to explore all kinds of notions, traditional as well as just off the design board.

www.DesignToFit.com
This site offers a variety of media, from books to DVDs and workshops to help you design clothes for yourself or your friends that really fit.

www.newarkdress.com
If you can't get to a fabric or craft store, this site is the place to shop. It's got everything you need from fabric to notions, patterns to thread—all on one site.

www.sew2000.com/dancingneedles
This is the place to go if you want to learn how to sew heirloom-quality garments for children.

Index